MANY WORLDS

MANY WORLDS

THE NEW UNIVERSE,
EXTRATERRESTRIAL LIFE,
AND THE
THEOLOGICAL IMPLICATIONS

EDITED BY

STEVEN J. DICK

TEMPLETON FOUNDATION PRESS

PHILADELPHIA AND LONDON

Templeton Foundation Press
Five Radnor Corporate Center, Suite 120
100 Matsonford Road
Radnor, Pennsylvania 19087

Typeset by Nesbitt Graphics, Inc., Glenside, PA
Printed by Versa Press, East Peoria, IL

Library of Congress Cataloging-in-Publication Data
Many worlds: the new universe, extraterrestrial life, and the theological implications / edited by Steven J. Dick.
   p. cm.
   ISBN 1-890151-37-8 (alk. paper) — ISBN 1-890151-42-4 (pbk.: alk. paper)
   1. Religion and science—Congresses. 2. Cosmology—Congresses. 3. Life on other plants—Congresses. I. Dick, Steven J.
BL241.M255 2000
291.2'4—dc21

00-020804

Printed in the United States of America

00 01 02 03   04   05   06   10 9 8 7 6 5 4 3 2

CONTENTS

INTRODUCTION

At the dawn of a new millennium it is striking to consider how much our world view has changed in the past 1000 years. In AD 1000 the geocentric cosmology of Aristotle and Ptolemy dominated intellectual thinking, then centered in Islamic civilization. The ancient Greek view was soon to be passed via the Arabs to the Latin West, where it met head on with Christianity, following which Thomas Aquinas and others made heroic efforts to reconcile the religious and the scientific understanding of the world. Human destiny, as immortalized in Dante's *Divine Comedy*, was defined by the unchangeable heavens above, the corruptible Earth below, and the threatening inferno within. Less than three centuries later, all that changed with the Sun-centered universe of Copernicus, which made the Earth a planet and the planets Earths, plunging European thought into a crisis from which it arguably has not yet emerged.

But that dethroning of the Earth pales in significance to the startling upheavals in world view unveiled in the past century. One hundred years ago, the entire universe was believed to be a few thousand light years across; now that extent is measured in billions of light years. Then the universe was believed to be static; now it is seen as expanding and evolving, and cosmic evolution is the watchword from the Big Bang to the present. Although the Earth had long been dethroned from the center of the solar system, our Sun and its retinue of planets was believed to be near the center of our galaxy, which many thought constituted the entire universe. Now, billions of galaxies are known to float in an Einsteinian space-time, which has no center. And the greatest question of all remains: are we, in all the universe, alone as sentient beings? An increasing number of scientists from many fields believe the answer is no, and that the last vestige of anthropocentrism is rapidly fading, any day to be overthrown by the discovery of extraterrestrial life.

Given these upheavals in our world view, we might have thought that the dialogue between science, philosophy, and religion would be crackling with synergistic ideas. Instead, some still question whether such a dialogue should even take place. Despite sporadic communication among these disciplines, there have been very few attempts at a "Cosmotheology" that takes the astounding facts of the new universe into account. Nor does this volume, based on a small meeting sponsored by the John Templeton Foundation in November 1998, have any such grandiose ambitions. Rather, it is a preliminary reconnaissance of the issues surrounding theology and the new world view, addressed by scholars from a wide array of disciplines. Here, the reader will find a variety of approaches and a variety of answers that can hardly be characterized as systematic. So it must be for any reconnaissance, and the result, while stimulating in itself, demonstrates how much remains to be done.

One may immediately ask, Why bother with the theme of Theology and the New Universe? Arthur Peacocke, both a biochemist and an Anglican priest, expresses one point of view in this volume when he says "any theology—any attempt to relate God to all-that-is—will be moribund and doomed if it does not incorporate this perspective [of cosmic evolution] into its very bloodstream." Although some may argue with this sentiment, it is a guiding principle of many, though not all, the authors in this volume. In Sir Martin Rees' essay, England's Astronomer Royal writes that cosmologists may not have much that is new to contribute to the dialogue between science and religion, although cosmology may say much about the role of terrestrial life. At the other end of the spectrum, Nobel biochemist Christian de Duve argues in his essay that science, especially biology, "urgently calls for an informed and unbiased dialogue" among science, philosophy, and religion. Physicist and author Paul Davies observes that "if it turns out to be the case that the universe is inherently biofriendly . . . then . . . the scientific, theological, and philosophical implications will be extremely significant."

The reader will also find in this volume a difference of opinion as to how much our concepts of God need to be modified in the light of what we know about the universe. Freeman Dyson writes that the modern universe "has not changed the age-old mystery of God's relation to the physical universe," that God is beyond the limits of our understanding and unlikely to be impressed with our efforts to read his mind. On the other hand, Lee Smolin boldly claims that "the old idea of an outside Creator and Knower has served its purpose and may now be relegated to history." Rather than a creator who stands eternally outside his creation, the "creative being, the knowledge of all its manifold variety, and that world itself, are one and the same thing." Similarly, I argue that, just as Aristotle's celestial-terrestrial dichotomy of the universe was abandoned after two millennia, so cosmotheology may have to abandon the 4,000-year-old supernatural God of the ancient Near East in favor of a "natural God" inside the universe. Even if we retain our traditional concepts of God, doctrines of particular religious traditions may be affected in ways that are also discussed in these pages.

Any volume such as this, which proposes to treat the relation of science and religion, must be well grounded in science. The authors of Parts I and II provide a foundation for Part III in this respect, as well as drawing philosophical and theological lessons themselves. Part I focuses on what lessons might be learned with the latest knowledge of the origin and evolution of life. After discussing some of the lessons of life, Christian de Duve immediately draws a sharp distinction between two possibilities: that of the French biochemist Jacques Monod, who in his book *Chance and Necessity* (1971) argued that "the universe was not pregnant with life, nor the biosphere with man," and the point of view (which de Duve prefers) that the pregnancy erroneously negated by Monod is in fact "the outcome of very special features built into the natural structure of the universe." De Duve views life as a "cosmic imperative," with all that implies for philosophy and theology. Physicist Paul Davies and biophysicist Bernd-Olaf Küppers both stress the informational aspects of the origin of life, and both return in the end to the question of chance and necessity. Davies concludes that if life and intelligence are freak accidents as some believe, then bleak atheism may be justified; however, if life arises as an "automatic and natural part of an ingeniously biofriendly universe" (as he believes), then "atheism would seem less compelling and something like design more plausible." Küppers, while not accepting Monod's claim that life is a lottery, also believes de Duve's cosmic imperative for life goes too far in the direction of determinism; consideration must be given to the historical circumstances under which evolution takes place, an exercise requiring an analysis of the generation and transformation of the boundaries that encode the blueprint of the living organism. Christopher McKay, a NASA scientist and expert on Mars, argues that these questions may only be answered when extraterrestrial life is discovered. He explores strategies for a successful search based on the principles of astrobiology in an essay that also extends the discussion from theology to environmental ethics.

Part II broadens the scope of the conversation to cosmic evolution. Indeed, what Arthur Peacocke calls the "genesis for the third millennium" is the theme that underlies the entire book. Sir Martin Rees lays out the panoply and grandeur of cosmic evolution, extending even to the evolution of other universes that may compose what he terms an infinite and eternal "multiverse." Theoretical physicist Lee Smolin discusses how natural selection of universes may play a role in cosmic evolution and posits a cosmological theory in which all scientific questions are explicable in terms of the history of the universe, whose laws may "result from natural and comprehensible processes of self-organization." Peacocke examines in considerable detail the stages and mechanisms of evolution for what they reveal about nature, humanity, and God. For Peacocke, the dynamic nature of the living world impels us to re-introduce the notion of a "semper Creator," who "creates in and through the process of natural order." Philosopher John Leslie tackles the significance of the fact that the universe seems to be fine tuned in life-permitting ways. This has suggested to some people that many universes exist with widely varying characteristics; among these, only appropriately tuned universes could be observed by anyone, as Brandon Carter's "anthropic principle" reminds us. Leslie comments that any observed fine tuning might, however, have resulted from "divine selection of our universe's properties." He defends a neoplatonic theory of God, implying, among other reasons, that the universe exists because it is ethically better that it exist.

Part III addresses most directly many of the questions commonly associated with theological implications of extraterrestrial life. With his usual knack for innovative thinking, physicist Freeman Dyson demonstrates that we need not leave Earth to assess the effects of different world views; alien worlds exist, in a deeply physiological sense, all around us. They are inhabited by people with neurological impairments such as autism—and the lesson to be learned from trying to imagine them is humility. From the extraterrestrial perspective, astronomer Jill Cornell Tarter, who heads the Project Phoenix Search for Extraterrestrial Intelligence, believes that an extraterrestrial message, unambiguously decoded, might be "a missionary campaign without precedent in terrestrial history," leading to the replacement of our diverse collection of terrestrial religions by a "universal religion." Alternatively, a message that indicates long-lived extraterrestrials with no need for God or religion might undermine our religious world view completely. Ernan McMullin, a priest and philosopher at the University of Notre Dame, and George Coyne, the Jesuit director of the Vatican Observatory, provide reflections from within the Christian tradition, in particular addressing how the astronomical world view might affect particular dogmas such as Incarnation and Redemption. "Coping with the reality of the Stranger," McMullin reminds us, "has always been a challenge for the theologians of the Book." Coyne points out that the God of Scripture and tradition is not an explainer but a lover—and that anthropocentrism need not imply exclusivity. In the closing essay, as an astronomer and historian of science I argue that it is time to take cosmotheology seriously, for religion to take into account what we know about the universe, no matter where it may lead us in our conceptions of God and in the revision of religious doctrines. Following that line of reasoning, we can only wonder where theology will be at the dawn of the next millennium.

A recognized limitation of this volume is that it is Western-centric. The majority of Earth's population is non-Western, non-Christian, and not necessarily imbued with the values we take for granted, and we must not ignore the multiplicity of our world in the new millennium. The new universe has implications for all areas of human thought and for all the world's cultures. A logical next step is a discussion of these implications for non-Western thought.

The meeting that served as the basis for this volume took place on November 22–24, 1998, in Lyford Cay, Nassau, The Bahamas. I thank Paul Davies, the meeting chair and co-organizer; Mary Ann Meyers, senior fellow of the Templeton Foundation, who also did much of the essential work of organization; and Sir John Templeton, the Foundation's creator, who attended the sessions and without whom the meeting would not have taken place. It goes without saying that the stimulating ideas and cooperation of the authors were essential for this volume. It was the consensus of the group that these discussions should reach beyond the confines of a small island; if this volume stimulates further discussion, it will have served its purpose.

I close with the stirring words of Christian de Duve: "The advances of biology have revolutionized the view we have of ourselves and our significance in the world. Many myths have had to be abandoned. But mystery remains, more profound and beautiful than ever before, a reality almost inaccessible to our feeble human means."

Steven J. Dick
Washington, D.C.

PART I
ORIGIN AND EVOLUTION OF LIFE

CHRISTIAN DE DUVE

Christian de Duve, who shared the 1974 Nobel Prize in Physiology or Medicine for pioneering work on cell structure and function, has devoted his career to studying the biochemistry of life. A native of Belgium, he studied at the Catholic University of Louvain where he earned an M.D., Ph.D., and advanced master's degree in chemical sciences. After postdoctoral fellowships at the Medical Nobel Institute in Stockholm and Washington University in St. Louis, he was appointed a lecturer in physiological chemistry on the Faculty of Medicine of the Catholic University of Louvain in 1947, becoming emeritus professor in 1985. Since 1962, he has shared his time between his Belgian alma mater and the Rockefeller University in New York, where he was named Andrew W. Mellon professor in 1974, reaching emeritus status in 1988. Dr. de Duve is the founder of the International Institute of Cellular and Molecular Pathology in Brussels, served as its president director from 1974 to 1991, and now is a member of the Institute's board of directors. Dr. de Duve has served on many advisory boards and committees. He is a member of numerous academies and learned societies, including the U.S. National Academy of Sciences, the American Philosophical Society, and the Royal Society. He holds sixteen honorary degrees from universities in Europe, South America, Canada, and the United States. He is the author of some 375 scientific papers and three books; the most recent is *Vital Dust: Life as a Cosmic Imperative.*

LESSONS OF LIFE*

CHRISTIAN DE DUVE

The twentieth century will be remembered for some of the most decisive breakthroughs in the history of human knowledge. Physics and cosmology captured the limelight in the first half of the century with the discovery of atomic structure, elementary particles, relativity, quantum mechanics, galaxies, the expanding universe, and the Big Bang. The awesome exploitation of nuclear power stands as the most epoch-making application of this new knowledge. The second half of the century belongs to biology, with elucidation of the key features of cell structure and function, the double-helical conformation of DNA, and the genetic code, leading to unprecedented mastery over life.

These revolutionary advances in science, especially those in biology, have affected in a profound manner our understanding of the nature, origin, and destiny of humankind—concerns traditionally addressed largely by philosophy and religion. The current situation urgently calls for an informed and unbiased dialogue between the two groups of disciplines. In this essay, I review briefly some of the most important notions that have been disclosed by recent biological discoveries, examine critically the evidence put forward in their support, and attempt to derive what lessons, if any, they hold for philosophy and religion. I do so from the vantage point of my own limited expertise in the life sciences. A more complete coverage of many of the topics discussed may be found in a recent book.[1]

*I am greatly indebted to my friend Neil Patterson for many useful suggestions in the writing of this chapter and to Larry Martin, who had severely, but constructively, criticized an earlier version. Neither, of course, bears any responsibility in the ideas expressed.

THE NATURE OF LIFE

A major lesson to be derived from our newly acquired understanding is that life is explainable in terms of the laws of physics and chemistry. This, of course, is the central postulate on which the scientific study of life rests. As such, it is a working hypothesis that guides and justifies our investigations, not a dogmatic a priori statement. While this is true historically, the present state of our knowledge makes the hypothesis into something as close to established fact as can be affirmed within the self-imposed boundaries of science.

We truly understand the basic processes that support life, and we successfully explain them in physical and chemical terms. The best proof that our explanations are both correct and sufficient is provided by the powerful achievements of biotechnology. The old concept of living organisms made of matter "animated" and goal-directed by some special force or "vital spirit" must be abandoned. Vitalism and finalism no longer are accepted by the vast majority of scientists.

THE UNITY OF LIFE

Another affirmation that may now be made with considerable confidence is that all known living organisms, be they bacteria, protists, plants, fungi, or animals, including humans, descend from a single ancestral form of life, from which they have inherited a number of shared key properties. All known organisms are made of one or more cells. All cells are constructed out of the same building blocks assembled into the same kinds of polysaccharides, lipids, proteins, nucleic acids, and other general biological substances. All cells manufacture their constituents by the same processes. They all use similar mechanisms to derive energy from their environments and convert it into useful work. There are differences, of course. But the mechanisms, whether tied to sunlight, respiration, or anaerobic fermentation, boil down to similar electron exchanges, proton potentials, and phosphate-linked group transfers. Most important, all living organisms use the same language; they obey the same genetic code.

Already strongly supported by those common properties, the unity of life is incontrovertibly proven by the close similarities among the amino-acid sequences of proteins that perform the same functions in different organisms and among the nucleotide sequences of the nucleic acids that code for these proteins. Such similarities are found universally and enforce the conclusion that the molecules—and therefore the organisms to which they belong—are derived from a common ancestor. Comparative sequencing can even serve for reconstructing filiations among organisms. The underlying assumption—subject to many refinements—is that the degree of sequence dissimilarity between two homologous molecules, which corresponds roughly to the number of genetic modifications they have undergone independently, is a measure of the evolutionary distance separating their owners from their last common ancestor. This technique is now used on a large scale. In the resulting reconstructions, the human species clearly appears as one among millions of terminal twigs on the tree of life—the outcome, like every other living species, of a very long evolutionary history. The evidence supporting this view is overwhelming.

THE ORIGIN OF LIFE

According to most experts, life arose naturally by way of processes entirely explainable by the laws of physics and chemistry. However, there is no definitive proof of this statement, since the origin of life is not known. The alternative theory, that life was launched on its course by a special act of creation, cannot be excluded; but this theory, in the light of compelling evidence, now appears gratuitous and heuristically sterile. The naturalist explanation is consistent with the explainability of life itself and is supported by all available data.

Organic radicals and molecules, some identical with the building blocks of life, are found in meteorites, comets, and even interstellar dust. Some of the steps whereby such substances can arise spontaneously and interact to form more complex compounds under plausible "prebiotic" conditions have been reproduced in the laboratory. Key stages in the development of life—the so-called "RNA world" is one—have been recognized. Reconstructing life in the test tube is still a distant goal but not, in the view of many scientists, an unattainable one.

An apparent corollary of the naturalistic explanation of life's origin is that life was bound to arise, in a form basically similar to its form on Earth, under the physical-chemical conditions that prevailed where and when it was born—presumably on Earth, a little less than four billion years ago. This opinion, which is shared by most biochemists, runs counter to the view, popularly accepted in many other circles, that life is the product of a highly improbable combination of chance events, so improbable as to be almost certainly unique in the entire universe.

With only a single instance of life known, discrimination between the two contrasting views can be based only on theoretical assessments. The deterministic explanation is supported by the fact that life must have arisen by way of chemical reactions. Chemistry deals with strictly reproducible processes that depend on the statistical behavior of trillions of molecules of different kinds and that leave little, if anything, to chance. Under specified conditions, chemical reactions always follow the same course. Such must have been the case of the reactions responsible for the emergence of life. Furthermore, a very large number of steps must have been involved in this process. The spontaneous appearance in a single shot, or even in a small number of steps, of something as complex as even the most primitive living cell is utterly impossible. Given the laws of probability, a process involving a large number of steps could have come to fruition only if, on average, the probability of each individual step had been reasonably high. Had this not been the case, the succession of steps leading to life most likely would have aborted before reaching a stage where self-support and self-perpetuation were ensured.

A deterministic view of the origin of life does not necessarily imply that life is widespread in the universe. It only means that life is as frequent—or as rare—as the physical-chemical conditions under which it must obligatorily arise. Should such conditions be so improbable as to be unique in the whole universe, then life, although the product of highly deterministic processes, would also be unique, and the consequence, albeit indirectly, of a highly improbable combination of circumstances. This is not a question for the biologist to answer. All that can be said is that the majority of cosmologists believe that there must be, in our galaxy alone, as well as in others, many celestial bodies with a history similar to that of planet Earth. If they are right, then the deterministic view leads to the conclusion that life is indeed widespread, a normal manifestation of matter in many sites of the universe, a cosmic imperative. Perhaps space exploration techniques will some day be sufficiently refined to settle this point.

THE HISTORY OF LIFE

Modern biology has confirmed and fleshed out in clear molecular terms Darwin's fundamental intuition that the evolution of life is driven by natural selection, acting after the fact in merely passive fashion, to sift accidentally arising genetic variants according to their ability to survive and produce progeny under prevailing environmental conditions. A basic tenet of this concept is that the variations offered to natural selection are induced by causes that are unrelated, except in a strictly fortuitous manner, to the evolutionary advantages their effects may entail. It rules out any form of directionality imposed on the evolutionary process by some hidden guiding principle and is consistent with the rejection of vitalism and finalism already mentioned. It is supported by all we know of evolution as it takes place today and by all the findings of molecular biology.

This concept seems to imply that the course of evolution was ruled entirely by chance, a point often invoked in support of the view that humankind, like every other living species, owes its emergence to a very unlikely succession of accidental events, devoid of any sort of significance. Even if there should be many other foci of life in the universe, it is argued, the probability that any one would evolve into conscious, intelligent beings is extremely low. Hence the view that humankind is most likely unique in this respect and that even its appearance on Earth is a highly improbable event that could very well never have happened, were it not for an extraordinary combination of circumstances.

This inference is not necessarily correct. Chance does not exclude inevitability. However improbable an event may be, it always can be made to occur almost obligatorily—within acceptable limits of time and space—by giving it a sufficient number of opportunities of taking place. As a simple example, take a seven-digit lottery number. Its likelihood of coming out in a single drawing is one in ten million. But with ten million drawings, the probability becomes two in three. And with one hundred million drawings, the probability of the number coming out is 9,999.5 in 10,000, close to certainty. This fact is of little help to lottery players, but it is highly relevant to the evolutionary lottery, to the extent that given events depend on the occurrence of a given mutation in an individual exposed to a given set of environmental conditions. Considering, on the one hand, the constraints imposed on the number of possible mutations by the sizes and structures of genomes and, on the other, the number of individuals at risk and the durations involved, one concludes that mutations rarely act as limiting factors in evolution.

This view is supported by what we know of evolution in action. Consider, for example, the many instances of drug-resistant pathogens and pests that have appeared in less than fifty years. This perspective also renders more easily understandable the many cases of evolutionary adaptation—such as mimicry, for example—that are often invoked in favor of the intervention of some guiding factor in evolution.

If the view outlined above is correct, the natural variability of biological populations, although due essentially to fortuitous factors, most often is rich enough to provide for a wide spectrum of contingencies. Thus, the decisive role in evolution would most often be played by the screening effect of the environment on the mutations. This still leaves chance a major influence. It is important, in this connection, to distinguish between horizontal and vertical evolution. Horizontal evolution leads to diversity without significant change in body plan; it is dominated by contingency. Vertical evolution, the kind that leads to complexity, is much more stringently constrained. Given the opportunity and here comes the chance factor, evolution is bound to lead to increasing complexity. In animal evolution, the direction toward increasingly complex polyneural networks appears strongly favored by the fact that a more effective brain is advantageous under any circumstance. Thus, if life exists elsewhere in the universe, the likelihood that it may produce intelligent forms, some perhaps more advanced than the human form, is far from negligible.

That this possibility deserves to be seriously entertained threatens one of our most cherished beliefs, a cornerstone not only of many religions, but also of humanism in general, whether religiously inspired or not: the conviction that humankind occupies a central position in a universe somehow constructed around it, if not for it. I shall come back to this.

THE BRAIN-MIND PROBLEM

Another "ism" that has fallen victim to the advances of biology is dualism. There can be little doubt that mental states emerge naturally from the functioning of complex assemblages of neurons in certain parts of the brain, especially the neocortex. All the findings of neurobiology and of neuropathology converge to support this statement. The Cartesian notion of mind, or "spirit," as an entity distinct from the body and of a different nature, which somehow controls the body by way of the brain and helps it interact with the outside world, must be abandoned. As I have argued elsewhere, this notion is not only incompatible with experimental observations, it is logically flawed. If brain and mind are different in essence, how does the brain generate mind and how does the mind, in turn, influence the brain? Of what essence is the bridge between the two entities?

In the opinion of many experts, the monistic view implies that human behavior is no more than the reflection of neuronal activities over which individuals have no control. Driven to its extreme conclusion, this view denies the existence of free will and, hence, of moral responsibility. The conviction we have of possessing these traits is depicted as an illusion, fostered by natural selection because it favored the cohesion and survival ability of the groups that entertained it. Oddly enough, even the most ardent advocates of this notion hesitate to drive it to its logical conclusion. Belief in free will, they tell us, although now recognized as an illusion, should nevertheless not be abandoned since we are unable ever to know the hidden processes that determine the decisions we assume we make freely. Ignorance creates uncertainty and thereby the feeling of freedom. Furthermore, belief in freedom somehow acts as a self-fulfilling process, in the sense that this belief, or rather its neuronal basis, becomes part of decision making.

This position, besides being intellectually shaky, leaves out the fact that consciousness itself is a subjective experience of which there is as yet only a phenomenological account but no objective explanation. The possibility that it may depend on properties not included in the physical descriptions of matter arrived at so far cannot be excluded. Neither can it be ruled out that mind, as an emanation of polyneuronal activities, has the ability to influence the course of these activities, at least in certain cases, to exercise free will. Is the phrase "mental power" just an image, part of the illusion? Or does it correspond to some unknown process? This question is most often shirked by neurobiologists, a majority of whom consider even raising it a dangerous concession to extrasensory perception, spoon bending, and other claims of "metascience." Such an attitude strikes me as overly cautious. Science is strong enough to entertain hypotheses that do not fit with fashionable trends, provided the hypotheses can be subjected to rigorous testing.

Monism, like materialism, is most often understood in a reductionist fashion that, when properly considered, appears as a residue of Cartesian dualism. The notion of "mere matter" is invoked, matter itself being defined in terms of the properties (solidity, inertia, and brute submission to the laws of physics and chemistry) that distinguish it from spirit. This is wrong. What monism truly means is not that we must somehow squeeze spirit into our traditional concept of matter, but that we must enlarge the definition of matter to include those properties that used to be attributed to spirit. It must be remembered that the senses whereby the human brain apprehends the surrounding world were refined by natural selection as tools of survival, not of knowledge. Only recently has this become evident, thanks to the development of physical instruments that extend the range of our senses and to conceptual tools that allow theoretical processing of the information gathered by these instruments. The glimpses of the "real" world revealed to us in this way have turned out to be so strange as to be utterly beyond the grasp of those who have not been introduced to them by long and arduous training. Even the experts have difficulties translating from their language—most often mathematical—to a more familiar mode of representation.

The capacity to approach reality in this manner is, at least on Earth, an exclusive property of human beings, acquired in the past few million years of evolution thanks, probably, to a remarkable development of the brain, especially the neocortex. This realization raises the question of what might be the impact of further brain development on the ability to investigate and understand nature. A second question concerns the significance of other forms of interaction—besides rational discourse—between the human brain and reality: artistic expression, moral judgment, intuitive apprehension, meditation, or mystic contemplation. Could there be several means of cognition each adapted to a facet of ultimate reality and perhaps each capable of further improvement through additional development of certain areas of the brain? These and other such questions cannot be answered in the present state of our knowledge and perhaps never will be. But they remind us that the relationship between brain and mind is an unsolved problem.

THE FUTURE OF LIFE

One last lesson of biology: evolution is far from over. According to cosmologists, our planet should remain able to bear life for about another five billion years before being engulfed in the fiery expansion of the dying sun. What can happen in such an enormous stretch of time is entirely beyond our imagination. Whatever the future may bring, humankind is most unlikely to remain at a standstill during all that time. It will either disappear or evolve. In either case, we are not the ultimate achievement of evolution, only a transient stage. The old anthropocentric view of a human-focused universe must be abandoned, even in its recent reformulation in the so-called "anthropic principle."

It would be surprising if in the future development of life on Earth, vertical evolution toward greater complexity did not continue to take place, perhaps leading to beings endowed with considerably sharper means of apprehending reality than we possess. Such beings could arise by further extension of the human twig, but they do not have to. There is plenty of time for a humanlike adventure to start all over again from another twig and perhaps go further than did the human adventure.

LESSONS OF LIFE FOR PHILOSOPHY AND RELIGION

Creationism, vitalism, finalism, dualism, and anthropocentrism have all been left by the wayside by the progression of modern biology. For scientists, the scenery is deeply gratifying in its austere and coherent beauty. But to others, the message may seem disquietingly bleak, because it questions a number of familiar notions, rooted in the biblical tradition and still entertained and propagated in more or less literal form by the major monotheistic religions. Aware of the potential conflicts, many philosophers and theologians have begun reflecting on how basic beliefs can be reconciled with the findings of science. This necessary reappraisal will not be easy, considering the intricate network of social structures that has been knit around the churches by centuries of shared faith and aspirations. In this exercise, the scientist can only point to what is now established beyond reasonable doubt or at least highly probable. Such has been the purpose of my brief survey. As to extrapolating from science to philosophy, scientists are poorly trained for such a venture and generally shy away from it. Here, for what they are worth, are a few suggestions.

A first notion to be singled out is that we belong to a universe capable of giving rise to life and mind. This affirmation would seem like a mere statement of the obvious, were it not for the widely publicized view that life and mind are freak products of a highly improbable combination of chance circumstances most unlikely to occur any time, anywhere. This attitude was summed up by Jacques Monod when he wrote, "The Universe was not pregnant with life, nor the biosphere with man."[2] This statement challenges evidence. The facts are that the Universe has given birth to life and the biosphere has given birth to humans. To affirm that those two births took place without pregnancies amounts to invoking miracles, which is certainly not what the great French biologist had in mind.

Miracles, in the form of special creative acts of God, are what religions traditionally invoke to account for the existence of life and mind in the universe. The lesson of modern biology is that such interventions were not needed and probably did not occur. Life and mind most likely developed through purely natural events rendered possible by the prevailing physical-chemical conditions or perhaps even imposed by these conditions. As the defenders of the anthropic principle have pointed out in great detail, these occurrences require an extraordinary degree of fine tuning of many key properties of the universe. The "pregnancy" that was erroneously negated by Monod is in fact the outcome of very special features built into the natural structure of the universe.

Some contemporary physicists, including Rees and Smolin, two other contributors to this volume, minimize the significance of this fact by assuming that our universe is not unique. They see it as a part or as an evolutionary product of a large set of universes—a "multiverse" in the suggestive terminology proposed by Rees—that display a wide array of physical properties. Lost in this ocean of "nonpregnant" universes, ours would be no more than the odd one that happened, by chance, to have the right combination of properties for life and mind to arise. Intriguing as they are, these theories do not in any way diminish the overwhelming significance of our universe as it exists. Whichever way they appeared, and whatever the probability of their emergence, life and mind are such extraordinary manifestations that their existence can only be a telling revelation of ultimate reality. Even diluted by trillions of lifeless universes, ours remains supremely meaningful. The anthropic principle is correct in this respect, except for its anthropocentric connotation.

A second major lesson of modern biology concerns the humble status of our species, which, far from being the ultimate goal of creation it has long been thought to be, now appears as a transient link or perhaps even a side branch in a long evolutionary process very likely to give rise some day to beings much more advanced than we are. There also is a real possibility that beings with mental attributes similar or superior to ours exist elsewhere in the universe. Although these possibilities have not been verified in reality, they deserve sufficiently serious consideration to be incorporated into our new world view. The resulting picture is not, however, as negative as is maintained by those who see in the findings of science reasons for denigrating the human species.

Even though we may not be the final product of evolution, our emergence nevertheless represents a watershed. Contrary to what I call the "gospel of contingency," popularized by a number of contemporary thinkers, the human species is not the meaningless outcome of chance events in a pointless universe. For the first time in the history of life, beings exist that have access, albeit in a very primitive and rudimentary fashion, to the reality behind the appearances, including the nature of matter, the structure of the universe, the basic mechanisms of life, the historical processes through which these entities have arisen and evolved, and especially abstract notions, such as truth, beauty, goodness, and love. Although apprehended only dimly, these abstractions are the closest we can get with our feeble means to the ultimate reality to which many give the name of God. No doubt, the beings with expanded mental powers who are likely to succeed us one day will see this reality more clearly. But the glimpses we are afforded already are immensely rewarding.

Also important and unique to the human condition is the acquisition of moral responsibility. Although disputed by some neurobiologists and philosophers, the feeling we have of being in command of our own actions and of being responsible for them is not likely to be abandoned, even by those who question its authenticity. It is an indispensable foundation of our societies. Far from yielding to the advances of science, our responsibility is made increasingly important by those advances, to the extent that they are giving us increasingly effective means of shaping the future of our planet, of the living world, and of our own species. To wield wisely the immense powers with which science in the twentieth century has endowed humankind will be the main concern of coming generations.

CONCLUSION

The advances of biology have revolutionized the view we have of ourselves and our significance in the world. Many myths have had to be abandoned. But mystery remains, more profound and more beautiful than ever before, a reality almost inaccessible to our feeble human means.

NOTES

1. C. de Duve, *Vital Dust* (New York: Basic Books, 1995).
2. J. Monod, *Chance and Necessity*, trans. A. Wainhouse (New York: Knopf, 1971), 145–146.

Paul C.W. Davies

Paul Davies is a British theoretical physicist based in South Australia and the author of more than twenty books. He obtained a doctorate from University College, London in 1970 and was a research fellow at the Institute of Theoretical Astronomy in Cambridge until 1972, when he was appointed lecturer in mathematics at King's College, London. In 1980, he was offered the chair of theoretical physics at the University of Newcastle upon Tyne. He is currently visiting professor of physics at Imperial College, London. Dr. Davies' research has been mainly in the field of quantum gravity and cosmology. His books, *The Physics of Time Asymmetry* (1974) and *Quantum Fields in Curved Space* (1981), written with former student Nicholas Birrell, remain standard texts for researchers. He has made several important contributions to the theory of black holes and cosmological models. His interests, however, spread much wider, ranging from particle physics to astrobiology. He is currently working on the problem of biogenesis and the role of cosmic impacts on the early development of life. For many years, he has pursued the broader philosophical and theoretical implications of science through books and lectures, work for which he was awarded the 1995 Templeton Prize for Progress in Religion. His best known text on the subject is *The Mind of God* (1992). He was for several years a columnist for *The Economist* and *The Australian*. He devised and presented a highly successful series of science documentaries on BBC Radio 3, two of which were published in book form as *The Ghost in the Atom* and *Superstrings: A Theory of Everything?* Dr. Davies is a Fellow of the Institute of Physics, the Australian Institute of Physics, The World Economic Forum, and the World Academy of Arts and Science. His most recent book is *The Fifth Miracle: The Search for the Origin of Life* (Allen Lane The Penguin Press, 1998).

Biological Determinism, Information Theory, and the Origin of Life

Paul C.W. Davies

Four hundred years ago, the Roman Catholic church burned Giordano Bruno at the stake for heresy. Among other things, he proposed the existence of an infinite number of inhabited worlds. Since this ran counter to the doctrine of man as God's supreme and special creation, Bruno was undermining a key tenet of the Christian faith at that time. I argue that the church got it exactly wrong. If life is widespread in the universe, it gives us more, not less, reason to believe in cosmic design. My discussion centers on the notion of biological determinism: given the right conditions, life inevitably will form after a sufficiently long time, and once life gets started, it will very probably progress toward intelligence. Thirty years ago, in spite of the popularity of science fiction stories about aliens, belief in extraterrestrial life was widely ridiculed by scientists. Today the pendulum has swung back, and biological determinism is the prevailing philosophy at NASA, among SETI researchers, school children, journalists, and even the rich and famous.[1]

The basic thrust of my argument is to refute the oft-repeated claim that "life is written into the laws of physics." There is absolutely no evidence that the laws of physics we know at present "contain" life, still less intelligence; indeed, there are powerful arguments that they cannot. This does not mean, however, that biological determinism must be wrong; only that if it *were* true, it would require something more than the normal laws of physics. I am not implying the "something more" must be anything as crude as a miracle or the guiding hand of an interventionist deity. However, if it turns out that the universe is inherently biofriendly, so that biological determinism is in fact correct, then I believe the scientific, theological, and philosophical implications will be extremely significant.[2]

. . . .

HYPOTHESES FOR THE ORIGIN OF LIFE

Panspermia

Traditionally, there have been two hypotheses for the existence of life beyond Earth: biological determinism and panspermia. Although the scientific consequences are similar in both cases, the philosophical and theological implications are vastly different. The panspermia hypothesis proposes that life can travel from one planet to another. If this process were efficient enough, life might spread across the galaxy, and even between galaxies. The ultimate origin of life is left unexplained, but the theory is consistent with a unique chance event of exceedingly low probability. In 1872, Lord Kelvin, an early proponent of panspermia, conjectured that the collision of an astronomical body with a planet might displace much debris, and thus "many great and small fragments carrying seed and living plants and animals would undoubtedly be scattered through space." In an address to the British Association in Edinburgh, Kelvin surmised that some of these fragments eventually would reach other planets and infect them with life:

> Because we all confidently believe that there are at present, and have been from time immemorial, many worlds of life besides our own, we must regard it as probable in the highest degree that there are countless seed-bearing meteoric stones moving about through space. If at the present instant no life existed upon this earth, one such stone falling upon it might ... lead to its becoming covered with vegetation.[3]

Shortly afterwards the Swedish chemist Svante Arrhenius developed a rather different theory (and also coined the term panspermia). [4] Arrhenius imagined that microbes might traverse interstellar space, propelled by the pressure of starlight. In this way, bacteria from one planet might reach another and seed it with life. In recent years, Fred Hoyle and Chandra Wickramasinghe have elaborated Arrhenius's theory by proposing a role for comets as both incubators of life and efficient delivery systems.[5] Further elaborations along these lines have been published by Christopher McKay.[6] A rather different idea of panspermia was suggested (perhaps not entirely seriously) by Francis Crick and Leslie Orgel, who conjectured that life might have been spread around the galaxy as a deliberate strategy by an advanced civilization using interstellar projectiles.[7] A major objection to Arrhenius's theory is the radiation hazard of outer space, especially the ultraviolet component of starlight. Experiments suggest[8] that the interstellar transport of viable microbes is highly unlikely, although not strictly impossible. A related hypothesis that life might travel between planets within a given star system, but not across interstellar space, in the rocky ejecta of asteroid and comet impacts is more plausible, and it has received attention in relation to the possible cross-contamination of Earth and Mars.[9]

Although the discovery that life had spread, for example, from Earth to Mars or vice versa through a panspermia mechanism, would be extremely interesting scientifically, it would have no significant philosophical or theological implications. In recent years, we have learned that the biosphere extends deep into the Earth's crust.[10] Perhaps it also extends to neighboring planets, although the chances of it extending to other star systems would seem to be exceedingly small. However, we would learn nothing new about life except its resilience in extreme environments. Finding terrestrial-type life on Mars would be entirely consistent with a unique and purely accidental origin for life. It would not be possible to conclude from such a discovery that the origin of life was more than a highly unlikely chemical fluke.

By contrast, suppose life were discovered on Mars and found to use biochemistry very different from terrestrial life. For example, it might employ molecules with the opposite chirality, i.e., its nucleic acids and amino acids would be the mirror images of ours. Or it might use a completely different genetic code, or a different "alphabet" of amino acids, or perhaps different sorts of molecules altogether. It may then be possible to conclude that Earth life and Mars life had independent origins. If life has happened at least twice in one star system, it would exist in vast abundance across the galaxy, and in all other galaxies. We would conclude that we inhabit a biofriendly universe. Since the consequences of an independent origin of life are so momentous, the possibility of cross-contamination of Earth and Mars is extremely frustrating. It may be that Mars is the only other planet we shall be able to explore in the foreseeable future, and the likelihood of interplanetary panspermia probably would compromise any attempt to demonstrate an independent origin.

Biological Determinism

Strong and Weak Biological Determinism. Let us distinguish between strong and weak versions of biological determinism. Strong determinism is captured by the oft-repeated phrase that life is written into the laws of physics. In other words, in a suitable chemical mixture under appropriate physical conditions, the laws of physics favor the production of molecules that are biologically relevant. Sidney Fox, one of the pioneers of biogenesis research, has explicitly claimed this in relation to the formation of peptide bonds in the production of proteins.[11] If Fox's point of view were correct, the effect would be to fast-track lifeless chemicals toward life, by heavily weighting the odds in favor of certain specific end states, i.e., living states. Life would form to order, like crystallization. If we envisage a soup of chemicals, and the near-infinite range of possible reactions, there will be a vast decision tree of molecular arrangements open to the mixture. Only a few tiny twiglets on this tree will lead to life. Strong biological determinists suggest that preferential chemical affinities serve to entice the participating molecules along the appropriate pathway through this tree until life is attained.

In the weak form of biological determinism, life emerges with a high degree of predictability, not because of the operation of explicitly biofriendly laws, but as a result of a general propensity for matter and energy to self-organize and self-complexify. The underlying mechanism for weak determinism might be the possibility that relatively simple high-fidelity replicating molecules form quite readily, because the laws of physics and chemistry fortuitously encourage their production. Once produced, molecular Darwinism could evolve these molecules toward more complex and familiar replicators, e.g., nucleic acids. Alternatively, there may exist as yet undiscovered principles of complexity, organization, and information flow consistent with the underlying laws of physics, but not reducible to them. These principles might create with high efficiency certain biologically useful physical states.

The Role of Information Theory. It is helpful to evaluate the plausibility and philosophical implications of strong and weak biological determinism in the light of information theory. Several authors (e.g., Loewenstein,[12] Küppers,[13] Yockey[14]) have stressed the informational aspect of life. Molecules like DNA and RNA can be considered a genetic databank, and reproduction viewed as the copying and propagation of information. Biologists agree that a gene is a set of *instructions*, e.g., for the assembly of a protein. A gene therefore represents not just information but *semantic* information (there is a context, or molecular milieu, which can *interpret* the information as a coded "message"). The living cell thus resembles a digital computer in its logical architecture. The genetic code, which converts nucleic acid data into protein data, provides a clear example of the power of software control in the organization of life processes. In short, life is an information processing and propagating system. Viewed this way, the problem of biogenesis is not so much a matter of exotic chemistry but of the origin of biological information. The traditional emphasis on chemistry as an explanation for life commits the classic fallacy of confusing the medium with the message. It is the origin of the message that needs explaining. Expressed starkly, how does hardware write its own software?

The subject of information theory is still in its infancy; indeed, information as a concept remains ill-defined and crops up in different guises in different subjects (thermodynamics, relativity, quantum mechanics, genetics). The most refined analysis is algorithmic information theory, whereby the information content of a physical state or system is quantified in terms of the complexity of the shortest algorithm or computational program that can simulate or describe it.[15]

In discussions of biogenesis, words like "order," "organization," "complexity," "chaos," "randomness," and "entropy" are often used in a sloppy and sometimes contradictory manner. This has led to much confusion about the nature of biological complexity and the way in which it might have emerged. In particular, order and organization are often employed synonymously, even though they can refer to opposite properties. Entropy is often not defined, which can lead to ambiguity since there are several inequivalent forms of entropy in use, all of them relevant to life. Arguments rage over alternative theories consisting of little more than a play on words rather than well-defined scientific concepts. Algorithmic information theory has the great advantage that it yields precise definitions for the above concepts, so it enables hypotheses to be properly framed and tested.

Applying information theory to biological determinism exposes severe problems with the strong version of determinism.[16] To see why, first note that if a physical state, or the output of a computer program, contains any patterns or regularities, then the program will be shorter than the state or output. In other words, the output is algorithmically compressible. If the output is not compressible, then it is random and patternless. Chaitin's theorem proves that the output of an algorithmic process cannot be more complex than the input.[17] A state with a high algorithmic information content has few patterns and is not very compressible. By contrast, a state with a high degree of regularity has a low algorithmic information content. A good example of the latter is a crystal, which has a periodic structure and so contains little information.

Since genomes are informational macromolecules, they had better not contain substantial regularities! If genome sequences were ordered (i.e., displayed patterns), genes would be deprived of information content, and so they would contain redundant matter that would be an encumbrance to life. To serve as information-rich structures, the base-pair sequences need to be essentially random. This conclusion comes as a surprise to many people, who mistakenly think that the arrangement of atoms in, say a molecule of DNA is highly ordered, whereas in fact order and randomness are opposite properties, as the algorithmic definition shows so clearly.

Now it is a fundamental theorem of algorithmic information theory, which can in fact be traced back to Gödel's incompleteness theorem of logic, that randomness cannot be proved. However, it is possible to disprove that a given sequence is random, simply by displaying an algorithmic compression of it, i.e., a more compact expression that generates the sequence. Therefore, just because a base-pair sequence in DNA looks jumbled and chaotic does not mean it is definitely random; there may be subtle patterns buried in the sequence that escape our notice. It is possible, but highly unlikely, that DNA is actually an information-poor structure masquerading as an information-rich one, and there is a hidden formula that links the members of the base-pair sequence. But few scientists would make a case for this, and there are powerful arguments against such a "conspiracy."[18]

For example, consider the structure of the DNA molecule, the famous double helix that when unraveled resembles a ladder, with the sequence of rungs (the base pairs) determining the information content. Chemistry determines the weak bonding between the two molecules that constitute each base pair (the two halves of each rung) and also the affixment of the bases to the two "handles" of the molecule. But there are no chemical bonds between adjacent rungs. As a result, any sequence of base pairs is as good as any other, as far as the laws of physics and chemistry are concerned. The bases are indifferent to what sequence they adopt. Indeed, nature exploits this very versatility, for by capitalizing on random alterations of the sequences, it is able to incrementally "climb Mount Improbable."[19] If chemistry were too restrictive and deterministic, open evolution would be impossible.

According to the strong determinism hypothesis, a genome (not necessarily nucleic acid) has a high probability of forming spontaneously as a consequence of the laws of physics. However, as shown, this cannot be the case. The laws of physics merely map input states into output states: they cannot add information on the way. The algorithmic information content of the (known) laws of physics is very low, i.e., the laws of physics are simple. Therefore, they cannot alone inject the complexity necessary for a structure like a random genome. Moreover, laws of physics are by definition general; they cannot contain implicit within them specific states of matter, such as information-rich macromolecules. Contrast this with crystallization, where the periodic crystal structure does indeed form deterministically, because its geometric form *is* implicit in the laws of physics. In the case of the crystal there is no information paradox, because crystals have low algorithmic information content and so can form predictably from simple initial states under the action of simple deterministic laws.

It is true that simple states can sometimes evolve into complex states in physics, but the complexity comes either from the boundary conditions or from the amplification of random fluctuations (i.e., deterministic chaos). It is certainly possible, therefore, for randomness to emerge spontaneously in accordance with deterministic laws. However, this consideration is not relevant to the formation of genomes for the following reason. Although the base sequences of RNA or DNA are random, they are not arbitrary. They belong to an infinitesimally small subset of all possible random sequences.

Let me illustrate this crucial point by considering not the gene but the protein that it specifies. The sequence of base pairs in DNA translates into the sequence of amino acids in the protein. In a typical short protein, there will be about 10^{130} different possible combinations of amino acids, of which a given protein will be just one such combination. Although slight variations in the sequence may not compromise the chemical efficacy of the protein—we do not seek a unique amino acid sequence—nevertheless only an exceedingly small subset of the 10^{130} possible sequences represent biologically useful molecules. The point is that a given protein has a very tightly specified function and hence a very tightly specified structure. We conclude that biologically relevant macromolecules simultaneously possess two vital properties: *randomness* and *extreme specificity*. A chaotic process could possibly achieve the former property but would have a negligible probability of achieving the latter.

At first sight this seems to make a genome an impossible object, unattainable by either known laws or chance. But this conclusion obviously is too hasty. Clearly Darwinian evolution by variation and natural selection has what is needed to generate both randomness (information richness) *and* tightly specified biological functionality in the same system. The particular combination of chance and law represented by Darwinism thus explains the dual properties of a genome. The problem as far as biogenesis is concerned is that Darwinism can operate only when life (of some sort) is already going. It cannot explain how life starts in the first place. From the foregoing discussion, it should be clear that no law of physics (at least of which we are familiar) *on its own* can do so either. So the strong form of biological determinism is refuted.

Strong determinists often remark that since the building blocks of life (e.g., amino acids) are easy to make and likely to be common throughout the universe, life also should be common throughout the universe. But our discussion exposes the fallacy of this reasoning. Just as bricks alone do not make a house, so biological building blocks alone do not make a living organism. The trick is to connect the building blocks together in the very, very specific sequences that represent biological relevance. That step is not explained by chemistry.

If strong biological determinism were true, it would be astounding. It would imply that *atomic* processes include a built-in bias favoring *organisms*, i.e., that the laws of atomic physics effectively contain within themselves a blueprint for life. There would have to be a link between the basic interatomic forces, and the final complicated macroscopic product—a functioning organism. But as I have argued, no such link is apparent in the sequences of DNA, proteins, and so forth. In any case, what would be the nature of such a link? How could the simple, basic mathematical laws of physics know about complex, specific, information-laden entities like living cells? That would be mind-boggling if true. The laws of nature may appear ingenious, but surely they can't be that contrived?

When it comes to weak determinism the situation is less clear-cut. One popular theory of biogenesis is molecular Darwinism,[20] which asserts that biogenesis is a case of "Darwinism all the way down." According to this theory, an ensemble of entities does not have to satisfy the conventional definition of life in order for Darwinian-type evolution to occur. All that is needed is replication, variation, and selection. These criteria could be satisfied by a chemical soup. Suppose a small replicator molecule first forms by pure chance, with a reasonable probability, in such a soup. The population of replicators then multiplies exponentially and undergoes random variations. By definition, the fastest replicators will predominate over the other variants. In a changing environment, evolutionary change will drive onward, perhaps to greater complexity and organization, eventually to the point at which something like life as we know it emerges.

To assess the plausibility of this molecular evolution scenario, consider the following three points:

1. Very little is known about the range of possible molecules that may act as replicators, or how simple they could be. Known organic replicators (e.g., RNA) are all exceedingly complex and unlikely (in the extreme!) to form by chance.

2. It is not enough to produce a replicator molecule per se; it is also necessary for a significant subset of variations of the replicator to also be replicators, or molecular evolution could not proceed.

3. A perfect replicator cannot evolve; evolution needs variation, which implies copying errors during replication. However, if the copying fidelity falls too low, the information content of the molecule will leak away faster than natural selection can inject it, and the process will cease. This is known as Eigen's error catastrophe.[21] As far as replicators from known living organisms are concerned, the simpler the molecule, the less accurate is the copying. This is because accurate copying requires complex molecular machinery. For nucleic acids with less than about 2,500 base pairs, an error catastrophe appears to be unavoidable. Thus, simple replicators containing just a few dozen atoms, of the sort that might form by chance in a chemical soup, would seem to be *extremely* vulnerable to the error catastrophe. The problem is, a genome smaller than this cannot code for the enzymes needed to facilitate the replication process itself. So for nucleic acid based life, the threshold of complexity at which it can even get started is already enormously high, and exceedingly unlikely to emerge by chance.

However, we do not know that the first replicators were nucleic acids or anything remotely like them. Life may have started with some other type of chemical structures (e.g., impure crystals[22]) from which nucleic acids and proteins emerged as byproducts and eventually took over. If this basic scenario is correct, it is conceivable that in nature, fortuitously, there do exist simple replicators of some sort that simultaneously (i) satisfy condition 2 above, (ii) avoid an error catastrophe, and (iii) form by chance with a reasonable probability in a plausible prebiotic medium. Thus, the key question confronting weak biological determinists favoring this scenario is: what is the probability that a functioning replicator, possessing enough complexity to satisfy the above three conditions, will form by chance? In the present state of our knowledge, the answer would still seem to be "exceedingly small," but the question remains open.

Informational Laws. In the second possible version of weak determinism, as yet unknown informational laws operate to create information-rich molecules. This seems to be what Eigen is suggesting when he writes, "Our task is to find an algorithm, a natural law that leads to the origin of information."[23] That is, these laws serve to actually inject information into a physical system, rather than to just shift it about, as is the case with conventional laws of physics. Is this possible? Nobody knows.

Mention of informational laws sometimes provokes accusations of vitalism or mysticism. Yet this seems to be little more than a knee-jerk reaction. Information theory is in its infancy. We recognize that information can be quantified and that it can move around—there exists information flow. There is no straightforward connection between information flow and matter flow. For example, in some situations in quantum field theory, energy may flow in one direction and information in the opposite direction. The dynamics of information have yet to be worked out; there is still no equivalent of Newton's laws of motion for information.

Since information depends on context, it is not a local quantity like mass or electric charge, so it does not rest easily with traditional concepts of dynamics that are all formulated in terms of proximate forces and local interactions. A future "info-dynamics" will link local and global properties of a system in a way that is unfamiliar in conventional physical theories. However, science has several examples in which additional organizing principles are invoked to augment local dynamics. These include Mach's principle in cosmology, cosmic censorship in general relativity, Mendel's laws of genetics, Feigenbaum's numerical relationships in chaos theory, and the quasi-universal properties of cellular automata. In all cases, the principles are consistent with, but not reducible to, the underlying laws of physics. For example, Feigenbaum's numbers are not related to the fundamental constants of physics, nor are Mendel's laws written into the laws of physics. But there is nothing magic or mystical about these principles.

To discover whether such additional organizing principles or informational laws might be relevant to biogenesis, let us explore the interface of quantum mechanics, classical mechanics, and quantum computation. Since information can certainly be quantified, the question arises of whether it is conserved. There is a widespread belief that it is (or at least that information cannot increase in a closed system). However, physicists do not agree about whether information invariably is a conserved quantity.[24] With thermodynamic information, belief that information is a nonincreasing function of time can be rigorously confirmed (at least in a statistical sense); it is equivalent to the second law of thermodynamics. But what about information in other contexts? In quantum mechanics, the basic unit of information is the qubit. It has unusual properties and is unlike the conventional "bit" of classical information theory. The relationship between qubits and bits, when a quantum system "goes over" into a classical system (i.e., the wavefunction "collapses") remains obscure.[25]

We do not know what form of information is relevant to biology, so the crucial question of whether biological information is conserved or not remains open. However, I offer a concluding speculation. Since the creation of a genome primarily is a problem about the emergence of information, or software, from hardware, it is essentially a computational or combinatorial problem—how matter discovers a tiny subset of structures from a vast range of possible, but biologically useless, molecular combinations. Quantum computation is known to be exponentially more efficient than classical computation. Might this hint at an underlying quantum aspect in biogenesis and imply that biological information may have more to do with qubits than bits?

Philosophical and Theological Implications

The philosophical and theological implications of the competing scenarios for the origin of life are starkly different and bear strongly on the possibility of life on other worlds. As Jacques Monod has pointed out, all physical processes are a combination of chance and necessity.[26] By chance one really means contingency, while necessity refers to what most physicists call deterministic law. If chance was the dominant factor, then it is easy to compute that the probability of a known organism forming from random molecular shuffling is absurdly small.[27] Even if one restricts the analysis to the formation of a single small protein, the odds against one such molecule forming anywhere in the observable universe are negligible. This has led many scientists who favor a chance origin for life (which includes Monod) to declare that we are alone in the universe and that the search for extraterrestrial life is pointless.

At the other end of the spectrum are the biological determinists, such as Christian de Duve, who believe that life will inevitably emerge given enough time and suitable conditions.[28] In other words, the emergence of life is a preordained consequence of the laws of nature. Biological determinists do not deny that chance plays a part, only that, at the end of the day, the "cosmic dice" are overwhelmed by the odds in favor of life forming. Although we do not know how many

Earthlike planets there are (and there is disagreement over just how like Earth an Earthlike planet must be in this context), recent astronomical evidence suggests that they may be rather common.[29] If so, and if biological determinism is true, then it is likely that the universe is teeming with life.

It is possible to take a middle position and attribute a large but not stupendous measure of luck to the formation of the appropriate organic molecules, with the difference made up by law, so that life is fairly but not overwhelmingly likely. In this case, there might be a few but not many planets per galaxy with life on them. However, this middle position is rather contrived. Since there is no obvious connection between the processes that bring about the formation of life and the processes that bring about the formation of Earthlike planets, it would be a remarkable coincidence if the two sets of numerics were tuned to each other in this way. If the two processes are independent, then we might expect extraterrestrial life to be either everywhere or nowhere (unless spread by a panspermia mechanism). Expressed differently, on the spectrum that lies between total chance at one end and complete determinism at the other, only an exceedingly tiny window would correspond to sparse life. If the truth lies to the deterministic side of that window, life will be common; and if it lies much to the chance side, it will have happened only once in the observable universe.

By "the observable universe" I mean, roughly, a Hubble volume, this being more or less the limit of our instruments. Some cosmological models provide for a spatially infinite universe with an infinity of stars and planets. In this case extraterrestrial life would be certain; i.e., it occurs with probability one, however small is the probability that life will form, so long as it is nonzero.[30] However, the average distance between inhabited planets generally is immensely greater than a Hubble length, and we would not expect to ever observe an alien biosystem.

I argue that on the spectrum between chance and determinism (or certainty), the closer to determinism the truth lies, the more reason we have to feel "at home in the universe" (to borrow Stuart Kauffman's evocative phrase[31]) and the more circumstantial evidence there would be for some sort of meaning, purpose, or design in nature. I am certainly not the first person to claim this relationship. The link between contingency and atheism has been articulated most eloquently by Monod in his famous book *Chance and Necessity*. He writes, "Man at last knows that he is alone in the unfeeling immensity of the universe, out of which he has emerged only by chance."[32] More recently, Stephen Jay Gould has linked a willingness to believe in the progressive nature of evolution with quasi-religious yearning.[33] Gould's own atheism urges him to resolutely deny any form of biological determinism, since it smacks of the guiding hand of God smuggled into science under the guise of a law of nature. I think both Monod and Gould are absolutely right to perceive bleak atheism in the scenario that life and intelligence are freak accidents, unique in the cosmos. But the flip side is also true. If it turns out that life does emerge as an automatic and natural part of an ingeniously biofriendly universe, then atheism would seem less compelling and something like design more plausible.

NOTES

1. In an interview in the *New York Times* (10 February 1999), Microsoft's Bill Gates is quoted as saying, "It seems quite likely that there's lots of life in the universe."

2. Most of what follows in this essay is based on the more extended discussion given in my book *The Fifth Miracle: The Search for the Origin of Life* (London: Allen Lane, 1998).

3. S. Arrhenius, *Worlds in the Making* (London: Harper, 1908), 216.

4. Arrhenius, *Worlds in the Making*.

5. F. Hoyle and N.C. Wickramasinghe, *Lifecloud* (London: Dent, 1978).

6. C. McKay, "Promethean Ice," *Mercury*, 25 (1996), 15.

7. F. Crick, *Life Itself: Its Origin and Nature* (New York: Simon & Schuster, 1981).

8. P. Weber and M. Greenberg, "Can Spores Survive a Million Years in the Radiation of Outer Space?" *Nature*, 316 (1985), 403; J. Koike et al., "Survival Rates of Some Terrestrial Microorganisms Under Simulated Space Conditions," *Advanced Space Research*, 12 (1992), 4721; G. Horneck et al., "Long-term Survival of Bacterial Spores in Space," *Advanced Space Research*, 14 (1994), 1041.

9. H.J. Melosh, "The Rocky Road to Panspermia," *Nature*, 332 (1988), 687; "Swapping Rocks: Exchange of Surface Material Among the Planets," *The Planetary Report*, 14 (1994), 16; K. Nealson et al., *Mars Sample Return: Issues and Recommendations* (Washington: National Academy Press, 1997); C. Mileikowsky et al., "Natural Transfer of Viable Microbes in Space," *Icarus*, in the press (1999); Davies, *The Fifth Miracle*, chap. 10.

10. T. Gold, *The Deep Hot Biosphere* (New York: Copernicus, 1999).

11. S. Fox and K. Dose, *Molecular Evolution and the Origin of Life* (New York: Marcel Dekker, 1977).

12. See, for example, W. Loewenstein, *The Touchstone of Life* (New York: Oxford University Press, 1998).

13. B.-O. Küppers, *Molecular Theory of Evolution* (New York: Springer-Verlag 1985).

....

14. H. Yockey, *Information Theory and Molecular Biology* (Cambridge: Cambridge University Press, 1992).
15. G.J. Chaitin, *Algorithmic Information Theory* (Cambridge: Cambridge University Press, 1990).
16. Yockey, *Information Theory.*
17. G.J. Chaitin, "Computational Complexity and Godel's Incompleteness Theorem," *ACM SIGACT News*, No. 9 (April 1971), 11.
18. Davies, *The Fifth Miracle,* chap. 10.
19. R. Dawkins, *Climbing Mount Improbable* (London: Viking, 1996).
20. Küppers, *Molecular Theory of Evolution.*
21. M. Eigen, *Steps Towards Life,* trans. P. Woolley (Oxford: Oxford University Press, 1992).
22. A.G. Cairns-Smith, *Seven Clues to the Origin of Life* (Cambridge: Cambridge University Press, 1985).
23. Eigen, *Steps Towards Life,* 12.
24. L. Susskind, "Black Holes and the Information Paradox," *Scientific American,* April 1977, 52.
25. G. Milburn, *The Feynman Processor* (Sydney: Allen & Unwin, 1998).
26. J. Monod, *Chance and Necessity*, trans. A. Wainhouse (London: Collins, 1972).
27. Yockey, *Information Theory.*
28. C. de Duve, *Vital Dust* (New York: Basic Books, 1995).
29. P. Halpern, *The Quest for Alien Planets* (London: Simon & Schuster, 1997).
30. Paul Davies, *Are We Alone?* (London: Penguin, 1995) Appendix 2.
31. S. Kauffman, *At Home in the Universe* (Oxford: Oxford University Press, 1995).
32. Monod, *Chance and Necessity,* 167.
33. S.J. Gould, *Life's Grandeur* (London: Jonathan Cape, 1996).

BERND-OLAF KÜPPERS

Bernd-Olaf Küppers has long focused his attention on basic questions of the natural science and the philosophy of science at the borders of physics, chemistry, and biology. His scientific interests cover a wide range of problems including the theory of biological information, the experimental and theoretical study of molecular evolution, and the epistemological questions of theory formation at the borders of physics and biology.

As a graduate of Göttingen University, where he studied physics, he went on to study with Nobel laureate Manfred Eigen and received a Ph.D. in biophysics from the Technical University of Braunschweig. From 1971 to 1993 he worked at the Max Planck Institute for Biophysical Chemistry in Göttingen. In 1993 Dr. Küppers held a distinguished professorship awarded by the Japanese government. Since 1994, he has been professor of natural philosophy at the Friedrich Schiller University in Jena.

Dr. Küppers is the author of some 100 scholarly papers and winner of the Woitschach Research Prize, awarded by the German Association of Science Foundation. He is a member of the *Deutsche Akademie der Naturforscher Leopoldina* and an external scientific member of the Centre of Human Studies at the University of Munich. He also has received a doctorate from Heidelberg University and an honorary doctorate from Nagaoka University of Technology in Japan.

Dr. Küppers is co-editor of the international journal *Philosophia naturalis,* and is a member of the advisory boards of several other international journals. He has written or edited nine books, including the monographs *Molecular Theory of Evolution* (Springer, 2nd edition, 1985) and *Information and the Origin of Life* (The MIT Press, 1990).

THE WORLD OF BIOLOGICAL COMPLEXITY: ORIGIN AND EVOLUTION OF LIFE

BERND-OLAF KÜPPERS

The problem of the origin and evolution of life represents one of the great challenges of contemporary science. In fact, it proves to be a scientific problem of tremendous complexity, which evokes numerous questions depending on the perspective that we adopt. For this reason we cannot expect to find a single answer to this fundamental problem. Instead, the solution may be to constitute a mosaic of quite different answers that some day may fit together into a coherent picture of the many-sided world of biological complexity.

Any investigation of the origin of life has to start from a basic classification of the facets of the problem. One has to distinguish between the origin of life as a historical event, with all its contingent characteristics, and the origin of life as a physical event, governed by natural laws. The first aspect deals essentially with the historical constraints under which evolution took place on the primordial earth. The second aspect is concerned exclusively with the general principles and the regular properties that are associated with the transition from nonliving to living matter. The physical aspect leaves open the question of which historical path life actually has taken during the early phase of evolution.

However, even if we choose to limit the problem of the origin of life to its physical roots, a variety of quite different questions can still be raised. First, we may ask how a material basis of living systems can originate. This question leads ultimately to the problem of the origin of biological macromolecules such as nucleic acids and proteins. Second, we may ask how macromolecules can organize themselves into complex hyperstructures similar to the living cell. Third, we may ask how such hyperstructures can differentiate and evolve to greater complexity.

These questions are obviously linked to different phases of the origin and evolution of life. The most primitive phase seems to be chemical evolution, which goes over into a phase of molecular self-organization and ends in biological evolution. All three phases together can be considered a gigantic process of material evolution that governs the origin of life. Since the transition from nonliving to living matter is assumed to be a quasi-continuous one, the three phases of evolution cannot be separated from each other in a strict sense. Thus, the above classification serves only to emphasize the fact that there are at least three levels of increasing complexity in evolution.

Despite the fact that there are important aspects of the problem of evolution still waiting for a solution, there is no limitation in principle of our understanding of the origin of life. The known laws of physics and chemistry seem to be sufficient to explain the origin of life as a regular event that takes place of necessity as soon as certain conditions are fulfilled. Physical considerations have led to the development of concepts that imply plausible mechanisms potentially involved in the first steps toward life. Actually, we have more physical models explaining the origin of life than we need, because experimental access limps behind theoretical progress and an experimental testing of all these highly sophisticated concepts is not possible at the moment.

Thus, the present state of our understanding of the origin of life is characterized by a controversial and still undecided debate about a wide variety of physical concepts rather than by a conceptual deficiency or an unbridgeable gap between physics and biology.

STRUCTURAL AND FUNCTIONAL COMPLEXITY

The most significant property of living matter is its extreme complexity, which has two basic aspects: one is structural, the other functional. The structural complexity can be seen directly in the tremendous complexity of biological macromolecules as made "visible" in the three-dimensional structure of those molecules. The functional complexity of living matter is a consequence of the specific organization of biological macromolecules, which is manifest at two levels. Biological macromolecules are long-chain molecules built up from only a few basic kinds of monomers. Thus, any macromolecule is characterized by its specific organization, i.e., by the unique pattern of its monomers. Conversely, the detailed sequence pattern determines the function of a macromolecule. Most of the functional properties of a living being are encoded in such patterns. The catalytically active proteins are the best examples of this kind of functional organization.

The integration of biological macromolecules to give complex aggregates constitutes the second level of molecular organization. At this level, certain self-reproductive and self-sustaining hyperstructures may arise, which could be considered possible precursors of the living cell.

Structural and functional complexity cannot be separated from each other, although functional complexity goes beyond structural complexity. For example, biological macromolecules of the same structural complexity as measured by their chain length can show dramatic differences in their functional capacity. In fact, as far as we know only a tiny fraction of all possible sequences of a macromolecule of given length possesses some functional property such as catalytic activity. The question of how some biologically relevant sequences become selected out of a tremendous number of physically equivalent structures is the well-known statistical problem of the origin of life.

The degree of functional organization is a criterion for the evolutionary stage that a system has reached. But how can we express the idea of functional organization in physical and chemical terms? Certainly, reaction rates or turnover numbers are suitable measures for the efficiency of a catalyst. But such measures, expressed by some number, are inadequate to characterize the kind of function that is associated with this catalyst. They do not allow us to draw any conclusions about the functional organization of living matter, just as a list of telephone numbers fails to tell us anything about life in a town.

We encounter a similar problem if we try to describe the function of a machine exclusively by physical and chemical terms. Again, the efficiency of a machine can be calculated precisely. But this does not tell us anything about its functional properties. The mere knowledge of the efficiency of a machine does not enable us to find out whether this machine is a steam engine or a motor car. Even if we had a complete description of the material properties of a machine, including the list of its components, driving forces, and energy supplies, it would not suffice to specify the machine's function. Rather, we would have to know the detailed arrangement of the components, i.e., the blueprint of the machine, to describe its function fully.

We can express this fact in another way by saying that the organization of a machine is characterized by a specific set of boundaries between the material parts of the system. In their specific form, the boundaries are constraints by which the physical laws are "compelled" to serve a specific purpose for which the machine has been designed. Expressed in an abstract manner: the boundaries act as a selection condition that narrows down the range of all possible physical processes to those that do actually go on in the system. Thus, boundaries play a key part in the understanding of functional complexity.[1]

COMPLEX BOUNDARIES

The idea of boundaries is borrowed from physics in which the boundaries denote the constraints of the system, such as the walls of a gas container or the movement of a bead on a wire. Moreover, in traditional physics the boundaries are considered to be contingent; that is, they are neither random nor determined by laws. They can be structured as they are, but they also can have some other structure. For example, if we change the walls of a gas container within reasonable limits, this will not have any serious influence on the existence and the characteristic features of the system itself.

In contrast to the boundaries of a simple system, the boundaries of a functional system such as a machine are exceptional because they are noncontingent properties of the system. This means that such systems depend critically on their boundaries and that even a marginal change in the boundaries may lead to the collapse of the system's functional properties. However, in the case of machines we normally do not speak of boundaries. Instead we use the term blueprint. A machine's blueprint is said to encode the information for its construction and thereby its function. Thus the terms "noncontingent boundaries" and "information" are equivalent terms in denoting the functional organization of a machine.

The general importance of the concept of boundaries becomes clear if we transfer the machine metaphor to the living organism. Obviously, the organism consists of a hierarchy of boundaries at all levels of complexity. At the phenotypic level, the boundaries are given by the interfaces between the whole and its parts, a relationship for which the machine's construction may be a good illustration. At the genotypic level, these boundaries are encoded in the detailed order of the monomers of an information-carrying nucleic acid molecule. In fact, the nucleic acid itself represents a boundary, i.e., a constraint under which the natural laws operate, and this constraint reduces the huge number of possible physical processes to the number of those that actually take place in the living system.

Michael Polanyi was the first to emphasize the importance of the concept of boundaries, which he claimed to be an irreducible property of living matter.[2] His main argument was that the boundaries encode the blueprint of the living organism and that this does not follow from natural laws, just as little as the blueprint of a machine follows from physics.

Polanyi's reasons for denying the possibility of a complete physical understanding of living systems cannot be refuted easily. Indeed, the concepts of function, purposiveness, and information do not seem to lie within the conceptual framework of physics. In traditional physics this is illustrated by the fact that the boundary conditions—like the walls of a gas container—are considered as contingent constraints to the system that themselves do not follow from physical principles.

Today, the traditional physical approach to biological systems has changed, and Polanyi's view is no longer tenable. Modern concepts of self-organization do attempt to explain the origin of specific boundaries from unspecific physical conditions. Within this framework, the evolution of specific boundaries is thought to start from some contingent initial state. By a dynamic feedback involving some internal mechanism of evaluation, the initial state modifies itself step by step until it gains the specificity and refinement that we associate with well-adapted living systems.

Thus, the genesis of a living being is reflected in the evolution of its boundaries. Since the complex hierarchy of boundaries is encoded in the genome, the genome and its information content represent the primary boundary of any organism. Finally, the problem of the origin of specific boundaries turns out to be equivalent to the problem of the origin of genetic information.

INFORMATION AND THE ORIGIN OF LIFE

It seems clear that the central aspects of living matter, such as organization, functionality, and purposiveness, can only be adequately approached within the framework of information science. Consequently, information science has become a powerful instrument in understanding life and its evolutionary origin.[3]

If we adopt the information-theoretical viewpoint, the problem of the origin of life has two fundamental aspects. One aspect concerns the

syntactic level of information and the selection of potential information carriers (DNA or RNA structures) with defined patterns (nucleotide sequences) out of a virtually unlimited number of physical alternatives. The other aspect concerns the semantic level of information
and the assignment of function to a specific pattern.

Again the dual classification of the problem is somewhat artificial
and is justified only by virtue of its aiding transparency. In a strict sense,
these two levels of information cannot be separated, although the
semantic aspect goes beyond the syntactic one. This is the information-
theoretical version of the relationship between structural and functional complexity.

The syntactic aspect of the origin of genetic information ultimately
is a statistical problem. For example, the smallest proteins in living organisms that are known to possess biological function are built up at
least of one hundred monomers. Even such small molecules have as
many as 10^{130} sequence alternatives. Thus, even for simple biomolecules, the information space possesses tremendous dimensions.

There are good reasons to assume that only a tiny fraction of all sequence alternatives of a biopolymer carry some biologically significant
function. Since under equilibrium conditions all sequences of a given
length have (nearly) the same expectation probability, the realization of
a prespecified pattern by pure chance is practically zero. The argument
of vanishingly small probability for the random origin of genetic information also applies to the random origin of a cellular machinery.[4]

For a long time the statistical problem of the origin of life seemed
to be an unsolvable riddle that indicated the existence of a creator or at
least of some cosmic plan. However, some years ago the statistical
problem proved to be solvable within the framework of the physics of
self-organization. Manfred Eigen was able to demonstrate that under
certain physical conditions a selective self-organization of biological
macromolecules occurs by which the range of all possible macromolecules is narrowed down to those whose information content is adapted
to the prevailing surrounding conditions.[5]

Eigen's theory deals with the general principles of selection and evolution at the molecular level. It integrates a number of concepts such as
those of information space, value gradient, quasi-species, and hypercy-
cles. A coherent presentation of this theory can be found elsewhere.[6]
The explanation of the origin of genetic information given by this theory is an explanation a posteriori; given a certain sequence pattern that

carries meaningful information, the theory explains how such a sequence could become selected out of a huge number of physical alternatives. However, the theory does not make any predictions about the detailed sequence pattern that will evolve. At best some very general statements are possible concerning the symmetry of the pattern, etc.

The limitations result from the fact that there are no physical rules or laws that allow a detailed prediction of the sequence pattern. On the contrary, the sequence pattern of a biologically meaningful piece of information seems to be random in the sense that such a pattern apparently fails to reveal any regularity. In fact, the aperiodicity of syntactic structure seems to be a necessary (not sufficient) prerequisite for an information carrier to encode meaningful information. Consequently, the theory of selective self-organization of matter provides only an explanation for the origin of semantic information as such, without saying anything about the actual information content embedded in these structures.

Of course, the actual information content is the result of the historical pathway that evolution has taken. Therefore, any physical explanation will run into limitations at this point. Nevertheless, the semantic details determine the functional complexity of the living organism, and the increase of this complexity in the course of evolution is a central problem that still requires a rigorous theoretical foundation.

HOW SHOULD THE SEMANTIC ASPECT OF INFORMATION BE APPROACHED?

Within the framework of the Darwinian concept of evolution, the increase of complexity is explained by means of plausibility arguments. For example, it seems to be plausible that systems of high complexity are better adapted to a complex environment than systems of low complexity, and for this reason the functional complexity of the organism gradually increases in evolution. This argument has been designed to close the theoretical gap mentioned above. Yet it has to presuppose the existence of a complex environment if it is not to lead to an impasse. Only within the framework of a given environmental complexity does the evolutionary origin of functional complexity become plausible.

If we translate the Darwinian mode of explanation into the language of information theory, then we have to replace the relationship between the evolving system and its environment with that of a sender and a receiver (or vice versa). According to the information-theoretical view, Darwinian evolution can be understood as a reciprocal interaction between sender and receiver, whereby the environment represents an external source of information that evaluates selectively the information accumulating in the genome. Thus, the evolving information carrier derives its information by selective interaction from the external source of information. This kind of information exchange between the genome and its environment finally leads to the origin of semantic information, i.e. purposive function.

The information-theoretical view of Darwinian evolution brings us back to the basic principle of context-dependence of information.[7] It can be formulated by two theses: information is never absolute but only relative; any information can only have a meaning with respect to some other information. The principle of context-dependence immediately leads to the following questions: How much information is necessary in order to understand some other information? How complex must the context of understanding be?

Clearly, a rigorous analysis of these questions requires a theory of semantic information, which seems to be an extraordinarily difficult task. The term "semantics" refers to the meaning of information. But the meaning of information always depends on the context of understanding between sender and receiver. In fact, the meaning is determined by the interpretation of the information through the receiver.

Obviously, any interpretation involves the historical and singular properties of the interaction between sender and receiver. Thus, the meaning of information is always coupled to some aspect of mutual understanding between sender and receiver that is unique. However, the natural sciences deal with events that can be described by general rules or laws. But how can we expect to have a general rule or law for specifying something that is unique?

There is only one way out of this dilemma: we have to approach the unique from a *network* of general perspectives. Any general aspect yields an incomplete picture of the object under investigation. This is an unavoidable consequence of the methodological approach of abstraction. But by the superposition of more and more general aspects, the object finally regains its unique properties. In other words, the unique aspects of any given structure "crystallize" out of the network of its general aspects when we look at this structure from more and more different sides.

Previously there have been three approaches to the semantic aspect of information. The first approach was put forward by Yehoshua Bar Hillel and Rudolf Carnap within the concept of artificial language.[8] Following the original idea of Claude Shannon and Warren Weaver that the basic nature of information is to reduce uncertainty, they used the degree of novelty as a measure of the content of information. The second approach is to measure the semantics of information by its pragmatic relevance. The pragmatic theory of semantic information is commonly encountered in information science.[9] Recently, a third approach to the semantics of information has been developed on the basis of algorithmic information theory.[10] This concept makes use of the plausible fact that meaningful information can only be encoded in aperiodic patterns.

The algorithmic approach to the semantics of information has far-reaching consequences for our understanding of information-generating systems. For one thing, it can be demonstrated by means of the theory of Turing machines that the complexity of the information-carrying contents represents a threshold value that cannot be crossed by any kind of information-generating process.[11] This theory proves that no machine exists that can generate any information of a complexity greater than that laid down in the machine's own informational structures (impossibility of a perpetual-motion machine of the third kind).

This result also may throw a new light on the problem of the origin and evolution of genetic information. In particular, it raises the question of whether natural evolution could break through the complexity barrier and thus violate the principle of context-dependence. Does natural evolution have the properties of a perpetual motion machine of the third kind? If we answer no, then we have to conclude that the initial complexity of the world must have been very high from the beginning to allow the evolution of complex living beings.[12]

The difficulties encountered in reaching an unambiguous conclusion are due to the fact that the idea of complexity itself is highly ambiguous. It usually refers to quite different aspects of reality, such as structures, functions, and relationships. In particular, algorithmic complexity is an instrument to describe the complexity of genetic programs. However, it is an open question whether this concept also can be applied to the phenotypic aspects of biological complexity.

Although the first steps toward a theory of semantic information already have led to deep insights into the origin and evolution of semantic information, we are still far from having reached solid theoretical ground.

PHILOSOPHICAL IMPLICATIONS

The information-theoretical approach to living matter also throws a new light on some philosophical questions in biology. First, information theory defines life differently from the usual physical ones:

$$Life = Matter + Information$$

At the first glance, this definition looks a little strange. The concept of information is normally used in human communication, and its application to matter seems to indicate a categorical mistake. However, we should remember that the original concept of information is linked— as the word suggests—to that of form. Following Aristotelian thinking, matter and form are inseparable from each other, so that the above definition is altogether in accordance with the standards of the natural sciences. Moreover, if we replace the concept of information with that of boundary conditions, then the information-theoretical definition of life can be immediately translated into the well-established language of physics. As outlined, the boundaries determine the shape, i.e., the form (and information) of a system.

The above definition agrees with the generally accepted view of modern biology that there is no sharp borderline between the nonliving and the living. This in turn has an important epistemological consequence: any theory of life has to introduce a criterion that demarcates those states that are denoted as "living" states from all other states. Normally this criterion is chosen according to the degree of material complexity to be explained by the theory. In any case, it is inevitable that through the demarcation criterion a normative element is introduced into the theory.

We need to take into account this normative aspect when attempting to assess the explanatory capacity of a theory of the origin of life. This underlines once more our earlier statement that any scientific understanding of the origin and evolution of life depends on the perspective we adopt.

Another central philosophical question is that of the relationship between chance and law in the origin and evolution of life. Even among biologists, this question is a matter of strong current controversy. Paradigmatic for the present discussion are the extreme and opposite positions that have been taken by Jacques Monod[13] and Christian de Duve.[14] Monod over-emphasizes the role of chance in the evolution of life, whereas de Duve accentuates the dominant role of natural law. According to Monod, life is the singular result of a highly improbable win in a lottery of nature, whereas de Duve argues that life occurs with deterministic regularity so that its occurrence is inevitable.

Any scientific explanation that uses the hypothesis of singular chance, as put forward by Monod, comes into a basic conflict with scientific standards. Nevertheless, Monod raised an important point. If we translate his basic argument into the language of information science, he claimed essentially that there is no link between the syntactic and the semantic aspects of information. According to this view, the semantics stand in a contingent relationship to the syntax, and the semantics are considered to be an irreducible epiphenomenon of the syntax.

Monod's argument becomes clearer if we demonstrate it at the level of human language. Let us consider a poem by Goethe. From a syntactic point of view, the pattern of letters that constitute the poem seems to be random. In fact, the randomness is expressed by the aperiodicity of the pattern, and this aperiodicity seems to be a necessary condition for coding any meaningful information.

However, the statement that the sequence of letters in a poem by Goethe is random refers exclusively to the property of the pattern. It says nothing about the origin of this pattern. In fact, from all possible sequence alternatives, this special pattern, which represents Goethe's poem, was selected by Goethe to express the information he wished to transmit. Thus, the sole origin of this pattern is in the creativity of Goethe's mind.

In a similar way the genetic program for a living being seems to resemble a grandiose poem of nature. Monod strictly denied the existence of a designer, or of a divine plan, or of a universal algorithm that could have generated the prototype of a meaningful blueprint. Therefore, he found himself forced to make the assumption that the existence of meaningful information, as encoded in living matter, is a pure epiphenomenon of random biopolymers. Moreover, the randomness of those sequence patterns was interpreted by Monod as a proof of his assertion that life is a pure product of chance.

In opposition to the chance hypothesis stands the thesis of strong physical determinism. According to this view, the known laws of nature are assumed to be necessary and sufficient for the generation of life. Thus, life will necessarily occur anywhere in the universe where physical conditions are similar to those on Earth. However, in an unlimited universe we will find such conditions an unlimited number of times.

In de Duve's view, life turns out to be a cosmic imperative. But is this actually reasonable? Let us suppose that the same physical conditions are given that once prevailed on the prebiotic Earth. And let us suppose that living matter arises as a direct consequence of natural laws. Would this mean that life as we know it today is a reproducible event like other physical events? Our answer must be "no." Above all, life is characterized by specific information content that reflects the specific history of its evolution. Although the evolution of this information is subject to the laws of physics and chemistry, the detailed structure of the information reflects the influence of the historical circumstances under which evolution took place.

The mere fact that a dynamic system follows deterministic laws does not justify the claim that the genesis of those systems is exactly reproduced somewhere else. Otherwise the world would be full of steam engines. The view of strong determinism is untenable because it deals with the physical aspect of the origin of life in a dogmatic way. It leads to an overinterpretation of the concept of sufficiency in physical laws by ignoring the influence of history on evolution. Seen from the standpoint of cosmic imperative, the selective feature of our dynamical world is completely lost.

Nevertheless, we may ask how far the historical aspect itself could become the subject of physical explanation. In answer, we must refer again to the concept of boundaries. As demonstrated, the history of a system is reflected in the structure of its boundaries. In traditional physics the boundaries play a subordinate role, in that they are regarded as contingent constraints of the system; in other words, the origin of the boundaries is not the subject of the explanation.

With regard to explanation of the phenomenon of life, the boundaries themselves move into the center of physical explanations. According to modern theory of self-organization, the boundaries develop step by step from unspecific initial conditions. In the future we may derive from the concept of self-organization a general theory of historicity that describes the main principles of the generation and transformation of boundaries. However, the fine structure of any historical pathway will be beyond a lawlike explanation, because the evolution of life must include an unlimited number of bifurcation points that are governed by chance.

Finally, it is a characteristic of the concept of self-organization that any explanation of the boundaries has to start from some other boundaries, which take on the role of initial conditions. Thus, from a physical point of view, the question of the ultimate origin of boundaries necessarily leads into an unending regression cycle. With this epistemological problem, the question of the origin of life seems to be open for metaphysical speculations in the same sense as the initial conditions of the evolution of the universe give rise to manifold speculations about the causal determination of its origin.

NOTES

1. B.-O. Küppers, "Understanding Complexity," in A. Beckerman, H. Flohr and J. Kim, eds., *Emergence or Reduction?* (Berlin: Walter de Gruyter, 1992).
2. M. Polanyi, "Life's Irreducible Structure," *Science,* 160 (1968), 1308.
3. B.-O. Küppers, *Information and the Origin of Life* (Cambridge: MIT Press, 1990).
4. E. Wigner, "The Probability of the Existence of a Self-Reproducing Unit," in E. Shils, ed., *The Logic of Personal Knowledge: Essays in Honor of Michael Polanyi* (Glencoe, IL: Free Press, 1961).
5. M. Eigen, "Self-Organization of Matter and the Evolution of Biological Macromolecules," *Naturwissenschaften,* 58 (1971), 465.
6. B.-O. Küppers, *Molecular Theory of Evolution* (Heidelberg: Springer, 1983).
7. B.-O. Küppers, "The Context-Dependence of Biological Information," in K. Kornwachs and K. Jacoby, eds., *Information: New Questions to a Multidisciplinary Concept* (Berlin: Akademie Verlag, 1995).
8. Y. Bar Hillel and R. Carnap, "Semantic Information," *British Journal for the Philosophy of Science,* 4 (1953), 144.
9. D.M. McKay, *Information, Mechanism and Meaning* (Cambridge: MIT Press, 1969).
10. B.-O. Küppers, "Der semantische Aspekt von Information und seine evolutionsbiologische Bedeutung," *Nova Acta Leopoldina,* 294 (1996), 195.
11. Ibid.
12. Ibid.
13. J. Monod, *Chance and Necessity,* trans. from French, Austryn Wainhouse (New York: Knopf, 1972).
14. Ch. de Duve, *Vital Dust* (New York: Basic Books, 1995).

CHRISTOPHER P. MCKAY

Christopher P. McKay has been a planetary scientist in the Space Science Division of NASA's Ames Research Center since 1982. A graduate of Florida Atlantic University, where he majored in physics, he completed his Ph.D. in 1982 in astrogeophysics at the University of Colorado. Dr. McKay's field work and expeditions include Antarctica, the Siberian arctic permafrost regions, the Gobi Desert, the Lechuguilla Cave in New Mexico, the Canadian Arctic, the Atacoma Desert in Chile, and the Negev Desert in Israel. Associate editor of *Planetary Space Science,* he is a member of the United States Committee for the International Permafrost Association. The author of some 175 scientific papers and the editor of four books, Dr. McKay has helped identify promising locations and approaches for finding evidence of past Martian life. His latest volume (with P.J. Thomas and C.F. Chyba) is *Comets and the Origin and Evolution of Life* (1997).

ASTROBIOLOGY: THE SEARCH FOR LIFE BEYOND THE EARTH

CHRISTOPHER P. MCKAY

Astrobiology has within it three broad questions that have deep philo-sophical as well as scientific import.[1] These are the origin of life, the search for a second genesis of life, and the expansion of life beyond Earth. It may seem unusual that NASA, the U.S. space agency, should be the leader in these areas of research. But indeed the answers to these questions will be found in space, and the astrobiology program com-bines earth, life, and space sciences in addressing these questions. We know enough already that we can frame answerable questions, we even have working hypotheses, and we are developing tools that can extend our reach into the expansiveness of space. We are, to use Churchill's memorable phrase, at "the end of the beginning" of our quest. It is timely then for the science community to look beyond its borders and engage the broader academy and public in a discussion on the nature of astrobiology.

WHY ASTROBIOLOGY MATTERS

We are confident that our experiences in the physics laboratory can be extrapolated over billions of years and over unimaginably small and large length scales. Thus, we can truly see the physical universe in a grain of sand. Not so for biology. To understand the scope and diver-sity of life in the universe may well require that we search the cosmos just as understanding the diversity of life on Earth only came with ex-ploration of the entire planet. At issue here is more than merely catego-rizing the cosmic menagerie. The answer to many basic questions re-lated to the nature of the universe and the form of the laws of physics depends on the search for life elsewhere.

Such questions include: Is life everywhere like Earthlife, implying that life is a phenomenon critically dependent on the particular laws of physics, chemical elements, and ecological environments that life on Earth utilizes? Or are there myriad patterns for life proving thereby that any conceivable universe will sustain life of one sort or another? Is self-awareness a common property of life and does it always follow the same physical, chemical, and social patterns? Do intelligent life forms elsewhere construct symbolic models of the universe that are congruent with our mathematics, science, and philosophy; supporting the argument that understanding comes from accessing another realm of Platonic ideals—a realm common to all intelligent beings? The questions dealing with the basic structure of the universe, its apparent design for life as we know it, and the unfathomable ability of humans to fathom the universe can only be answered adequately when we find other life forms and other intelligences—or conclude, after an exhaustive search, that they are not there to be found.

The search has begun, and by necessity it is a search that takes us off the Earth both literally and through the aid of telescopes. Nonetheless, everything we know about life we have learned on Earth and it therefore provides the framework within which we craft our search strategy. Thus, in the next section I review what we know about life on Earth and what are the immediate questions that arise from our studies of life. Next I turn to Mars, the most likely target for a search for a second independent example of life. I then consider how life from Earth might expand to Mars and the ethical considerations associated with such an activity. Finally, I discuss the implicit philosophical basis of our approach to astrobiology.

LIFE AS WE KNOW IT

Of the everyday phenomena that science has sought to investigate and understand, life is one of the most readily observed and yet most challenging to explain. By studying life on Earth and investigating the fossil record we have developed a mostly empirical understanding. A summary of the main points follows.

Only One Example of Life on Earth
All organisms examined to date have the same basic biochemical and genetic makeup and are related by common descent. The basic biochemical similarity of living things is one of the profound results of bi-

FIGURE 1
PHYLOGENETIC UNITY OF LIFE

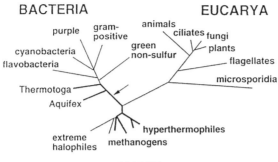

A phylogenetic tree showing the relatedness of all life on Earth. The arrow indicates the probable location of the common ancestor to all extant life on Earth.

ology. The great diversity of life forms on Earth are really just morphological variations on a single fundamental biochemistry.[2] Every life-form on Earth carries RNA and DNA that use just 5 nucleotide bases. The proteins that constitute the machinery of biochemistry are based on twenty left-handed amino acids. The essential biomolecules of life are these nucleotide bases and amino acids, plus a few sugars, from which polysaccharides are constructed, and some simple alcohols and fatty acids that are the building blocks of lipids.

Not only do all organisms on Earth share the same basic genetic code, but they all show clear evidence, in this code, of shared descent. Certain conserved portions of the genetic material can be found in all life forms and therefore can be used to make a universal tree of life showing the evolutionary relationship among all organisms. This is the phylogenetic unity of life shown in Figure 1. Life on Earth is divided into three main groups: the eucarya, the bacteria, and the archaea. The eucarya include the multicellular life forms encompassing all plants and animals. The bacteria are the familiar bacteria including intestinal bacteria, common soil bacteria, and the pathogens. The archaea are a class of microorganisms that are found in unusual and often harsh environments such as hypersaline ponds and hydrogen rich anaerobic sediments.

Life on Earth Is a Material System
This material system undergoes the Darwinian evolution of reproduction, mutation, and selection. Clearly a precise definition of life would

help unravel the origin of life on Earth and would be the first step toward a fundamental theory of life that could be generalized to life elsewhere. Despite the observed unity of biochemistry and the universality of the genetic code, no single definition has proven adequate in describing life.[3] Many of the attributes that we would associate with life, for example, self-replication, self-ordering, and response to environmental stimuli can be found in nonliving systems: fire, crystals, and bimetallic thermostats, respectively. Furthermore, there are various and peculiar life forms such as viruses and giant cell-less slime molds that defy even a biological definition of life in terms of the cell or the separation of internal and external environments. To resolve this problem, the most useful definition of life is that it is a material system that develops Darwinian evolution: reproduction, mutation, selection. This answers the question of what does life do.

Minimal Requirements for Life[4]
The list of requirements include energy, mostly supplied by sunlight; carbon; liquid water; and a few other elements, notably N, P, and S. Of these, water in the liquid state is the one that is rare on the other planets. Energy is required for life from basic thermodynamic considerations. Typically on the Earth, this energy is provided by sunlight, that is a thermodynamically efficient (low entropy) energy source. Some limited systems on Earth can derive their energy from chemical reactions (e.g., methanogenesis,[5] $CO_2 + 4H_2 \rightarrow CH_4 + 2H_2O$) and do not depend on photosynthesis. On Earth these systems are confined to locations where the more typical photosynthetic organisms are not able to grow, and it is not clear if an ecosystem that was planetary in scale or survived over billions of years could be based solely on chemical energy. There are no known organisms that can obtain their metabolic energy from thermal gradients, the way a heat engine does, or from electomagnetic fields, the way an electric motor does. Many organisms derive their metabolic energy by consuming other organisms, ultimately consuming primary producers.

On Earth, carbon is the backbone molecule of biochemistry, but life almost certainly requires other elements as well. Known life forms utilize a vast array of the elements available on the surface of the Earth. However, this does not prove that these elements are absolute requirements for life. Among the elements other than carbon, nitrogen, phosphorus, and sulfur are probably the leading candidates for the status of required elements.

Liquid water is the quintessential requirement for life on Earth. Liquid water is the solvent in which biochemical reactions take place and the water molecules themselves interact with many biochemicals in ways that influence their properties. Sunlight, carbon, and the other elements required for life are common in the solar system. What appears to be the ecologically limiting factor for life on other planets is the occurrence of liquid water. Thus in our solar system and beyond, the search for life may be, for all intents and purposes, equated with a search for liquid water.

With only one example of life to study, it is perhaps not surprising that we do not know what is particular and what is universal in biochemistry. For example, evolution could occur using an information storage mechanism that is not DNA/RNA based. There have been suggestions of living systems based on chemistries completely different to biology on Earth. Popular suggestions include substituting ammonia for water or silicon for carbon. Although speculations of alien biochemistry are intriguing, no specific experiments directed toward alternate biochemistry have been designed. Thus, we have no strategies for where or how to search for such alternate life or its fossils. In the future we may develop general theories for life based on observations of many and diverse life forms. Basing our current theories and search strategies on the one type of life we know should be considered a practical limitation and not a fundamental issue.

Life Appeared Rapidly after Formation of the Earth

The origin of life remains a scientific mystery. Despite impressive advances in the abiological synthesis of important biomolecules since the early work of Miller,[6] the processes that lead to life have not been duplicated in the laboratory. The record of the events on Earth have been destroyed and there is a scarcity of data. There is, however, an abundance of theories. W.L. Davis and I have compared the published theories for the origin of life and the applicability of each of these theories to the possible origin of life on Mars.[7] Figure 2 shows a diagrammatic representation of the theories for the origin of life.

While we do not know how life originated on the Earth, there is good evidence as to the timing. The end of the accretionary phase for the formation of the inner planets is believed to have been about 3.8 Gyr ago. The oldest direct fossil evidence for life is 3.5 Gyr old[8] (Figure 3), and there is persuasive isotopic evidence for life at 3.9 Gyr ago.[9] The oldest fossils on Earth include microfossils and stromatolites—layered

FIGURE 2
CLASSIFICATION OF CURRENT THEORIES FOR THE ORIGINS OF LIFE

Theories for the Origins of Life

Extraterrestrial Origins of Life

Terrestrial Origins of Life

Random Panspermia

Directed Panspermia

Organic Origins

Inorganic Origins

Clay Organisms

Organic Energy Source

Nonorganic Energy Source

Exogenous Delivery of Organics

Endogenous Production of Organics

Hetero-trophic Organisms

Photo-synthetic Organisms

Chemo-synthetic Organisms

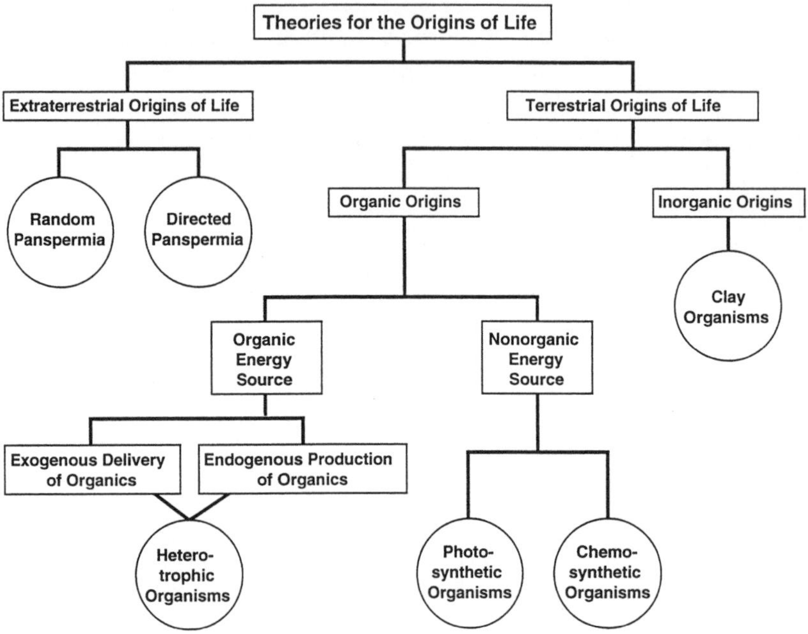

sedimentary structures produced by microorganisms. The major events in the history of life on Earth (and Mars) are shown in Figure 4.

It is likely that the high impact rate during the accretion would have rendered the surface of Earth and Mars uninhabitable.[10] It is not

FIGURE 3
EARLIEST FOSSIL EVIDENCE FOR LIFE ON EARTH

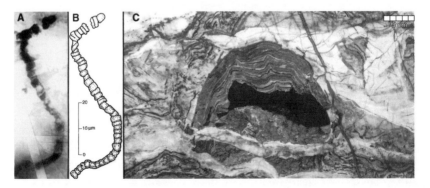

A 3.5 billion-year-old stromatolite and associated microfossil.

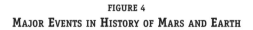

FIGURE 4
MAJOR EVENTS IN HISTORY OF MARS AND EARTH

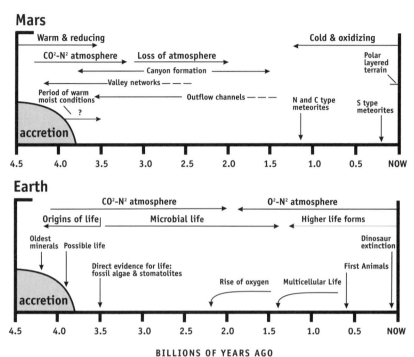

The period of moist surface conditions on Mars may have corresponded to the time during which life originated on Earth. The similarities between the two planets at this time raises the possibility of the origin of life on Mars.

known when the last life-threatening impact occurred, but it is likely that the Earth was not suitable for life much before 3.8 Gyr ago. The early evidence for life suggests that the time required for the appearance of life was brief. If the sediments at 3.9 Gyr are taken as evidence for life, it suggests that, within the resolution of the geological record, life arose on Earth as soon as a suitable habitat was provided that must then have been at least 100 Myr before the end of the accretion.

Microscopic Life on Earth until High Levels of Oxygen
As recognized by A.H. Knoll,[11] the buildup of oxygen was the key variable in the evolution of complex multicellular life on Earth and could vary considerably on other habitable planets. Following Knoll, we identify the rise of oxygen and concomitant development of tissue

multicellularity as the rate-determining critical step in the evolution of intelligence.[12] All other steps are rapid by comparison. Oxygen levels on the Earth appear to have increased about 2.2 Gyr ago, but present levels were not reached until much later. The rise of multicellular life about 600 Myr ago appears to be correlated with, and is thought to be contingent on, the rise of free oxygen to power metabolism.

Oxygen buildup appears to have been controlled by the competing forces of biological production of oxygen and its geological removal. Oxygenic photosynthesis could have plausibly originated quite early on the Earth.[13] However, the oxygen produced would have been consumed by volcanic gases and organic recycling—and thus the first indication of oxygen in the atmosphere is about 2 Gyr after the origin of life (see Figure 4). Mars, with a much thinner ocean, reduced volcanism, and no plate tectonics to power global recycling of sediments, may have experienced the rise of oxygen much earlier than the Earth.[14] Similarly, other planets with differing geology might take longer to show a buildup in atmosphere oxygen.

Technological Intelligence

By the time technological intelligence arose on the Earth, the Sun was halfway through its expected lifetime. Technological intelligence, defined as the ability to communicate over interstellar distances, arose on the Earth only in the present millenium, some 5 Gyr after the formation of the Sun and the planetary system. The Sun has an expected lifetime of 10 Gyr before it becomes a red giant and consumes the Earth. The Earth may become uninhabitable in only a few hundred million years as the continuing brightening of the Sun results in Venuslike conditions.

QUESTIONS

Perhaps equally as important as what we know about life are the outstanding questions about it. In the context of astrobiology, I list the main questions as follows.

- How did life on Earth originate?
- What aspects of biochemistry are invariant?
- Is there life on other planets?
- Are there other intelligent life forms in the cosmos?
- What is the future role of life in the evolution of the cosmos?

MARS: THE SEARCH FOR A SECOND GENESIS

The discovery of a second genesis of life would be of scientific and general interest. There are currently three independent programs directed toward a search for a second type of life: laboratory synthesis of self-replicating systems, the search for life on Mars and Europa, and SETI. The second of these I consider here.

Although the Viking results indicated that the Martian surface is dry and lifeless, the orbital images, such as Figure 5, showed clear evidence that liquid water flowed on the surface of Mars in the past. From a biological perspective the existence of liquid water, by itself, motivates the question of the origin of life on Mars.[15] Fluvial features indicative of the slow stable flow of liquid water are not consistent with the present Martian climate and are thus evidence that Mars had a thicker warmer atmosphere early in its history. Mars and Earth may have been comparable worlds, both containing liquid water, during the early history of the solar system, during the time life first appeared on Earth.

The hypothesis that Mars was more Earthlike during its early history and then experienced a change that made it the cold desert world we observe today is corroborated by the twelve meteorites on Earth thought to have come from Mars. Eleven of the twelve Martian meteorites are relatively young, having formed on Mars between 200 and 1,300 million years ago. Their chemical structure indicates that they formed under conditions similar to the cold, dry, oxidizing environment of Mars today. However, one specimen known as ALH84001 is old, having formed on Mars about 4.5 Gyr ago under warm, reducing conditions. There are even indications that it contains Martian organic material. This rock formed during the time period when Mars is thought to have had a warm, wet climate capable of supporting life— even if the fossil evidence in the meteorite remains debatable.

The potential origins of life on Mars can best be approached by analogy to Earth because of the indications that the environments on Earth and Mars were similar during the time in which life first appeared on Earth. This approach is necessary because there is no consensus theory for the origins of life on Earth. This comparative approach to the origins of life assumes that the development of life is a fundamental and reproducible process and will occur given suitable chemical and physical conditions. The universal requirement common to all the theories for the origins of life is liquid water. The direct evi-

FIGURE 5
ORBITAL IMAGES OF MARS

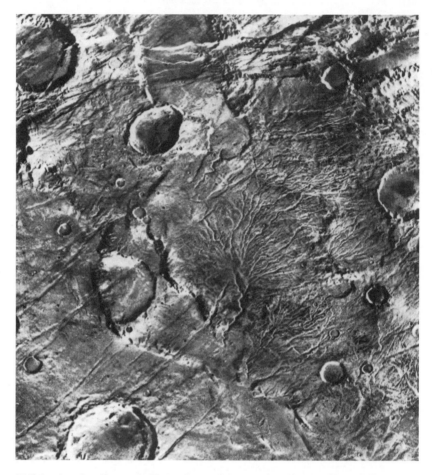

Well-developed valley network in the ancient cratered terrain. These valleys were probably formed under a significantly warmer climate—presumably caused by a denser atmosphere—than the present Mars. This evidence for the stability of liquid water in the Martian surface 3.8 Gyr ago is the primary motivation for considering the possible origin of life on Mars.

dence of liquid water on early Mars is consistent therefore with all theories for the origins of life.

The search for fossils on Mars would focus on microfossils and stromatolites (Figure 3). Stromatolites are an important form of fossil evidence of life because they form macroscopic structures that could be found on Mars. It is therefore possible that a search for stromatolites near the shores of an ancient Martian lake or bay could be conducted in the near future. Expecting microbial communities to have formed stromatolites on Mars is not entirely misplaced geocentricism. The properties of a microbial mat community that result in stromatolite formation need only be those associated with photosynthetic uptake of CO_2. There are broad ecological properties that we expect to hold on Mars even if the details of the biochemistry and community structure of Martian microbial mats were quite alien compared with their terrestrial counterparts. Within stromatolites, trace microfossils sometimes can be found.

While convincing fossils from Mars would show that there had been life present on that planet they would not by themselves provide evidence of a second genesis. It is possible that life on Mars and Earth share a common origin. Life could have been carried from Earth to Mars and vice versa. To determine if Martian life was indeed a second genesis requires that we analyse the biochemicals of an actual Martian organism—either dead or alive. Access to Martian biomaterial may be possible if it has been preserved in the southern polar permafrost.

HUMANS, ETHICS, AND EXPANSION OF LIFE BEYOND EARTH

One of the new questions in the astrobiology program is what is the potential for survival and biological evolution beyond the planet of origin? In our solar systems, Mars provides the best target for biological survival and evolution beyond the Earth. Indeed, the observation that Mars was once a habitable world leads us to ponder how Mars became a cold harsh desert and to speculate under what conditions, natural or artificial, it could be restored to a habitable state. Could humans play a role in restoring Mars to life, and restoring life to Mars? If it is possible, should such a thing be done? These questions deal with the future of life and the role of humans in that future.

The physics of restoring Mars to habitable conditions is straightforward.[16] The fundamental challenge is that of warming up a world by a few tens of degrees Celsius—similar to what we are doing on the Earth. The ethical aspects of ecosynthesis on Mars are less clear. Historically, environmental ethics had focused on Earth with the understandable conflation of nature and biology that results. It is not clear then how one extends our principles of environmental ethics from Earth to Mars. For example, consider A. Leopold's "Land Ethic": "A thing is right when it tends to preserve the integrity, stability, and beauty of the biotic community. It is wrong if it tends to do otherwise."[17] How do we apply this to Mars on which there is no biotic community? Do we preserve nature on Mars and value it just because it "is"?

As an alternative view, consider the first two tenets of *Deep Ecology*.[18] First, the well-being of nonhuman life on Earth has value in itself. This value is independent of any instrumental usefulness for limited human purposes. Second, richness and diversity in life forms contribute to this value and is a further value in itself. Would a rich and diverse biosphere on Mars have value? More value than the fascinating but dead world we explore today?

Considering the possibility of ecosynthesis on Mars forces us to realize that on Earth nature is equivalent to life, but beyond the Earth this is not the case. We must generalize our approach to environmental ethics.[19]

IMPLICATIONS OF ASTROBIOLOGY

From our discussion, it is clear that the search for life beyond the Earth is based on the assumption that our experience of life on Earth is typical for the cosmos—the Copernican principle. We assume that we are not unique and that similar events have occurred numerous times in numerous places. The Copernican principle is well established only for stars and elements. We know that the chemical elements found in our solar system exist elsewhere and we know that our Sun is not an unusual star. We may be just beginning to establish the existence of planets around other stars completing another step in the train of logic. The Copernican principle is not established with respect to biology, culture, or ethics. In this context, the question "Are we alone?" is a deep philosophical question.

That we must look beyond the Earth to address these questions is clear. In a fundamental way we seek to place the Earth, life, and most important our unique role as intelligent beings on this Earth in the broader context. In the past we have sought answers to these questions from pure logic or through spiritual revelation. Now, for the first time, we can begin a direct investigation that may construct a framework within which we may find the answers to these questions.

NOTES

1. Astrobiology is a program within NASA. Program updates and further background information are available through the NASA Web Site at www.nasa.gov.
2. A.L. Lehninger, *Biochemistry* (New York: Worth, 1975).
3. There exists extensive discussion in the literature on this topic. See C.P. McKay and W.L. Davis, "Planets and the Origin of Life," in P. Weissman, L. McFadden, and T. Johnson, eds., *Encyclopedia of the Solar System* (San Diego: Academic Press, 1999), 899–922.
4. The list of requirements for life used here is from C.P. McKay, "Urey Prize Lecture: Planetary Evolution and the Origin of Life," *Icarus*, 91 (1991), 92–100.
5. T.O. Stevens and J.P. McKinley, "Lithoautotrophic Microbial Ecosystems in Deep Basalt Aquifers," *Science*, 270 (1995), 450–454.
6. The original work was published in S.L. Miller, "A Production of Amino Acids under Possible Primitive Earth Conditions," *Science*, 117 (1953), 528–529. For a recent review see S.L. Miller, "The Prebiotic Synthesis of Organic Compounds as a Step Toward the Origin of Life," in J.W. Schopf, ed., *Major Events in the History of Life* (Boston: Jones and Bartlett, 1992) 1–28.
7. W.L. Davis and C.P. McKay, "Origins of Life: A Comparison of Theories and Application to Mars," *Origins of Life and Evolution of the Biosphere*, 26 (1996), 61–73.
8. J.W. Schopf, ed., *Earth's Earliest Biosphere: Its Origin and Evolution* (Princeton, N.J.: Princeton University Press, 1983); J.W. Schopf, "Microfossils of the Early Archean Apex Chert: New Evidence for the Antiquity of Life," *Science*, 260 (1993), 640–646; J.W. Schopf and B.M. Packer, "Early Archean (3.3-billion to 3.5-billion-year-old) Microfossils from Warrawoona Group, Australia," *Science*, 237 (1987), 70–73.
9. M. Schidlowski, "A 3,800-Million-Year Isotopic Record of Life from Carbon in Sedimentary Rocks," *Nature*, 333 (1988), 313–318; S.J. Mojzsis, G. Arrhenius, K.D. McKeegan, T.M. Harrison, A.P. Nutman, and C.R.L. Friend, "Evidence for Life on Earth before 3,800 Million Years Ago," *Nature*, 384 (1996), 55–59.
10. N.H. Sleep, K.J. Zahnle, J.F. Kasting, and H.J. Morowitz, "Annihilation of Ecosystems by Large Asteroid Impacts on the Early Earth," *Nature*, 342 (1989), 139–142.
11. A.H. Knoll, "The Precambrian Evolution of Terrestrial Life," in M.D. Papagiannis, ed., *The Search for Extraterrestrial Life: Recent Developments* (Dordrecht: Reidel, 1985), 201–211.
12. C.P. McKay, "Time for Intelligence on Other Planets," in L. R. Doyle, ed., *Circumstellar Habitable Zone* (Menlo Park: Travis House Publications, 1996), 405–419.
13. C.P. McKay and H. Hartman, "Hydrogen Peroxide and the Origin of Oxygenic Photosynthesis," *Origins of Life*, 21 (1991), 157–163.
14. C.P. McKay, "Oxygen and the Rapid Evolution of Life on Mars," in J. Chela-Flores and F. Raulin, eds., *Chemical Evolution: Physics of the Origin and Evolution of Life* (Dordrecht: Kluwer, 1996), 177–184.
15. C.P. McKay, "The Search for Life on Mars," *Origins of Life and Evolution of the Biosphere*, 27 (1997), 263–289.

16. C.P. McKay, O.B. Toon, and J.F. Kasting, "Making Mars Habitable," *Nature*, 352 (1991), 489–496: C.P. McKay, "Bringing Life to Mars," *Scientific American Presents*, 10 (1) (Spring 1999), 52–57.
17. A. Leopold, *A Sand County Almanac*, (New York: Ballantine Books, 1966).
18. A. Naess, "The Shallow and the Deep, Long-Range Ecology Movement: A Summary," *Inquiry*, 16 (1973), 95–100.
19. C.P. McKay, "Does Mars have Rights? An Approach to the Environmental Ethics of Planetary Engineering," in D. MacNiven, ed., *Moral Expertise* (London and New York: Routledge, 1990), 184–197.

PART II
HUMANITY'S PLACE IN COSMIC EVOLUTION

MARTIN J. REES

One of the world's leading theoretical astrophysicists, **Martin J. Rees**, England's Astronomer Royal, was for many years the director of Cambridge University's famed Institute of Astronomy. Since 1992 he has been the Royal Society Research Professor at Cambridge and an official fellow at King's College, Cambridge. A graduate of Cambridge, where he studied at Trinity College, he took an undergraduate degree in mathematics and earned a Ph.D. in theoretical astronomy in 1967. He was a fellow of Jesus College, Cambridge, a research fellow at California Institute of Technology, and a staff member of Cambridge University's Institute of Theoretical Astronomy before becoming a professor of astronomy at the University of Sussex in 1972. Dr. Rees has lectured around the world and been a visiting professor at Caltech, Harvard, and the Institute for Advanced Study in Princeton, as well as a Regents Visiting Fellow at the Smithsonian Institution. He has served as president of the International Astronomical Union's Commission on High Energy Physics, the Royal Astronomical Society, and the British Association for the Advancement of Science and is currently a trustee of the British Museum. Dr. Rees was knighted by Queen Elizabeth II in 1992. He has won a dozen major scientific prizes, including, most recently, the Bowser Prize of Philadelphia's Franklin Institute, and holds honorary degrees from seven universities. A member of the editorial boards of a number of leading scientific journals, he has published some 350 research papers and three technical books. His latest volume is *Before the Beginning* (1997).

LIFE IN OUR UNIVERSE AND OTHERS: A COSMOLOGICAL PERSPECTIVE

MARTIN J. REES

I am diffident about contributing to a volume with a theological slant, especially as scientists so often reveal themselves as naive in this arena. A further reason for diffidence is that despite my enthusiasm about the progress and prospects in cosmology, I am dubious that cosmologists have much that is new to contribute to the dialogue between cosmology and religion. Modern developments are clearly relevant to naive "creationism" and to the "arguments from design" of nineteenth-century natural theology. Moreover, the progress in elucidating the underlying laws leaves less room either for "vitalism," or for "animist" concepts of the spirit world. But do they really have an impact on more sophisticated world views?

It is interesting to note that E.O Wilson, in his brilliant recent book *Consilience*, regards deism (though not of course theism in general) as "a problem in astrophysics"![1] In my view there is little qualitative change in the interface between cosmology and religion since Newton's time. Modern concepts of the scale of our universe—in time and space—do nonetheless change our perceptions of the likely role of terrestrial life. I shall address these questions from a cosmological perspective and venture into more speculative territory by raising the question of whether there could be, beyond our observable universe, other domains governed by different physical laws.

THE COSMIC CONTEXT: ORIGIN OF ATOMS, STARS, AND PLANETS

I take my text from Darwin's famous closing words of the *Origin of Species*: "Whilst this planet has been cycling on according to the fixed law of gravity, from so simple a beginning forms . . . most wonderful have been, and are being, evolved." Cosmologists aim to trace things back before Darwin's "simple beginning"—to set our solar system in a grander cosmic context, traceable right back (we believe) to a Big Bang.

Stars and the Periodic Table

Our Sun is four and one-half billion years old, but less than half of its central hydrogen has so far been used up: it will keep shining for a further five billion years. It will then swell up to become a red giant, large and bright enough to engulf the inner planets, and to vaporize all life on Earth. After this red giant phase, some outer layers are blown off, leaving a white dwarf, a dense star no larger than the Earth, that will shine with a dull glow, no brighter than the full Moon today, on whatever remains of the solar system.

To conceive these vast timespans—future as well as past—a metaphor helps. Suppose you represent the Sun's life by a walk across America, starting in New York when the Sun formed, and reaching California ten billion years later, when the Sun is about to die. To make this journey, you would have to take one step every two thousand years. All recorded history would be just a few steps. Moreover, these steps would come just before the half-way stage that is somewhere in Kansas, perhaps—not the high point of the journey. This perspective has an impact on how we should see our species. The progression toward diversity has much further to go. Even if life is now unique to the Earth, there is time for it to spread from here through the entire galaxy, and even beyond. We may be nearer to the simple beginning than to any endpoint of evolution.

Astrophysicists can compute, just as easily, the life cycle of a star that is half, twice, or ten times the mass of the Sun. Smaller stars burn their fuel more slowly. Stars ten times as heavy as the Sun—the four blue Trapezium stars in Orion, for instance—shine thousands of times more brightly, and consume their fuel more quickly. We can check our theory by observing other stars like the Sun, which are at different stages in their evolution. Having a single snapshot of each star's life is not a fatal handicap if we have a large sample, born at different times, available for study.

Heavy stars expire violently, by exploding as supernovae. The nearest supernova of modern times was seen in 1987. On February 23–24, a new bright star appeared in the southern sky that had not been visible the previous night. Astronomers have studied this particular supernova, how it fades and decays. They have even found, on images taken before the explosion, that the precursor was a blue star of about twenty solar masses.

Supernovae fascinate astronomers because they offer a chance to test theories of this dramatic and complicated phase in the life of stars. These stellar explosions, occurring thousands of light years away, played a fundamental part in shaping everyone's environment: they created the mix of atoms of which we, and the Earth, are made.

When a heavy star has consumed its available hydrogen, its core contracts and heats up, until the helium can itself react. When the core helium is itself all consumed, the star contracts and heats up still more, releasing energy via a succession of reactions involving progressively heavier nuclei: carbon, oxygen, silicon, and so forth. Material gets processed further up the periodic table. For stars heavier than about 8 solar masses, this continues, each step releasing further energy, until the core has been transmuted into iron. But it is an iron nucleus more tightly bound than any other. The star then faces an energy crisis, it cannot draw on any further nuclear sources.

The consequences are dramatic. Once the iron core gets above a threshold size (about 1.4 solar masses), it suddenly collapses down to the size of a neutron star. This releases enough energy to blow off the overlying material in a colossal explosion—a supernova. Moreover, this material has by then an "onion-skin" structure, the hotter inner layers have been processed further up the periodic table. The debris thrown back into space contains the mix of elements. Oxygen is the most common, followed by carbon, nitrogen, silicon, and iron. There are traces of the others. Moreover, the proportions agree with those observed on Earth. At first sight, the heavier atoms might seem a problem. The iron nucleus is more tightly bound than any other, and it is only number 26 in the periodic table. It takes an input of energy to build up the still heavier nuclei. But a very hot blast wave that blows off the outer layers can produce small traces of the rest of the periodic table, right up to uranium.

The oldest stars were formed about ten billion years ago from primordial material that contained only the simplest atoms—no carbon, no oxygen, and no iron. Chemistry would then have been a very dull subject. And there could certainly have been no planets around these first stars. Why are carbon and oxygen atoms so common here on Earth, but gold and uranium so rare? The answer—one of the undoubted triumphs of twentieth-century astrophysics—involves stars that exploded before our solar system formed. Our galaxy is like a vast ecosystem, recycling gas through successive generations of stars, gradually building up the entire periodic table. Before our Sun even formed, several generations of heavy stars could have been through their entire life cycles, transmuting pristine hydrogen into the basic building blocks of life: carbon, oxygen, iron, and the rest. We are literally the ashes of long-dead stars.

Planets?

One fascinating question is whether there are planets orbiting other stars. "Catastrophist" ideas on planet formation long ago fell from favor, astronomers now suspect planetary systems to be common because protostars, as they contract from rotating clouds, spin off discs of dusty gas around them. The dusty cloud in Orion, although denser than most of the expanses between the stars, is still very rarified. For a region in this cloud to become a star, it contracts so much that its density rises by a billion billion. Any slight spin would have been amplified during the collapse (a cosmic version of the well-known spin up when an ice skater pulls in his or her arms) until centrifugal forces prevented all the material from joining the star. Protostellar discs have been observed in Orion and are the natural precursors of planetary systems. They are dense enough that dust particles would collide frequently with each other, sticking together to build up rocky lumps; these in turn coalesce into larger systems, which merge to make planets. Our solar system formed in this way, and there is every reason to expect many other stars to be orbited by retinues of planets. Fully-formed planets orbiting other stars are, however, harder to detect that their precursor discs. But a real astronomical highlight of the late 1990s has been the discovery of compelling indirect evidence for planets. This evidence comes from the detection of the wobble they induce in the motion of the central star. In 1995 two Swiss astronomers found that the Doppler shift of 51 Pegasi, a nearby star resembling our Sun, was varying sinusoidally by 50 m/sec. They inferred that an orbiting planet weighing one thousandth as much was circling it at 50 km/sec, causing the star to pivot around the combined center of mass.

Several more planets have been discovered by astronomers in California. But the planets inferred so far are all big ones like Jupiter. They may be the largest members of other planetary systems like our own, but individual Earthlike planets would be a hundred times harder to detect. The observed "Jupiters" are also closer to their parent stars than Jupiter is to our Sun. These other solar systems are not like ours. But this probably is a selection effect; it would need more sensitive measurements, and a longer timespan of observations, to detect the smaller-amplitude and slower wobble induced by a heavy planet in an orbit like Jupiter's.

The actual layout of our solar system is the outcome of many accidents. In particular, our Moon was torn from Earth by a collision with another protoplanet. The odd spin of Uranus (around an axis in the plane of its orbit) may indicate another large collision. The craters on the Moon bear witness to the violence of Earth's early history, before the planetesmals had been depleted by impacts or coalescence. Space probes that have now visited the planets show that they (and their larger moons) are highly distinctive worlds. There is no reason to expect other solar systems to have the same configurations or same numbers of planets.

Planets on which life could evolve, as it did here on Earth, must be rather special. Their gravity must pull strongly enough to prevent the atmosphere from evaporating into space; they must be neither too hot nor too cold and therefore the right distance from a long-lived and stable star. There may be other special circumstances required. For example, Jupiter has been claimed to be essential to life on Earth because its gravity "scoured out" the asteroids and reduced the rate of catastrophic impacts on Earth; also, the tides induced by our large Moon may have stimulated some phases in evolution. But even if there are extra requirements like this, planetary systems are (we believe) so common in our galaxy that Earthlike planets would be numbered in millions.

As a foreigner, I follow the U.S. space programs with immense interest and general admiration. I am depressed at NASA's vast commitment to the space station, but delighted that a search for Earthlike planets has become a main thrust of the space program. This is a long-range goal that will require vast optical interferometers in space, but it will stimulate much excellent science on the way. And once a candidate has been found, several things could be learnt about it. Suppose an astronomer forty light years away had detected our Earth; it would be, in Carl Sagan's phrase, a "pale blue dot," seeming very close to a star (our Sun) that outshines it by many million. If Earth could be seen at all, its light could be analyzed and would reveal that it had been transformed (and oxygenated) by a biosphere. The shade of blue would be slightly different depending on whether the Pacific Ocean or the Eurasian land mass was facing us. Distant astronomers could therefore, by repeated observation, infer the Earth was spinning and learn the length of its day, and even infer something of its topography and climate.

LIFE ON OTHER PLANETS?

What fascinates people most—and what motivates NASA's interest—is whether there is life out there. Even when a planet offers a propitious environment, what is the chance that simple *organisms* emerge? Life on earth has occupied an immense variety of niches. The ecosystems near hot sulphurous outwellings in the deep ocean bed tell us that not even sunlight is essential. We still do not know how or where terrestrial life began. Was it in Darwin's "warm little pond," or deep underground, or even in dusty molecular clouds in space?

And what were the odds against life getting started? We still do not know whether life's emergence is natural, or whether it involves a chain of accidents so improbable that nothing remotely like it has happened on another planet anywhere else in our galaxy. That is why it would be so crucial to detect life, even in simple and vestigial forms, elsewhere in our solar system—on Mars or under the ice of Europa. If it had emerged twice within our solar system, this would suggest that the entire galaxy would be teeming with life. That momentous conclusion would follow provided that the two origins were indeed independent. That is an important proviso: for instance, if meteorites from Mars could impact on the Earth, maybe we are all Martians; conversely, Mars could have been seeded by reverse traffic from the Earth. If an Earthlike planet could be detected in orbit around another star, its light could be analyzed and would reveal that it had been transformed (and oxygenated) by a biosphere.

But there is another issue about which the uncertainties are perhaps even greater. Even when simple life exists, we do not know the chances that it evolves toward intelligence.

The year 2000 marks the fourth centenary of the death of Giordano Bruno, burnt at the stake in Rome, and an early believer in inhabited worlds. Ever since his time, this belief has been widely shared, but there has been little firm evidence. Only in the past four years of the twentieth century, have we known for sure that "worlds" exist in orbit around other stars. But even if innumerable planets exist, we are little closer to knowing whether any of them harbor anything alive. This question is one for biologists, not for astronomers. It is much more difficult to answer, and there seems no consensus among the experts.

Systematic scans for artificial signals are a worthwhile gamble, despite the heavy odds against success, because of the philosophical import of any detection. A manifestly artificial signal—even if we could not make much sense of it—would convey the momentous message that intelligence was not unique to the Earth and had evolved elsewhere, and concepts of logic and physics were not peculiar to the "hardware" in human skulls. The nearest potential sites are so far away that signals would take many years in transit. For this reason alone, transmission would be primarily one-way. There would be time to send a measured response, but no scope for quick repartee!

The most common idea is that contact might be achieved via radio signals. There are ongoing searches for transmissions that might be artificial in origin. But this is not the only option; narrowly beamed lasers are another possibility. It is already technologically possible for us to proclaim our presence over distances of many light years by either of these techniques.

We still do not know the odds against life getting started. Even when simple life exists, we do not know the chances that it evolves toward intelligence. Intelligent life could be natural, or it could have involved a chain of accidents so surpassingly rare that nothing remotely like it has happened anywhere else in our galaxy. And even if intelligence exists elsewhere, it may be enjoying a purely contemplative life and doing nothing to reveal itself. Absence of evidence would not be evidence of absence.

The odds may be stacked so heavily against life that there is none anywhere else in our part of the universe. Some may find it depressing to feel alone in a vast inanimate cosmos. But I react in quite the opposite way. It would in some ways be disappointing if searches for extraterrestrial signals were doomed to fail. But if our Earth were the sole abode of life in our galaxy, we could view it in a less humble cosmic perspective than it would merit if our universe already teemed with advanced life forms.

BACK TO THE BEGINNING: OUR UNIVERSE ON LARGE SCALES

Evidence for Cosmic Evolution

I have described how the atoms of the periodic table are made—that we are stardust or, if you are less romantic, the "nuclear waste" from the fuel that makes stars shine. But from where did the original hydrogen come? To answer this question, we must extend our horizons to the extragalactic realm. Our Milky Way, with its hundred billion stars, is just one galaxy similar to millions of others visible with large telescopes.

And we can now see a vast number of galaxies, stretching to immense distances very far back. One amazing picture taken with the Hubble Space Telescope shows a small patch of sky, a thousandth of the area covered by a full Moon. It is densely covered with faint smudges of light—each a billion times fainter than any star that can be seen with the unaided eye. But each is an entire *galaxy*, thousands of light years across, which appears so small and faint because of its huge distance.

What is most fascinating about this picture is not the record-breaking distance in itself, but the huge span of time that separates us from these remote galaxies. They are being viewed when they have been only recently formed. They have not yet settled down into steadily spinning pinwheels like Andromeda. Some consist mainly of glowing diffuse gas that has not yet condensed into individual droplets, each destined to become a star. Their stars have not had time to manufacture the chemical elements. These newly formed galaxies would not yet harbor planets, and presumably no life.

Astronomers can actually *see* the remote past. But what about still more remote epochs, before any galaxies had formed?

Did everything really start with a so-called Big Bang? This phrase was introduced into cosmology by Fred Hoyle as a derisive description of a theory he did not like. Two strong lines of evidence have firmed up the case for a Big Bang (the undignified name has stuck). First, the weak microwaves that make even intergalactic space slightly warm have now been measured, at many different wavelengths to a precision of one part in ten thousand. The spectrum fits a black body very precisely. The errors are smaller than the thickness of the line. This spectrum is just what you would expect if these microwaves are indeed an afterglow of a pregalactic era when the entire universe was hot, dense, and opaque. The expansion has cooled and diluted the radiation, and stretched its wavelength. But this primordial heat is still around—it fills the universe and has nowhere else to go!

And there is a second line of evidence. When the entire universe was squeezed hotter than a star, there would be nuclear reactions. Astrophysicists have calculated these and found they fit with the proportions of helium and deuterium that are measured.

Astronomers can actually *see* the remote past and infer (via the microwave background and the helium abundance) what the universe was like at still earlier stages. But how much of this should we believe? I think the extrapolation back to the stage when the universe had been expanding for *a few seconds* (when the helium formed) deserve to be taken as seriously as, for instance, what geologists or paleontologists tell us about the early history of our Earth. The inferences of the latter are just as indirect (and less quantitative).

Sometimes cosmologists are asked, Is it not absurdly presumptuous to claim to know anything, with any level of confidence, about our entire universe? My response would be that it is complexity, and not sheer size, that makes things hard to understand—a star is simpler than an insect, for instance. In the primordial fireball, everything must have been broken down into its simplest constituents. The early universe really could be less baffling, and more within our grasp, than the smallest living organism. It is biologists, trying to understand the layer on layer of intricate structures in an animal, who face the toughest challenge. The origin of life is at least as challenging as the origin of matter.

Futurology

In about five billion years the Sun will die and the Earth with it. But will the universe go on expanding forever? Or will the entire firmament eventually recollapse to a "big crunch"?

The answer depends on how much the cosmic expansion is being decelerated by the gravitational pull that everything in the universe exerts on everything else. It is straightforward to calculate that the expansion can eventually be reversed if there is, on average, more than about 5 atoms in each cubic meter. That does not sound like much. But if all the galaxies were dismantled and their constituent stars and gas spread uniformly through space, they would make an even emptier vacuum— 1 atom in every 10 cubic meters—like one snowflake in the entire volume of the Earth.

That's fifty times less than the critical density, and at first sight this seems to imply perpetual expansion, by a wide margin. But it is not so straightforward. Astronomers have discovered that galaxies, and even entire clusters of galaxies, would fly apart unless they were held together by the gravitational pull of about ten times more material than we actually see. Cosmologists denote the ratio of the actual density to the critical density by the Greek letter omega. There is certainly enough dark matter around galaxies to make omega = 0.2 (remember that what we see is only a fiftieth). There is almost certainly enough dark matter, mainly in galactic halos and clusters of galaxies, to contribute twenty percent of the critical density. Until recently, we could not rule out several times this amount—comprising the full critical density at omega = 1— in the space between clusters of galaxies. But it now seems that, in toto, dark matter does not contribute more than an omega of about 0.3. It seems that expansion of our universe will be never ending. Moreover, the dominant mass-energy could be in some even more exotic form than the dark matter—maybe even latent in empty space. The odds now favor perpetual expansion.

Emergence of Complexity from a Simple Big Bang

It may at first sight seem mysterious that our universe started off as a hot amorphous fireball and ended up manifestly far from equilibrium. Temperatures now range from those of the blazing surfaces of stars (and their even hotter centers) to the night sky only 3 degrees above absolute zero. This is not, however, contrary to the second law of thermodynamics. It is actually a natural outcome of cosmic expansion and the workings of gravity.

Because of the expansion, there is no time for all reactions to attain equilibrium. At high temperatures, everything tends to turn into iron, as inside a hot star. But that (fortunately) did not happen in the early universe, because it cooled too quickly for the reactions to go to completion. Instead, the material emerged with proportions of hydrogen and helium that actually accord well with what we observe.

And, even more important, *gravity renders the expanding universe unstable to the growth of structure*, in the sense that even very slight initial irregularities would evolve into conspicuous density contrasts. Eventually the overdense regions stop expanding and condense into gaseous protogalaxies that fragment into stars. Ever since the beginning, gravity has been amplifying inhomogeneities, building up structures, and enhancing temperature contrasts—a prerequisite for emergence of the complexity that lies around us ten billion years later, and of which we are part.

The Initial Conditions

The way that slight initial irregularities in the cosmic fireball evolve into galaxies is in principle as predictable as the orbits of the planets, which have been understood since Newton's time. But to Newton, some features of the solar system were a mystery. He showed why the planets traced out ellipses; it was, however, a mystery to him why they were "set up" with their orbits almost in the same plane, all circling the Sun in the same way. In his *Opticks* he writes:

blind fate could never make all the planets move one and the same way in orbits concentrick.... Such a wonderful uniformity in the planetary system, must be the effect of providence. This coplanarity has only now been understood—it's a natural outcome of the Solar System's origin as a spinning protostellar disc.

Indeed, we have pushed the barrier back from the beginning of the solar system to the first second of the Big Bang. But—and this is my reason for the flashback to Newton—*conceptually we are in no better shape than Newton was.* He had to specify the initial trajectories of each planet. Our calculations of cosmic structure need to specify, at some early time like one second, a few factors:

1. The cosmic expansion rate "tuned" so that the universe neither recollapsed very quickly nor expanded so fast that gravity could not form bound structures such as galaxies.
2. The proportions of ordinary atoms, dark matter, and radiation in the universe.
3. The character of the fluctuations—large enough to evolve into structures but not to invalidate the overall uniformity.
4. The constants of microphysics.

We have pushed the causal chain far further back than Newton did, but we still reach a stage when we are reduced to saying "things are as they are because they were as they were."

Any explanation for these numbers (1–4) must lie still earlier in cosmic history—not just the first second but the first tiny fraction of a second. What is the chance, then, of pushing the barrier back still further?

The Uncertain Physics of the First Microsecond

I was confident in tracing back to when the universe was a second old. The matter was no denser than air; conventional laboratory physics is applicable and is vindicated by the impressive evidence of the background radiation, helium, and so forth. But for the first trillionth of a second every particle would have more energy than even CERN's new accelerator will reach. The further we extrapolate back, the less confidence we have that known physics is either adequate or applicable. So we lose our foothold in experiment.

Incidentally, I am uneasy about how cosmology is sometimes popularized. Authors—academic cosmologists are at fault even more than professional communicators—do not always distinguish between things that are quite well established and those that are still speculative. And sometimes an unwarranted triumphalism creeps in. If cosmologists claim too often to be "stripping the last veil from the face of God," or making discoveries that "overthrow all previous ideas," they will surely erode their credibility. It would be prudent as well as seemly to rein in the hyperbole. Otherwise journalists have to become as sceptical in assessing scientific claims as they already are in assessing politicians.

The formative instants of our universe were plainly crucial, and there have been some important insights. No theories of this ultra-early time are yet, however, firm enough to have much predictive power.

The cosmic expansion rate presents a special mystery. The two eschatologies of perpetual expansion or recollapse to a crunch seem very different. But our universe is still expanding after ten billion years. A universe that recollapsed sooner would not have allowed time for stars to evolve, or even to form. On the other hand, if the expansion were too much faster, gravity would have been overwhelmed by kinetic energy and the clouds that developed into galaxies would have been unable to condense out. In Newtonian terms the initial potential and kinetic energies were very closely matched. How did this come about? And why does the universe have the large-scale uniformity that is a prerequisite for progress in cosmology?

The answer may lie in something remarkable that happened during the first 10^{-36} seconds, when our entire observable universe was compressed in scale by twenty-seven powers of ten (and hotter by a similar factor). Theoretical physicists have come up with serious (though still, of course, tentative) reasons why, at the colossal densities before that time, a new kind of "cosmical repulsion" might come into play and overwhelm "ordinary" gravity. The expansion of the ultra-early universe would then have been exponentially accelerated, so that an embryo universe could have inflated, homogenized, and established the fine-tuned balance between gravitational and kinetic energy when it was only 10^{-36} seconds old.

This generic idea that our universe inflated from something microscopic is compellingly attractive. It looks like something for nothing, but it is not really, because our present vast universe may in a sense have zero net energy. Every atom has an energy because of its mass—Einstein's Mc^2. But it has a negative energy because of gravity. We, for instance, are in a state of lower potential energy on the Earth's surface than if we were up in space. And if we added up the negative potential energy we possess because of the gravitational field of everything else, it could exactly balance our rest mass energy. Thus, it does not, as it were, cost anything to expand the mass and energy in our universe.

Cosmologists sometimes loosely express such ideas by saying that the universe can essentially arise from nothing. But they should watch their language, especially when talking to philosophers. The physicist's vacuum is latent with particles and forces, and it is a far richer construct than the philosopher's nothing. Theorists may, some day, be able to write down fundamental equations governing physical reality. But no physicist will ever tell us what breathes fire into the equations and actualizes them in a real cosmos.

POSSIBLE SCOPE AND LIMITS OF THEORY: ARE THERE OTHER UNIVERSES?

I have outlined in earlier sections how our carbon-based biosphere has slowly evolved on a planet orbiting a stable star. It is made of atoms that were themselves transmuted from hydrogen in earlier generations of stars. The hydrogen itself emerged from a hot Big Bang about 12 billion years ago.

Our universe had to provide the galaxies that form the backdrop to the emergence of stars, planets, and life. It had to possess many features—being long-lived, stable, and far from thermal equilibrium, for instance—that are prerequisites for our existence. Moreover, our emergence depended crucially on apparent fine tuning of the basic physical constants: the strengths of the fundamental forces, the masses of elementary particles, and so forth

There are various ways one can react. The most robustly dismissive attitude is that the basic numbers defining our universe, and the physical constants, must have some values, so we have no reason to be surprised at any particular value rather than another.

A more reasonable reaction to the coincidences is to invoke a kind of selection effect. Fishermen are not surprised (to use an old metaphor of Eddington's) to catch no fish smaller than the holes in their nets. It may seem irrational to be surprised that our universe has any particular property if we would not exist otherwise.

But even that does not seem quite enough. To say that we would not be here if things were otherwise need not quench our curiosity and surprise that our universe is as it is. John Leslie has given a nice analogy. Suppose you are facing execution by a fifty-man firing squad. The bullets are fired, and you find that all have missed their target. Had they not done so, you would not survive to ponder the matter. But realizing you were alive, you would legitimately be perplexed and wonder why.

It seems noteworthy, at the very least, that the physical laws governing our universe have allowed so much interesting complexity to emerge in it, especially as we can so readily imagine still-born universes in which nothing could evolve. If a "cosmic being" turned knobs to vary the key numbers and constructed a whole ensemble of universes, then clearly only one would be like our own, and we would not feel at home in most of them—that much is obvious. However, what is less trivial, and may be deeply significant, is that only a narrow range of hypothetical universes would allow any complexity to emerge.

These arguments pertain to basic physics and chemistry and cannot be as readily discounted as those of Paley concerning the fitness of animals and plants for their environment. Any complicated biological contrivance is the outcome of prolonged evolutionary selection, involving symbiosis with its surroundings but the basic laws governing atoms, stars, and the cosmos are given, and nothing biological can react back on them to modify them.

A Multiverse?

Some theologians would of course attribute the fine tuning to providence. John Polkinghorne, for instance, opines that "the universe is not just any old world," but it is special and finely tuned for life because it is the creation of a Creator who wills that it should be so.[2] But there is an alternative view: perhaps our Big Bang was not the only one. We may be part of an infinite and eternal multiverse within which new domains sprout into universes whose horizons never overlap. The fundamental forces—gravity, nuclear, and electromagnetic—freeze out as each universe cools down. The outcome of this cooling is somewhat arbitrary, like the patterns of ice on a pond or the way a magnet behaves when cooled. So different universes would end up governed by different physics and would evolve in distinctive ways. Other universes would be, in most versions of these ideas, completely disjoint from ours, and they will never come within the horizon of even our remotest descendents.

Our Big Bang would, in this perspective, be just one event in a grander structure; the entire history of our universe would be just an episode in the infinite multiverse. The multiverse could encompass all possible values of fundamental constants, as well as universes that follow life cycles of very different durations: some, like ours, may expand for much more than ten billion years; others may be stillborn because they recollapse after a brief existence, or because the physical laws governing them are not rich enough to permit complex consequences. In some universes there could be no gravity, or gravity could be overwhelmed by the repulsive effect of a cosmological constant (lambda), as it would have been during the early inflation phase of our own universe. In others, gravity could be so strong that it crushes anything large enough to evolve into a complex organism. Some could always be so dense that everything stayed close to equilibrium, with the same temperature everywhere. Some could even have different numbers of dimensions from our own.

Even a universe that was, like ours, long-lived and stable could contain just inert particles of dark matter, either because the physics precludes ordinary atoms from ever existing, or because they all annihilate with exactly equal numbers of antiatoms. Even if protons and hydrogen atoms exist, the nuclear forces may not be strong enough to hold the nuclei of heavy elements together; there would then be no periodic table and no chemistry.

The concept of an ensemble of universes of which ours is just one member (and not necessarily a typical one) is not yet in sharp theoretical focus. But it helps to explain basic (and previously mysterious) features of our universe, such as why it is so big, and why it is expanding. In the broader perspective of a multiverse, anthropic reasoning could acquire genuine explanatory force.

Let me add a semantic note about the definition of universe. The proper definition of universe is of course "everything there is." I argue here that the entity traditionally called the universe—what astronomers study or the aftermath of our Big Bang—may be just one of a whole ensemble, each one maybe starting with its own Big Bang. Pedants might prefer to redefine the whole ensemble as the universe. But I think it is less confusing, especially while the concept is so tentative and provisional, to leave the term universe for what it has traditionally connoted, even though this then demands a new word, the "multiverse," for the entire ensemble of universes.

Most universes would be less propitious for complex evolution than ours, but not necessarily all. We cannot conceive what structures might emerge in the distant future of our universe. Still less, therefore, can we envisage what might happen in a universe in which the forces differentiated into more than our familiar four, or where the number of dimensions was larger. Our universe could be impoverished compared with some others that could harbor vastly richer structures and potentialities beyond our imaginings.

The status and scope of such concepts, in the long run, will depend on the character of the (still quite unknown) physical laws at the very deepest level. If the physical constants were indeed uniquely fixed by a final theory, it would then be a brute fact that these universal numbers happened to lie in the narrowly restricted range that permitted complexity and consciousness to emerge. The potentialities implicit in the fundamental equations—all the intricate structures in our universe—may astonish us, but this reaction would be akin to the surprise mathematicians must sometimes feel when vastly elaborate deductions follow from innocuous-looking axioms or postulates.

Simple algorithms generally have dull outcomes, but a few do not. Consider, for instance, the Mandelbrot set. The instructions for drawing this astonishing pattern can be written in just a few lines, but it discloses layer on layer of varied structure however much we magnify it. Similarly, latent in the succinct equations of a final theory could be everything that has emerged in our universe, as it cooled from the initial Big Bang to the diffuse low energy world we inhabit.

But what we call the fundamental constants—the numbers that matter to physicists—may be *secondary consequences* of the final theory rather than direct manifestations of its deepest and most fundamental level. The multiverse may be governed by some unified theory, but each universe may cool down in a fashion that has accidental features, ending up governed by different laws (and with different physical constants) from other members of the ensemble. Anthropic arguments can be properly deployed to account for the physical constants in our universe. Indeed, this would be *the only way* to understand why these numbers did not have values that were very different.

Any final theory is still such a distant goal that we cannot yet assess how far our universe can be explained anthropically. However, we may be able to fathom the nature of the final theory even before we know its specific details.[3]

CONCLUSIONS

The frontiers of science are the very small, the very large, and most of all, the very complex. Cosmology involves them all. Theorists must elucidate the exotic physics of the very early stages, which entails a new synthesis between the cosmos and the microworld, and tell us whether there is a basis for the multiverse and for selection of physical constants. Such a theory may explain some aspects of the particles and governing forces that are so far "fed in" from experiment. If so, it would gain enough credibility that we would take seriously its predictions about how inflation occurred, whether our Big Bang would be the only one, and whether the other universes would be governed by different physics.

But cosmology also is the grandest of the environmental sciences, and its second aim is to understand how at least one Big Bang evolved, over ten billion years, into the complex cosmic habitat we find around us so that on at least one planet around at least one star, creatures evolved able to wonder about it all. And that is an unending quest barely begun.

By mapping and exploring our universe, using all the techniques of astronomy, we are coming to understand (to a degree that even a decade ago would have seemed impossible) our cosmic habitat, the laws that govern it, and how it evolved from its formative initial instants. But even more remarkably, we have intimations of other universes and can deduce something about them. We can infer the scope and limit of a final theory even if we are still far from reaching it—even if, indeed, it eludes our intellectual grasp forever.

NOTES

1. E.O. Wilson, *Consilience: The Unity of Knowledge* (New York: Alfred A. Knopf, 1998).
2. J. Polkinghorne, *Quarks, Chaos, and Christianity* (London: Triangle Press, 1994).
3. M. Rees, *Before the Beginning* (Perseus, 1997), esp. chap. 15.

LEE SMOLIN

Lee Smolin is a theoretical physicist who has made significant contributions to the search for a quantum theory of gravity. A professor of physics at the Center for Gravitational Physics and Geometry at Pennsylvania State University, he is one of a small number of scientists actively seeking to reconcile—or "unify"—general relativity, Einstein's theory of gravity, and quantum mechanics. Dr. Smolin began his studies in physics at Hampshire College, where he majored in natural philosophy, and then went on to Harvard University, where he earned his Ph.D. in theoretical physics in 1979. After postdoctoral work at the Institute for Advanced Study in Princeton, the Institute for Theoretical Physics at the University of California, Santa Barbara, and the University of Chicago, he joined the Yale faculty as an assistant professor of physics in 1984, and in 1988, he became an associate and then a full professor of physics at Syracuse University before accepting his current position at Penn State five years ago. He has been a visiting scientist at more than a dozen universities and institutes and given some fifty invited lectures to scientific audiences. The author of more than eighty scientific papers, he recently published *The Life of the Cosmos* in 1997.

Our Relationship to the Universe

Lee Smolin

Every scientist and philosopher must have had the experience of failing, when asked, to explain one's work in a few words. The theme of my essay stems from a comment of a friend, Saint Clair Cemin, a sculptor. Seeing him at a brunch, I complained about how badly I had done in an interview about my book, *The Life of the Cosmos.* He interrupted and said, "But the point of your book is very simple: it is just that the whole show of the universe is so extraordinary that even the absence of God would be God enough." Reinforced by this remark, I will describe a few ideas that are playing a central role in recent developments in theoretical physics and cosmology.

Any discussion of the implications of twentieth century science must start with the statement that this is a period of transition in our understanding of nature as great as any in our history. The Newtonian physics and cosmology were overthrown at the beginning of the century, but we are not yet done with the task of constructing its successor. We are making a lot of progress, and it has accelerated in recent years. On the observational side the results are stunning, as the detail with which we observe the evolution of our region of the universe is increasing exponentially. On the theoretical side, we have made much progress in the past fifteen years on uniting relativity and cosmology with the quantum theory so that the outlines of the replacement of Newtonian physics are in sight.

So while there is much work to do (and there is still the possibility we are completely wrong), I will hazard a statement of the seven main principles that underline the transition from the Newtonian to the next universe. What follows is a personal view of the implications of recent work of many scientists, many of whom may not agree with the way I put things.

1. No meaning can be given to the idea of a view of the universe from the point of view of an observer who is outside of it or who is not a participant in it.

This was not true of Newtonian physics, which was constructed explicitly as a description of the universe from the point of view of an outside observer. This was Newton's reason for basing the theory on an absolute conception of space and time according to which position and time have an absolute meaning that is accessible only to this outside observer. Of course, for Newton this observer was God, as he discussed at length in the scholium to his *Principia*. The contrary view, championed by Leibniz, is that there is no meaning to space, time, or any other property of anything in the world apart from its real relationships with other things in the world. Einstein's general relativity is a complete realization of Leibniz's view, and its experimental success is a repudiation of Newton's notion of absolute space and time. In any description of a closed universe that is consistent with general relativity, the physical properties of things in the world are defined only by relationships with other things, and they are only observable for observers inside the universe.

In quantum theory, the situation is more subtle. Many formulations of the interpretation of that theory depend on splitting the world into two parts: one contains the system to be described; the other contains the observer and his or her measuring instruments. Until recently it was not obvious how to reconcile this with the relational character of general relativity. However, recent developments show that this can be done, and in a way that leaves the basic moral of general relativity intact: there is no coherent notion of a view of the universe except that of an observer who is also part of and a participant in that universe.

Basing science on an imagined view of the universe from outside of it had one clear advantage: the knowledge held by such an omniscient outside observer could be imagined without contradiction to be both complete and unique. Neither is possible for the knowledge of any observer who is inside and a participant in the system. The view of any observer in the universe is necessarily incomplete, for two reasons. First, as an embodied observer in space and time, he or she sees what happens only when the light from those events reaches the observer. Different observers, situated differently in space and time, see some things to happen in a different order, and each sees the history only up to the information that reaches him or her at a particular time.

Furthermore, there are regions, such as black holes, that provide no information to many (but not all) observers.

Second, no observer can make a complete determination of his or her own state. Thus, observers cannot have a complete description of the whole universe if only because what they know completely must exclude the part of space they occupy.

A complete cosmological physics has no choice but to incorporate these limitations. The result is that a science based on what observers in the universe can actually observe necessarily must give up the notion of a unique and complete view of the universe for a plurality of many different, incomplete views.

2. In such a physics, the notion of the state of the universe as the complete description of physical reality must necessarily fragment into a pluralistic description composed of many states. Each of these corresponds to the view some observer inside the universe has of the rest. As each of these views is necessarily partial, so are each of these descriptions.

This does not mean that objectivity is impossible. On the contrary, the views of all the different observers are based on observations of the same universe. The whole point is that all the views, while each different and incomplete, are coherent. Indeed, as Leibniz expressed clearly in his monadology, and Bohr suggested less clearly in his writings, the laws of physics ultimately must be about the coherence of the different possible views of the universe.

This may seem like philosophy. But in fact recent developments in physics by Louis Crane, Carlo Rovelli, James Hartle, Murray Gellmann, Chris Isham, Fotini Markopoulou, and others show how a quantum theory of cosmology can be constructed that realizes this view exactly. Even in mathematics, an entire subject is devoted to the study of the modifications in logic required when the truth value of propositions about a system depends on the context defined by the relationship between the knower and the system. Called topos theory, it grew out of both category theory and intuitionalistic logic.

Topos theory shares an important idea with the approaches to quantum cosmology I mentioned; it rejects the Platonic notion that truth is about an eternal ideal realm in favor of the notion that any true statement is meaningful in a context that depends, above all, on time. Thus, it is becoming increasingly clear that rather than erasing time, as was believed by some previously, the combination of relativity and quantum theory requires that time be an essential and irreducible element, not only of our experience of reality, but of reality itself. Thus, we have the third principle.

3. The geometrization of time, according to which change in time is visualized by identifying time with a spatial dimension, is giving way to an algebraization of both time and space, in which each is constructed from a description of real causal processes and the notion that the universe evolves along a curve in a preexisting space of possible states is found to be both incoherent and unnecessary.

It is perhaps not surprising then that observations show us that we live in a universe whose description cannot be divorced from time.

4. The part of the universe we can observe is neither static nor eternal, as Newton supposed. Instead, it has a history, each stage of which is different from those previous, and it has apparently an origin.

In fact, measured on the time scales of geology and evolutionary biology, the observable universe is not very old. During this time, the galaxies, stars, and most of the elements were formed in processes that we are coming to understand as well as we understand the geological processes that have formed the surface of the planet on which we live.

We see evidence that everything we see has expanded from a condition not unlike that at the center of stars. If we look back farther, do we see an ultimate origin or do we see a time before our Big Bang? We do not know the answer, but there are plausible scenarios in which the part of the universe we see was created in a natural, physical process out of a previously existing region of space and time. Certainly there is no compelling scientific reason to regard the Big Bang as the beginning of time.

5. The universe we see is not in thermal equilibrium, so that, so far at least, the story of our universe is one in which nonequilibrium processes evolve structure and complexity.

We observe that spiral galaxies such as our own are steady state nonequilibrium systems in which the rates of their important processes, such as star formation and the transfer of energy and materials between stars and the interstellar medium, are determined by competing feedback loops, just as in biological and ecological systems. We have known for some time that life is possible on Earth because the biosphere is a nonequilibrium self-organized system; what is newer is that the surface of a planet may be out of equilibrium for cosmological time scales because it is embedded in a much larger nonequilibrium self-organized system, which is the disk of the galaxy. Whether this picture extends to larger scales of distance and time is still unknown, but it is becoming very plausible that nonequilibrium processes also were important for the formation of galaxies as well as structure on larger scales.

In the nineteenth century, many people worried that life was an anomaly in a universe that was close to, and rapidly returning to, a state of thermal equilibrium. This perspective was necessary to reconcile the existence of the observed structure with the wrong assumption that the universe was eternal. While we do not know the long-term future of our universe, we do know that it is largely far from equilibrium, and the time scale for reaching equilibrium, if not infinite, is certainly much longer than the present age of the universe. Thus, we can understand the existence of life, at least at the present nonequilibrium stage of the universe, as a natural consequence of the fact that the whole universe is out of equilibrium. Thus our present physics and cosmology present us with a universe that is in many respects hospitable to, rather than hostile, to life.

Whether the second law of thermodynamics must ultimately apply, or whether equilibrium will never be established, is the subject of disagreement. Certainly the standard forms of the second law do not apply to systems such as the universe that are dominated by gravitational forces and that live in a dynamical, rather than a fixed, spacetime. I believe that the application of the second law to cosmology rests on the invalid extensions of the notion of information, from a relational property that holds between two different subsystems of the universe to an absolute property that might characterize all of it.

6. Consistency alone does not determine the laws of nature.

That it would was the old Platonic dream that motivated generations of theoretical physicists, including myself. Now we have good evidence from string theory that there are many equally consistent formulations of laws of nature that unify, at least at the level of approximation so far studied, quantum theory with relativity and the other known forces. The result is the curious situation in which many theorists believe string theory has something to do with nature, but it is difficult to test because it comes in many different versions that lead to different predictions about the elementary particles. Recently there is evidence that these different versions of string theory describe different phases of some deeper theory. This means that there are physical processes by which a region of the universe can undergo a phase transition. The consequence is, however, not melting or freezing, but a modification in the properties of the elementary particles and forces that are observed.

I believe that many of the questions about the laws of nature will have explanations that involve history rather than *a priori* arguments from mathematics. That is, if there is choice about the laws of nature, at least in how they manifest themselves to us on scales we can observe, there must be a historical explanation for how those choices were made. This makes fundamental physics much more like biology than previously anticipated by most of us (although one can find anticipations of this in the writings of philosophers such as Diderot and Pierce.)

While certainly not demonstrated, the following is thus a genuine possibility.

7. The laws of nature we observe were not imposed on the universe from outside, but are the result of natural and comprehensible processes of self-organization.

Since Plato, the explanation for any structure of organization that we observed in nature was that it was imposed from the outside that system by some intelligent organizer. Thus, in the *Timaeus,* the Pilot imposes order on chaos, and in Newton the laws of Nature are imposed by God. This is a natural supposition for us, since constructing order from chaos is part of our biology. As makers of tools and dwellings, it is natural for us when we find some organization to ask who did it. When physics was mathematized, the notion of an eternally true law of nature took over to some extent the role of God: the laws imposed behavior on matter, but the laws were supposed to be eternal and immutable, as God was.

Darwin introduced for the first time a coherent alternative, according to which the incredibly intricate organization of living things could be understood as having arisen from a long history of self-construction from very simple beginnings, following processes that are both natural and comprehensible. In my opinion, this is an alternative not only for biology, but for all the evidences of organization that we observe, up to and including the properties of the elementary particles and the forces with which they interact. I found that it is possible to construct scenarios in which this kind of explanation accounts for many of the unanswered questions about the elementary particles.[1] Further, because they involve hypotheses about real historical processes, such theories are easily falsifiable, which is in contrast to theories about the elementary particles that rely only on platonic forms of explanation.

I believe that the different developments I have mentioned may make possible a cosmological theory in which our universe is understood completely as a system of relations that has evolved over time to reach its present state. In such a universe, all scientific questions will be explicable in terms of the history of relationships between real things in the world. There will be no need to posit anything external to the system of relations that are the universe, whether for purposes of either giving meaning to the properties of things in the world, or proscribing the laws they obey. Even the mathematics necessary to make this vision into science will be understood intuitionalistically, which means without the idealistic supposition that mathematics is about some ideal realm of eternal truth.

What are the implications for our view of ourselves and our relation to the world, were this to turn out to be our world? Clearly there is no less reason to feel awe when contemplating such a universe. In such a world there is much to wonder at, much to worship. But the object of our adoration will then be nothing outside and apart from the reality in which we live. For we will understand that an even greater possibility exists than that our world was created by a being that stands eternally outside of its creation. It is that the creative being, and the world itself are one and the same thing. And our understanding of our relation to it then begins with the realization that we are of it and that we, and all our knowledge, and all our wondering are also creations of it.

That we may be able to achieve a rational understanding of our universe that requires no outside pilot or observer does not mean that God is nonexistent. It only means that the old idea of an outside creator and knower has served its purpose and may now be relegated to history. But perhaps this is not such a tragedy, because the presence of such a God raised a problem of our alienation either from nature or its creator. Since they were distinct, we had to choose which we were; we could not be both of nature and of spirit. In the absence of such a God, we may perhaps discover a different notion of God, which is not different from its creation. Perhaps this will be a God enough.

NOTES

1. L. Smolin, *The Life of the Cosmos* (New York and Oxford: Oxford University Press, 1997). Author's note: Recently there has been definite progress on formulating both classical and quantum theories of cosmology in terms of the multiple views of observers inside the universe. See F. Markopoulou, "The Internal Description of a Causal Set: What the Universe Looks Like from the Inside, gr-qc/9811053," to appear in *Commun. Math. Phys.;* "Quantum Causal Histories, hep-th/9904009;" "An Insider's Guide to Quantum Causal Histories, hep-th/9912137." For a recent discussion of progress made in quantum gravity, see L. Smolin, *Physics World,* Dec. 1999. For the work of Saint Clair Cemin, see http://www.artnet.com/GalHome/FineArtThumbnails.asp.

4

ARTHUR PEACOCKE

Arthur Peacocke devoted the first twenty-five years of his career to teaching and research in the field of physical chemistry. His principal interest during the past twenty-five years has been in exploring the relation of science to theology. After going up to Oxford, where he was a scholar of Exeter College, he worked in the Physical Chemistry Laboratory, with Nobel laureate Sir Cyril Hinshelwood and earned a D.Phil. in physical biochemistry in 1948. For the next eleven years, he taught at the University of Birmingham and then returned to Oxford as a fellow and tutor at St. Peter's College from 1959 to 1973. In addition to publishing more than 125 papers and three books in his field, he served as editor of *Biopolymers,* the *Biochemical Journal,* and a series of monographs on physical biochemistry. While lecturing at Birmingham, Dr. Peacocke also studied theology and was ordained a priest in the Church of England in 1971. From 1973 to 1984 he was Dean (of chapel) of Clare College, Cambridge and then became founding director of the Ian Ramsey Centre at St. Cross College, Oxford, in 1985, a position he held until 1988. In 1995, he resumed the directorship of the Centre. A founder of the Science and Religion Forum in the United Kingdom, of the corresponding European society, and of the Society of Ordained Scientists, a new dispersed religious order, he was honorary chaplain of Christ Church Cathedral, Oxford, from 1989 to 1996 and is now an honorary canon. He was made a member of the Order of the British Empire by Queen Elizabeth II in 1993. The author of nine books exploring the relationship between science and religion, his most recent studies are *From DNA to Dean: Reflections and Explorations of a Priest-Scientist* and *God and Science: A Quest for Christian Credibility.* His forthcoming book is *The End of our Exploring: From the World of Science Towards God* (Oxford: One World, 2000).

The Challenge and Stimulus of the Epic of Evolution to Theology

Arthur Peacocke

Prologue

I begin with a story that recounts a dazzling vista, which we are the first generation of human beings to have vouchsafed to us. It might be called "Genesis for the Third Millennium." It is as follows:

There was God. And God Was All-That-Was. God's Love overflowed and God said: "Let Other be. And let it have the capacity to become what it might be—and let it explore its potentialities."

And there was Other in God, a field of energy, vibrating energy but no matter, space, time, or form. Obeying its given laws and with one intensely hot surge of energy—a hot Big Bang—this Other exploded as the universe from a point twelve or so billion years ago in our time, thereby making space.

Vibrating fundamental particles appeared, expanded, and expanded and cooled into clouds of gas, bathed in radiant light. Still the universe went on expanding and condensing into swirling whirlpools of matter and light—a billion galaxies.

Five billion years ago, one star in one galaxy—our Sun—attracted round it matter as planets. One of them was our Earth. On Earth, the assembly of atoms and the temperature became just right to allow water and solid rock to form. Continents and mountains grew and in some wet crevice, or pool, or deep in the sea, just over three billion years ago, some molecules became large and complex enough to make copies of themselves and so the first specks of life.

Life multiplied in the seas, diversifying and becoming more and more complex. Five hundred million years ago, creatures with solid skeletons, the vertebrates, appeared. On land, green plants changed the atmosphere by making oxygen. Then 300 million years ago, cer-

*tain fish learned to crawl from the sea and live on the edge of land,
breathing that oxygen from the air.*

*Now life burst into many forms—reptiles and mammals (and
dinosaurs) on land, flying reptiles and birds in the air. Over millions
of years, the mammals began to develop complex brains that enabled
them to learn. Among these were creatures who lived in trees. From
these our first ancestors derived and then, only 40,000 years ago, the
first men and women appeared. They began to know about themselves and what they were doing—they were not only conscious, but
also self-conscious. The first word, the first laugh was heard. The first
paintings were made. The first sense of a destiny beyond—with the
first signs of hope, for they buried their dead with ritual. The first
prayers were made to the One who made All-That-Is and All-That-
Is-Becoming. The first experiences of goodness, beauty, and truth but
also of their opposites, for human beings were free.*

That is what some have called "the epic of evolution." Whatever we
call it, it is a framework sufficiently now well established that it is now
impossible, literally inconceivable, for us to set ourselves back into the
temporal framework that has largely shaped theology, which for the
present purposes I take to be Christian theology. That framework is,
and has been for two millennia, that of the Bible which has by and
large been the cosmology of the Old Testament, represented explicitly,
but not only, in the early chapters of Genesis. The doctrine of creation
has been largely shaped by Genesis 1 (together with parts of the
psalms, prophets, and wisdom literature). Doctrines concerning human nature have depended strongly on the quite different mythical accounts of the Garden of Eden and of the Fall in Genesis 2 and 3, and
so consequently have understandings of the work of Jesus the Christ,
in particular, theories of atonement. And of course much more.

Since theology is, in principle, the relating of everything to God, it
is not surprising that the establishing of this evolutionary perspective
has been perceived as a challenge, and even as a threat, to received
Christian beliefs about God, nature, and humanity. I hope to show
that, far from being this latter, the scientific vista for the third millennium, or at least the twenty-first century, constitutes a stimulus to theology to become more encompassing and inclusive, but only if it radically alters its currently widely assumed paradigms, not excluding the
significance of Jesus the Christ.

To some, this might appear an iconoclastic program. But I remind readers that Christian theology has been at its most creative and most vital when it has faced the challenges of engagement with new systems of thought encountered in new cultural contexts: the Gentile, then the Hellenistic (mainly neo-Platonic), and later the Aristotelian in the twelfth and thirteenth centuries.

We are now living through the most fundamental challenge of all to Christian belief—the fundamental displacement of the basic understandings of nature and of humanity, and consequentially also of God, that are being provoked by that new scientific vista with which I began. Recently, the BBC radio morning news program invited listeners to name the "most significant *British* figure (it was the *BBC*, after all!) of the second millennium." You can imagine the list that emerged. In the first three or four, Shakespeare was nearly always included and very often Churchill but rarely scientists. Yet the intellectual history of the seventeenth and eighteenth centuries was transformed and dominated by the creative achievements of Newton. A fundamental transition occurred that is well documented and widely recognised.

Many scientists were shocked by this "dumbness" of the great British public and the lack of attention to Darwin outraged, in particular, Richard Dawkins (who recently lectured in Oxford on Universal Darwinism). His well-known ideologies apart, I do not think he was wrong in choosing Darwin to head the list. Yet to many the impact of Darwin, and even more so of Darwin*ism,* is looked at askance and with suspicion by many Christian believers.

But Darwin's uniquely eminent place in the history of biology is totally assured, for he propounded a plausible mechanism for the transformation of species: natural selection (the increasing predominance of forms able to produce and rear more progeny as the environment changes). He brilliantly, doggedly, and at great personal cost showed that the operation of this mechanism was the best explanation, and made most sense, of widely disparate data concerning the form, habitats, distribution, and behavior of an immense variety of living organisms. It was only really vindicated by the later discovery of the laws of heredity (to which Darwin did not have access), and, in the twentieth century, by the establishment of the statistics of the process; the direct observation of natural selection in vivo; the irrefutable evidence for the interconnectedness of all living forms from the universality of the (chemically arbitrary) genetic code (linking DNA nucleotide to amino acid sequences in proteins); and by the evidence of genealogical connections between widely diverse species, based on sequence relationships in genetic DNA and in particular proteins. No professional, informed biologist works honestly now on any other basis than on recognizing the historical connectedness of all living forms and of the role of natural selection in their mutual transformation over four and one-half billion years. As Theodosius Dobzhansky (an Orthodox Christian) notably affirmed: "Nothing in biology makes sense except in the light of evolution."[1]

Now, as my own Genesis story indicated, we also have a purely naturalistic, intelligible account from the cosmological and astronomical sciences of the development of our observable universe from a concentrated mass over the past twelve or so billion years. The two stories join up to give us the contemporary epic of evolution—a perspective of a universe in process from an original fluctuating quantum field, or quark soup, to the astonishing complexity of the universe, observed both from planet Earth, e.g., by the Hubble telescope, and on Earth itself, fecund with complex forms of life, if we will only desist from destroying them.

Any theology, any attempt to relate God to all-that-is, will be moribund and doomed if it does not incorporate this perspective into its very bloodstream. Yet much Christian theology simply tinkers apologetically with its beliefs at what seem vulnerable chinks in its armor, hoping that it will survive into what it hopes will be less challenging times. That is a recipe for extinction for it is with this evolving world that on the surface of planet Earth the tragicomedy of human existence is working itself out. We are part of nature, part of an evolving cosmos, indeed, we are stardust become persons!

Let us now look, in sequence, at stages in the life process and reflect on their significance for our understanding of nature, humanity, and God—and so their significance for theology.

STAGES OF THE LIFE-PROCESS AND THEIR SIGNIFICANCE

The Physical Origin of the Universe

Extrapolation backward in time on the basis of known physical relations and observations enables astronomers to trace the evolution of the universe back to when it was only a tiny fraction of a second old, in the form of a compressed fireball hotter than the center of the Sun. With varying degrees of confidence, cosmologists can go "back" further than that, but however far they go the universe was indisputably physical, consisting of matter-energy-space-time in its most basic forms (e.g., a fluctuating quantum field). From this all else has developed, hence it can at least be affirmed (and there will be *much* more to affirm) that all concrete particulars in the world, including human beings, are constituted of fundamental physical entities—whatever it is that current physics postulates as the basic building constituents of the world (remembering ultimately that matter and energy are interchangeable). This is a monistic view, and indeed an ontologically constitutively reductionist one, in the sense that everything can be broken down into fundamental physical entities and no extra entities are to be inserted at higher levels of complexity, (e.g., at that of living organisms—no vitalism, no *élan vitale,* and so forth).

This is entirely in accord with the biblical tradition that "the Lord God formed man from the dust of the ground"[2] and that Adam was told "you are dust and to dust you shall return."[3]

Such a *monistic* view of the constitution of all entities in the universe, including living organisms and human beings, does not mean that all in the long run is to be explained by fundamental physics. For what is significant about the temporal process, and about the relation of existing complex systems to their constituent units, is that the concepts needed to describe and understand each emerging level in the hierarchy of complexity are specific to and distinctive of these levels. Moreover, it is often the case that such concepts are not logically reducible to those used to describe their constituent parts, least of all those pertaining to the fundamental physical building blocks of the universe. When this is so and, in particular, when causal efficacy can be attributed to the way the "wholes" influence the behavior of the "parts," then we are justified in asserting that a new kind of reality has emerged at the higher level of complexity. Philip Clayton and I have dubbed this view "emergentist monism" to distinguish it from epistemologically anti-reductionist physicalism, which is held by many philosophers of mind. Life is emergent from the physicochemical, the psychological from the neurological, and personhood from the human-brain-in-the-human-body—all are levels of reality. This is a presupposition of what I have to say.

The Origin of Life

There is a complex, and unresolved, debate concerning the way there came into existence the earliest entities that could be called living and that could replicate complex structures that are maintained by incorporating molecules from their environment. It is over twenty years ago now that two Nobel laureates, Ilya Prigogine and Manfred Eigen, showed by irreversible thermodynamics and by stochastic molecular kinetics, respectively, that the transformation of certain, apparently inchoate, physicochemical systems into complex, self-copying systems is likely to occur under certain conditions. So much so that Eigen could affirm that:

> The evolution of life, if it is based on a derivable physical principle [as it has to be, to be consistent with physics and chemistry], must be considered to be an inevitable process despite its indeterminate course. . . . [It is] also sufficiently probable within a realistic span of time. It requires appropriate environmental conditions. . . . These conditions have existed on Earth. . . . There is no temporal restriction to the continuation of the evolutionary process, as long as energy can be supplied.[4]

The inability of scientists to find the precise mechanism of the origin of life has led some to become sceptical about even the possibility of life emerging on Earth or even in our galaxy without divine intervention. I think this pioneer thermodynamic and kinetic work shows this scepticism to be unwarranted and that the emergence of living organisms from nonliving matter is a natural phenomenon requiring no "God of the gaps" to intervene as a *deus ex machina* to ensure its occurrence. In my view, those investigators established the principle of the inevitability of the emergence of life on some planet, some galaxy, some time in the universe, but left open the details of when and how. For theists, the whole process is given its existence, with that potential capacity for life, by God (who is therefore not of the gaps). It is amusing to note, in spite of this, that Dawkins, in response to a claim (by Craig Ventor in the United States) to synthesize a living system using artificial genes, could assert, "Synthesising life in a test tube would be a blow to the religious view that there's something special about life" (*Independent*, 25 January, 1999).

The Duration of Evolution

The oldest rocks to contain fossils of living forms (prokaryotic cells, bacteria and cyanophytes, no nucleus) are three and one-half billion years old and since these are already very complex, the origin of life must be located in the first half billion years of the Earth's existence, of some four and one-half billion years. If the Earth was formed at midnight of the day before yesterday and each hour is equivalent to 100 million years, then life first appeared during yesterday morning.[5] Only at 6 pm *today* did calcareous (hard) fossils appear; at 6 to 7 pm on this second day, the seas fill with shelled creatures; at 8 pm fishes; at 9 pm amphibia appear on land; by 11:30 pm mammals and the first primates spread across the globe; monkeys and apes at 11:50 pm; in the last few minutes of this second day of the Earth hominids arise, and *only* on the last stroke of tonight's midnight bell would we see toolmaking *homo sapiens.*

During the eons before our emergence on Earth, hundreds of millions (if not billions) of species have come and gone, predecessors of perhaps as many as twenty million species still extant, and rapidly being diminished by human action. Theists who believe that the ultimate ground of all existence is God as Creator have to face new questions: Is it permissible to regard these myriads of species, other than *homo sapiens*, most of them now extinct, as simply byproducts in a process aimed at producing human persons? Or do they have value in themselves and for themselves to God as Creator? The process is so fecund and rich and the sheer variety and often intricate beauty of coordinated structures and functions so great, that surely we now have to escape from our anthropocentric myopia and affirm that God as Creator takes what we can only call joy and delight in the rich variety and individuality of other organisms *for their own sake*? Certainly the Hebrew scriptures encourage such a view. Psalm 104 depicts the Lord as caring for living creatures and delighting in their enjoyment of their vitality and the conclusion of the Priestly account of creation is "God saw *everything* that he hade made, and indeed, it was very good."[6]

Incidentally we have here the basis for an ecotheology that grounds the value of all living creatures in their distinctive value to God for their own sake, and not just as stages en route to humanity and for human exploitation and use.

The Mechanism of Biological Evolution—Natural Selection
This is the proposition that species are derived from one another by natural selection of the best procreators. In the words of Darwin:

> If under changing conditions of life organic beings present individual differences in almost every part of their structure . . . if there be, owing to their geometrical rate of increase, a severe

struggle for life . . . then . . . it would be a most extraordinary fact if no variations had ever occurred useful to each being's own welfare. But if variations useful to any organic being ever do occur, assuredly individuals thus characterised will have the best chance of being preserved in the struggle for life; and from the strong principle of inheritance, these will tend to produce offspring similarly characterised. This principal of preservation, as the survival of the fittest, I have called Natural Selection.[7]

In more up-to-date language, we would say today that the original mutational events in the DNA are random with respect to the future of the biological organism, even its survival, and that the biological niche in which the organism exists then filters out, in a lawlike, statistical manner by the processes of natural selection, those changes in the DNA which enable the organisms possessing them to produce more progeny. (We will refer again to the interplay of chance and law in this process).

There are no professional biologists who doubt that natural selection is a factor operative in biological evolution, and most would say it is by far the most significant one. Some, such as Dawkins, say it is all-sufficient. It can certainly be subtle in its operation and counterintuitive with respect to the degree of change and the complexity of new structures and functions it can effect. However, other biologists are convinced that it is not the whole story, and some even go so far as to say that natural selection alone cannot account for the formation of distinctly new species.

Some other factors which, it is claimed, must be taken into account:

- Evolution of evolvability (D.C. Dennett).
- Constraints and selectivity effected by self-organizational principles (S. Kaufmann and B. Goodwin).
- Genetic assimilation (C.H. Waddington).
- How an organism might evolve is a consequence of its state at any given moment (R.C. Lewontin).
- Innovative behavior of individual organisms in a particular environment (A. Hardy).
- Top-down causation through a flow of information from environment to the organism (D. Campbell).
- *Group* selection (D.S. Wilson and E. Sober).

- Long-term changes resulting from molecular drive (gene-hopping—G.A. Dover).
- Effects of the context of adaptive changes or even stasis (N. Eldredge).
- Recognition that much molecular evolutionary change is immune to natural selection (M. Kimura).

What is significant about all these processes is that they all operate entirely within a naturalistic framework and assume a basically Darwinian process also to be operating, while differing about its speed and smoothness. Moreover, the depiction of this process and "nature, red in tooth and claw" (a phrase of the poet Tennyson that actually predates the public proposal of Darwin) is a caricature. For, as many biologists have pointed out,[8] natural selection is not even in a figurative sense the outcome of struggle, as such—in spite of the language of Herbert Spencer (the survival of the fittest) unwisely borrowed by Darwin. Natural selection involves many factors that include better integration with the ecological environment, more efficient utilization of available food, better care of the young, more cooperative social organization, and better capacity of surviving such struggles as do occur, remembering that it is in the interest of any predator that its prey survive as a species.

Death of the individual member of a species is essential to survival of the species, as such, and to the species' ability to adapt to environmental changes and, if need be, to evolve into a new species. In evolution we are witnessing new life through death of the old, and believers in God as creating through this process have to accept that the biological death of the individual is the means whereby God has been creating new species, including ourselves. Biological death was this creative means eons before human beings appeared. Hence, we can no longer take Paul's "The wages of sin is death"[9] to mean that our biological death can be attributed to human sin, as has often been assumed in atonement theories. If we wish to rescue Paul's phrase, we would have to reinterpret it to refer to some kind of spiritual death as being the consequence of sin.

Furthermore, the believer in God as Creator has to view biological evolution through natural selection (and possibly through the other naturalistic processes I mentioned) as simply the means whereby God has been and is creating. There is no *prima facie* case, as I elaborate later, for postulating any special supposed intervention by God to understand what has been going on.

The Emergence of Humanity

The biological and historical evidence is that human nature has emerged only gradually by a continuous process from other forms of primates and humanoids and that there are no sudden breaks of any substantial kind in the sequences noted by paleontologists and anthropologists. This is not to say that the history of human culture is simply a smoothly rising curve. There must have been, for example, key turning points or periods in the development of speech and so of social cooperation and of rituals for burying the dead, with provision of food and implements, testifying to a belief in some form of life after death. These apparently occurred among the Neanderthals of the middle Palaeolithic even before the emergence of *homo sapiens* some 100,000 or so years ago, when further striking developments later occurred.[10] However, there is *no* past period for which there is reason to affirm that human beings possessed moral perfection existing in a paradisal situation from which there has been only a subsequent decline. All the evidence points to a creature slowly emerging into awareness, with an increasing capacity for consciousness and sensitivity and the possibility of moral responsibility and, the religions would affirm, of response to God (especially after the axial period around 500 BC). So there is no sense in which we can talk of a "Fall" from a past perfection. There was no golden age, no perfect past, no individuals, and no Adam or Eve from whom all human beings have now descended and declined and who were perfect in their relationships and behavior. We appear to be rising beasts rather than fallen angels—rising from an amoral (and in that sense) innocent state to the capability of moral and immoral action. Of course, the myths of Adam and Eve and of the Fall have long since been interpreted nonhistorically and existentially by modern theologians and biblical scholars.[11]

What is also true is that humanity manifests aspirations to a perfection not yet attained, a potentiality not yet actualized, but no "original righteousness." Sin as alienation from God, humanity, and nature is only too real and appears as the consequence of our very possession of that *self*-consciousness which always places ourselves at the egotistical center of the universe of our consciousness that has evolved biologically. Sin is about our awareness of our falling short from what God would have us be and is part and parcel of our having evolved into self-consciousness, freedom, intellectual curiosity, and the possession of values. The domination of Christian theologies of redemption, for example, by classical conceptions of the Fall as a past event urgently needs, it seems to me, to be rescinded and what we mean by redemption to be rethought if it is to make any sense to our contemporaries.

We all have an awareness of the tragedy of our failure to fulfill our highest aspirations; of our failure to come to terms with finitude, death, and suffering; of our failure to realize our potentialities and to steer our path through life. Freedom allows us to make the wrong choices, so that sin and alienation from God, from our fellow human beings, and from nature are real features of our existence. So the questions of not only who we are but even what we should be becoming and where we should be going remain acute for us.

Human Behavior

Human behavior thus comes into focus and our understanding of it has been enriched by the new sciences of sociobiology and behavior genetics. Sociobiology is the systematic study of the biological, especially genetic, basis of patterns of social behavior in socially organized species, including the human, and aspires to include even human culture in its purview. Behavior genetics aims to examine over a wide range the inheritance of many different behaviors in individual organisms, again including humanity. These studies do not necessarily have to be pursued with excessively reductionist ambitions, although that has certainly been the stance of many of its practitioners, e.g., E.O. Wilson, the founder of sociobiology. They cannot but influence our general assessment of human nature and of the genetic constraints and limitations under which free will operates. Theologians should acknowledge that it is this kind of genetically based creature God has actually created as a human being through the evolutionary process. The limits and scope, and perhaps even the procedures (see next section) of human thinking and action, clearly depend on our genetic heritage. However, that heritage cannot in advance determine the content of our thinking, for example, of our moral reasoning even if it is a prerequisite of our possessing these capacities. I think we must not, in this context, perpetrate the "genetic fallacy" *(mot juste!)* of explaining reductively the form of a human, cultural development in terms of its biological (or even cultural) origins. Just as science is not magic, so ethics, on the same grounds, is not genetics.

Even so, the Christian theologian does not have to enter this debate with destructive ambitions. For if God, as a scientifically sensitive theology affirms, is creating immanently through the evolutionary processes, it would not be inconsistent with such a theology for human moral awareness to have originated sociobiologically. But this is not to preempt the maturation of moral sensitivity of self-aware, reasoning persons whose emergence in the created order God can properly be posited as intending (as I hope to make clear). Furthermore, a distinctive role for the religious impulse of humanity can be discerned in this context. As Donald Campbell first put it:

> Committing oneself to living for a transcendent God's purposes, not one's own [or those of one's genetic kin], is a commitment to optimize the social system rather than the individual system. . . . It seems from cross-cultural surveys that belief in transcendent deities that are concerned with morality of human behavior toward other human beings occurs more frequently in more complex societies.[12]

Moreover, humanity could only have survived and flourished if it held social and personal values that transcended the urges of the individual, embodying selfish genes—and these stem from the sense of a transcendent Good.

Evolution and Human Rationality

Evolutionary biology can trace the steps in which a succession of organisms have acquired nervous systems and brains whereby they obtain, store, retrieve, and use information about their environments in a way that furthers their survival. Our sense impressions must be broadly trustworthy and so must the cognitive structures whereby we know the world, otherwise we would not have survived. In a nutshell, our cognitive faculties *qua* biological organisms must be accurate enough in their representations of reality to enable us to survive. In the case of human beings, these cognitive faculties include the representations of external reality we individually and socially make to ourselves and must have at least the degree of verisimilitude to facilitate survival in the external realities of our environments. The extent to which evolutionary biology actually helps us understand the cognitive processes whereby this reliable knowledge about the environment was acquired is still an open, indeed confused, question. However, there can be little doubt that there is a continuity in the evolution of *homo sapiens* between:

- Cognitive processes that allow a physically and relatively weakly endowed creature to survive against fiercer predators and in a variety of environments.

- Processes of ordinary common sense ratiocination applied in everyday life.
- Ability to think abstractly and to manipulate symbols in mathematics, art, science, music, and the multitudinous facets of human culture.

This gives us grounds for our confidence in the reality-referring capacity of the cognitive processes with which evolution has provided us. It warrants the postulating of the existence of a general rationality in *homo sapiens* that yields, for the purpose of living, reliable knowledge and justified belief. This approach goes back to Karl Popper, Konrad Lorenz, and especially to Donald Campbell, who first named it "evolutionary epistemology." It is a healthy corrective to the epidemic of relativism associated with postmodernism, for it supports the conviction that our cognitive processes can refer to reality—that which we cannot avoid taking account of in our diagnoses of our experience and (in science) of our experiments.

The Paradox of Human Nonadaptedness

Biological organisms evolve to be adapted to the environment on which they depend for existence and suitable awareness of which is essential to their survival, as we have just seen. Yet oddly enough, there are signs of a kind of misfit between human beings and their environment that is not apparent in other creatures. We alone in the biological world, it seems, individually commit suicide; we alone by our burial rituals evidence the sense of another dimension to existence; we alone go through our biological lives with that sense of incomplete fulfillment evidenced by the contemporary quests for self-realization and personal growth. Human beings seek to come to terms with death, pain, and suffering, and they need to realize their own potentialities and learn how to steer their paths through life. The natural environment is not capable of satisfying such aspirations nor can the natural sciences describe, accurately discern, or satisfy them. So our presence in the biological world raises questions outside the scope of the natural sciences to answer. Because we are capable of joys and miseries quite unknown to other creatures, we evidence a dis-ease with our evolved state, a lack of fit that calls for explanation, and if possible cure.

This alienation of human beings from nonhuman nature and from each other appears as a kind of anomaly within the organic world. As human beings widen their environmental horizons, so they experience this anomaly, this "great gulf fixed," between their biological past environment out of which they have evolved and that in which they conceive themselves as existing or rather that in which they wish they existed. We may well ask, Why has, how has, the process whereby living organisms successfully evolved, finely tuned to and adapted to their environments, failed in the case of *homo sapiens* to ensure this fit between lived experience and the environing conditions of their lives? It appears that the human brain has capacities that were originally evolved in response to an earlier environmental challenge, but the exercise of which now engenders a whole range of needs, desires, ambitions, and aspirations that cannot all be harmoniously and jointly fulfilled.

Such considerations raise the further question of whether or not human beings have identified what their *true* environment really is—that environment in which human flourishing is possible. There seems to be an endemic failure of human beings to be adapted to what they sense as the totality of their environment. This incongruity was eloquently expressed by that great nineteenth-century Presbyterian preacher Thomas Chalmers in his 1822 Bridgewater treatise:

> There is in man, a restlessness of ambition; . . . a dissatisfaction with the present, which never is appeased by all the world has to offer . . . an unsated appetency for something larger and better, which he fancies in the perspective before him—to all which there is nothing like among the inferior animals.[13]

Does not the human condition raise the profound question of what humanity's true environment really is and of the nature of that reality to which it must relate? Thus, it was that St. Augustine, after years of travail and even despair, addressed his Maker: "You have made us for yourself and our heart is restless till it rests in you."[14]

Extraterrestrial Life

I have said enough to show that if the chemical conditions were right on a planet of about the same age as the Earth, moving round a planet of about the age of our Sun, then it is probable that living forms of matter would have appeared on it; and with a lower nonzero probability, that intelligent creatures would have emerged by the operation of natural selection. The physical *form* of these living extraterrestrial intelligences would of course almost certainly be very different from ours. Such is the number of possible planets and stars of this kind (there are about 10^{10-12} stars in our galaxy [the Milky Way] alone and about 10^{11}

galaxies, so of the order of over 10^{20} stars) that the tiniest probability of extraterrestrial life still leads to a finite probability of its existence on the planet other than the Earth at some time.

Christians have to ask themselves (and sceptics will certainly ask *them)*, What can the cosmic significance possibly be of the localized, terrestrial event of the existence of the historical Jesus? Does not the mere possibility of extraterrestrial life render nonsensical all the superlative claims made by the Christian church about his significance? Would ET, Alpha-Arcturians, Martians, et al., need an incarnation and all it is supposed to accomplish, as much as *homo sapiens* on planet Earth? Only a contemporary theology that can cope convincingly with such questions can hope to be credible today.

GENERAL FEATURES OF EVOLUTION

Chance and Law

We have seen that there is a creative interplay of chance and law apparent in the evolution of living matter by natural selection. This interplay between chance, at the molecular level of the DNA, and law or necessity at the statistical level of the population of organisms tempted Jacques Monod, in *Chance and Necessity,* to elevate chance to the level almost of a metaphysical principle whereby the universe might be interpreted. He concluded that the "stupendous edifice of evolution" is in this sense rooted in "pure chance" and that therefore all inferences of direction or purpose in the development of the biological world, in particular, and of the universe, in general, must be false.

However, there is no reason why the randomness of molecular event in relation to biological consequence has to be given the metaphysical status that Monod attributed to it. The involvement of what we call chance at the level of mutation in the DNA does not, of itself, preclude these events from displaying regular trends and manifesting inbuilt propensities at the higher levels of organisms, populations, and ecosystems. To call the mutation of the DNA a chance event serves simply to stress its randomness with respect to biological consequence.

Instead of being daunted by the role of chance in genetic mutations as being the manifestation of irrationality in the universe, it would be more consistent with the observations to assert that the full gamut of the potentialities of living matter could be explored only through the agency of the rapid and frequent randomization that is possible at the molecular level of the DNA. This role of chance, or rather randomness at the microlevel, is what one would expect if the universe were so constituted that all the potential forms of organizations of matter (both living and nonliving) that it contains might be thoroughly explored. This interplay of chance and law is the basis of the inherent creativity of the natural order, its ability to generate new forms, patterns, and organizations of matter and energy. If all were governed by rigid law, a repetitive and uncreative order would prevail; if chance alone ruled, no forms, patterns, or organizations would persist long enough for them to have any identity or real existence, and the universe could never have been cosmos and susceptible to rational inquiry. It is the combination of the two that makes possible an ordered universe capable of developing within itself new modes of existence.

This combination, for a theist, can only be regarded as an aspect of the God-endowed features of the world. The way in which chance operates within this given framework to produce new structures, entities, and processes can then properly be seen as an eliciting of the potentialities that the physical cosmos possessed *ab initio*. One might say that the potential of the "being" of the world is made manifest in the "becoming" that the operation of chance makes actual. God is the ultimate ground and source of both law (necessity) and chance.

For a theist, God must now be seen as acting rather like a composer extemporising a fugue to create in the world through what we call chance operating within the created order, each stage of which constitutes the launching pad of the next. The Creator, it now seems, is unfolding the divinely endowed potentialities of the universe, in and through a process in which these creative possibilities and propensities (see next section), inherent by God's own intention within the fundamental entities of that universe and their interrelations, become actualized within a created temporal development shaped and determined by those selfsame God-given potentialities.

Trends and Directions in Evolution?

Can God be said to be implementing any purpose in biological evolution? Or is the whole process so haphazard, such a matter of happenstance, such a matter of what Monod and Jacob called *bricolage* (tinkering), that no meaning, least of all a divinely intended one, can be discerned in the process? Popper has pointed out that the realization of possibilities, which may be random, depends on the total situation within which the possibilities are being actualized so that "there exist weighted possibilities which are more than mere possibilities, but tendencies or *propensities* to become real" and that these *"are properties of the whole situation* and sometimes even of the particular way in which a situation changes"[15] (emphasis added). Propensities are simply the effects of the context on the outcomes of random events. I suggest that the evolutionary process is characterized by propensities, evoked by natural selection, toward increase in complexity, information processing and storage, consciousness, sensitivity to pain, and even self-consciousness (a necessary prerequisite for social development and the cultural transmission of knowledge down the generations). Some successive forms, along some evolutionary branch or twig, have a distinct probability of manifesting more and more of these characteristics. However, the actual physical form of the organisms in which these propensities are actualized is contingent on the history of the crossing of disparate chains of events, including the survival of the mass extinctions that have occurred (96% of all species in the permo-Triassic one).

Stephen J. Gould has interpreted the extraordinary fossils of very early (about 530 million years ago) soft-bodies fauna found in the Burgess Shale of the Canadian Rockies to represent a maximum in disparity of forms.[16] After this, he claims, there was a dramatic decline in the range of types (phyla) of species, that is, in disparity. On this basis he then so emphasizes the role of contingency in evolution that he can attribute no trends, let alone inevitability, toward the emergence of particular features in evolution. This interpretation of these fauna has now been strongly opposed by S. Conway Morris, an evolutionary paleobiologist, who has devoted his research life to the study of the Burgess Shale and related formations. He shows, in his book *The Crucible of Creation*, that disparity has *not* in fact diminished since that point.[17] Even more significantly, he demonstrates, with respect to Gould, what is widely accepted by evolutionary biologists, namely, the eminent role of *convergence* in evolution, whereby in independent lines and places similar solutions are found to the same kind of environmental challenges. Gould argues that if we were "to rerun the tape of life" from the time of the Cambrian explosion, we would then have a totally different biological world, from which anything remotely like humans would be absent. Morris says that this argument is based on a

> basic confusion concerning the destiny of a given lineage . . . versus the likelihood that a particular biological property or feature will sooner or later manifest itself as part of the evolutionary process.[18]

> For . . . animals (as well as plants and other organisms) often
> come to resemble each other despite having evolved from differ-
> ent ancestors. Nearly all biologists agree that convergence is a
> ubiquitous feature of life . . . [for] all organisms are under the
> scrutiny of natural selection. . . . [C]onvergence shows that in a
> real world not all things are possible.[19]

Morris cites, as an example of convergence, the sabre-toothed tiger of
the Northern Hemisphere, a close relative of the tiger and the panther,
and the very similar South American sabre-toothed "cat" that is in fact
a marsupial, related to the living kangaroos and opossums.

> Again and again we have evidence of biological form stumbling
> on the same solution to a problem. . . .
>   The reality of convergence suggests that the tape of life, to
> use Gould's metaphor, can be run as many times as we like and in
> principle intelligence will surely emerge. . . .
>   [T]he appearance of the nerve cell must be regarded as one of
> the great steps in the history of life . . . evolution is then set towards
> the development of brains, presumably intelligence, and perhaps
> consciousness . . . the first two steps—brains and intelligence—have
> been acquired at least twice in the history of animals, then an inves-
> tigation of these similarities between molluscs and vertebrates . . .
> will be rewarding in terms of our evolutionary understanding.[20]

Thus Morris, with superb illustrations and convincing detail, amplifies
and gives content to the notion of propensities and so of inbuilt trends
in biological evolution. Hence, providing there had been enough time,
a complex organism with consciousness, self-consciousness, and social
and cultural organization (that is, the basis for the existence of persons)
would have been likely,[21] because of the advantages in natural selection
of these characteristics, eventually to have evolved and appeared on the
Earth (or on some other planet amenable to the emergence of living
organisms)—although no doubt with a physical form very different
from *homo sapiens*. There can, it now appears (*pace* Gould), be overall
direction and implementation of divine purpose through the interplay
of chance and law without a deterministic plan fixing all the details of
the structure(s) of what emerges as possessing personal qualities.
Hence, the emergence of self-conscious persons capable of relating personally to God still can be regarded as an intention of God continuously creating through the processes of that to which God has given an
existence of this contingent kind and not some other.

Incidentally, I see no need to postulate any special action—any nonnatural agent pushing, pulling, or luring by some divine manipulation of mutations at the quantum level—to ensure that persons emerge in the universe and in particular on Earth. Not to coin a phrase, "I have no need of that hypothesis!"

The Ubiquity of Pain, Suffering, and Death

The ability for information processing and storage is indeed the necessary, if not sufficient, condition for the emergence of consciousness. This sensitivity to, this sentence of, consciousness' surroundings inevitably involves an increase in its ability to experience pain, which constitutes the necessary biological warning signals of danger and disease—and pain entails suffering in conscious creatures. Insulation from the surrounding world in the biological equivalent of three-inch nicked steel would be a sure recipe for preventing the development of consciousness.

New patterns can only come into existence in a finite universe (finite in the sense of the conservation of matter-energy) if old patterns dissolve to make place for them. This is a condition of the creativity of the process—of its ability to produce the new—which at the biological level we observe as new forms of life only through death of the old. For the death of individuals is essential for release of food resources for new arrivals, and species simply die out by being ousted from biological niches by new ones better adapted to survive and reproduce in them. So there is a kind of *structural* logic about the inevitability of living organisms dying and of preying on each other for we cannot conceive, in a lawful nonmagical universe, of any way whereby the immense variety of developing, biological, structural complexity might appear, except by utilizing structures already existing, either by way of modification (as in biological evolution) or of incorporation (as in feeding). The statistical logic is inescapable: new forms of matter arise only through the dissolution of the old; new life only through death of the old. So biological death of the individual is the prerequisite of the creativity of the biological order, in creativity which eventually led to the emergence of human beings.

Hence pain, suffering, and death, which have been called natural evil, appear to be inevitable concomitants of a universe that is going to be creative of new forms, some of which are going to be conscious and self-conscious.

Even so, the theist cannot lightly set aside these features of the created order. For any concept of God to be morally acceptable and coherent, the ubiquity of pain, suffering, and death as the means of creation through biological evolution entails that—if God is also immanently present in and to natural processes, then we cannot but infer that—in some sense hard to define *God*, like any human creator, suffers in, with, and under the creative processes of the world with their costly unfolding in time.

Rejection of the notion of the impassibility of God has been a feature of the Christian theology of recent decades. There has been an increasing assent to the idea that it is possible "to speak consistently of a God who suffers eminently and yet is still God, and a God who suffers universally. . ."[22] God, we find ourselves having tentatively to conjecture, suffers the natural evils of the world along with ourselves because (we can only hint at this stage) God purposes to bring about a greater good, namely the kingdom of free-willing, loving persons in communion with God and with each other.

A THEOLOGY OF AND FOR EVOLUTION

I urge that far from the epic of evolution being a threat to Christian theology, it is a stimulus to and a basis for a more encompassing and enriched understanding of the interrelations of God, humanity, and nature. An argument for the existence of God in Anglo-Saxon "physico-theology" (an eighteenth and early nineteenth century form of natural theology) was based on attributing to the direct action of God the Designer the intricacy of particular biological mechanisms. This argument collapsed when Darwin and his successors showed that this apparent design could evolve by a purely natural process based on scientifically intelligible processes. The beginning of the impact of Darwinism on theology is usually dated from the legend of the debate of the then Bishop of Oxford with T.H. Huxley at the meeting of the British Association for the Advancement of Science on Saturday, 30 June, 1860. I say legend because historical studies show that the story is mainly a later construct of Huxley and his biographers, for the impact of this now much-quoted event was not great at the time. No mention of it has been found in any publication between 1860 and 1880. After this, triumphalist accounts, on behalf of Huxley's science and for the independence of the profession of scientists, began to appear in various "Lives" and "Letters." So it is indeed a legend, and today often an icon, of the so-called conflict of religion and science, biology in particular, which we have all inherited. But even in the nineteenth century, many Anglican theologians, both evangelical and catholic, embraced positively the proposal of evolution. Of the former, one can think of Charles Kingsley, who in his *Water Babies* affirmed that God makes "things make themselves"; of the latter, we may instance Aubrey Moore, who in *Lux Mundi* in 1889 (a publication of a group of Oxford High Anglicans) wrote:

> Darwinism appeared, and, under the disguise of a foe, did the work of a friend. It has conferred upon philosophy and religion an inestimable benefit, by showing us that we must choose between two alternatives. Either God is everywhere present in nature, or He is nowhere.[23]

God and the World

Immanence. Such an emphasis on the immanence of God as Creator in, with, and under the natural processes of the world unveiled by the sciences is certainly in accord with all that the sciences have revealed since those debates of the nineteenth century. For a notable aspect of the scientific account on the natural world in general is the seamless character of the web that has been spun on the loom of time: the process appears as continuous from its cosmic beginning, in the hot Big Bang, to the present and at no point do modern natural scientists have to invoke any nonnatural causes to explain their observations and inferences about the past.

The processes that have occurred can, as we saw, be characterized as one of *emergence*, for new forms of matter, and a hierarchy of organization of these forms themselves, appear in the course of time. New kinds of reality may be said to emerge in time.

The scientific perspective of the world, especially the living world, inexorably impresses on us a dynamic picture of the world of entities and structures involved in continuous and incessant change and in process without ceasing. This impels us to re-introduce into our understanding of God's creative relation to the world a dynamic element that was always implicit in the Hebrew conception of a living God, dynamic in action—even if obscured by the tendency to think of creation as an event in the past. God has again to be conceived of continuously creating, continuously giving existence to what is new; that God is *semper Creator*; that the world is a *creatio continua*. The traditional notion of God sustaining the world in its general order and structure now has to be enriched by a dynamic and creative dimension—the model of God sustaining and giving continuous existence to a process that has an inbuilt creativity, built into it by God. God is creating at every moment of the world's existence in and through the perpetually endowed creativity of the very stuff of the world.

All of which reinforces this need to re-affirm more strongly than at any other time in the Christian (and Jewish and Islamic) traditions that in a very strong sense God is the immanent Creator creating in and through the processes of the natural order. The processes themselves, as unveiled by the biological sciences are God-acting-as-Creator, God *qua* Creator. The processes are not themselves God, but the *action* of God-as-Creator. God gives existence in divinely created time to a process that itself brings forth the new: thereby God is creat*ing*. This means we do not have to look for any extra supposed gaps in which, or mechanisms whereby, God might be supposed to be acting as Creator in the living world.

Panentheism.[24] Classical philosophical theism maintained the ontological distinction between God and creative world that is necessary for any genuine theism by conceiving them to be of different *substances*, with particular attributes predicated of each. There was a space outside God in which the realm of created substances existed. This substantival way of speaking has become inadequate for it has become increasingly difficult to express the way in which God is present to the world in terms of substances, which by definition cannot be internally present to each other. God can only intervene in the world in such a model. This inadequacy of classical theism is aggravated by the evolutionary perspective which, as we have just seen, requires that natural processes in the world need to be regarded as God's creative action. In other words, the world is to God, rather as our bodies are to us as personal agents, with the necessary caveat that the ultimate ontology of God as Creator is distinct from that of the world (pan*en*theism, not pantheism). Moreover, this *personal* model of embodied subjectivity (with that essential caveat) represents better how we are now impelled to understand God's perennial action in the world as coming from the inside, both in its natural regularities and in any special patterns of events. These three factors—the stronger emphasis on God's immanence in the world, the stressing (as in the biblical tradition) of God as at least personal, and the need to avoid the use of substance in this context—lead to a panentheistic relation of God and the world. Panentheism is, accordingly,

> The belief that the Being of God includes and penetrates the
> whole universe, so that every part of it exists in Him but (as
> against pantheism) that His Being is more than, and is not ex-
> hausted by, the universe.[25]

This concept has strong philosophical foundations and is scriptural, as
has been carefully argued by P. Clayton[26]—recall Paul's address at
Athens when he says of God that "In him we live and move and have
our being."[27] It is in fact also deeply embedded in the Eastern
Christian tradition.

The Wisdom (Sophia) and the Word (Logos) of God. Biblical scholars
have in recent decades come to emphasize the significance of the central themes of the so-called Wisdom literature *(Job, Proverbs,
Ecclesiastes, Ecclesiasticus,* and *Wisdom).* In this broad corpus of writings, the feminine figure of Wisdom *(Sophia)*, according to J.G. Dunn,
is a convenient way of speaking about God acting in creation, revelation, and salvation; Wisdom never becomes more than a personifica-
tion of God's activity.[28] This Wisdom endows some human beings, at
least, with a personal wisdom that is rooted in their concrete experiences and in their systematic and ordinary observations of the natural
world—what we would call science. But it is not confined to this and
represents the distillation of wider human, ethical, and social experiences and even cosmological ones, since knowledge of the heavens fig-
ured in the capabilities of the sage. The natural order is valued as a gift
and source of wonder, something to be celebrated. All such wisdom,
imprinted as a pattern on the natural world and in the mind of the
sage, is but a pale image of the divine wisdom—that activity distinctive
of God's relation to the world.

In the New Testament, Jesus came to be regarded as "the one who
so embodied God's creative power and saving wisdom (particularly in
his death and resurrection) that he can be identified as 'the power of
God and the wisdom of God' [1 Cor. 1.24]."[29]

That wisdom is an attribute of God, personified as female, has
been of especial significance to feminist theologians[30] one of whom
has argued, on the basis of a wider range of biblical sources, that the
feminine in God refers to all persons of the Christian Triune God.
Thus, Wisdom *(Sophia)* becomes "the feminine face of God expressed
in all persons of the Trinity."[31] In the present context, it is pertinent
that this important concept of Wisdom *(Sophia)* unites intimately the

divine activity of creation, human experience, and the processes of the natural world. It therefore constitutes a biblical resource for imaging the panentheism we have been urging.

So also does the closely related concept of the Word *(Logos)* of God, which is regarded[32] as existing eternally as a mode of God's own being, as active in creation, and as a self-expression of God's own being and becoming imprinted in the very warp and woof of the created order. It seems to be a conflation of the largely Hebraic concept of the "Word of the Lord," as the will of God in creative activity, with the divine *logos* of Stoic thought. This latter is the principle of rationality as both manifest in the cosmos and in the human reason (also named by the Stoics as *logos*). Again we have a panentheistic notion that unites, intimately, as three facets of one integrated and interlocked activity: the divine, the human, and (nonhuman) natural. It is, needless to say, significant that for Christians this *logos* was regarded as "made flesh"[33] in the person of Jesus the Christ.

A Sacramental Universe. The evolutionary epic, as I have called it for brevity, recounts in its sweep and continuity how over eons of time the mental and spiritual potentialities of matter have been actualized above all in the evolved complex of the human-brain-in-the-human-body. The original fluctuating quantum field, quark soup or whatever, has in some twelve or so billion years become a Mozart, a Shakespeare, a Buddha, a Jesus of Nazareth—and you and me!

Every advance of the biological, cognitive, and psychological sciences shows human beings as psychosomatic unities—that is, as persons. Matter has manifest personal qualities, that unique combination of physical, mental, and spiritual capacities. (I use "spiritual" as indicating relatable to God in a personal way.) For the panentheist, who sees God working in, with, and under natural processes, this unique result (to date) of the evolutionary process corroborates that God is using that process as an instrument of God's purposes and as a symbol of the divine nature, that is, as the means of conveying insight into these purposes.

But in the Christian tradition, this is precisely what its sacraments do. They are valued for what God is effecting instrumentally and for what God is conveying symbolically through them. Thus, William Temple came to speak of the "sacramental universe"[34] and we can come to see nature as sacrament, or at least, as sacramental. Hence, my continued need to apply the phrase of in, with, and under, which Luther used to refer to the mode of the Real Presence in the Eucharist, to the presence of God in the processes of the world.

This could be (and has been[35]) developed further in relation to the doctrine of the Incarnation and to the new valuation of the very stuff of the world, which ensues from those significant words of Jesus at the Last Supper: "This: my body" and "This: my blood"—referring, as it is often said in the Liturgy, to bread "which earth has given and human hands have made" and to "wine, fruit of the vine and work of human hands." But this is best considered in the light of how Jesus the Christ is to be regarded in the light of all the forgiving. To this we must now turn.

Humanity and Jesus the Christ in an Evolutionary Perspective

We have already seen that humanity is incomplete, unfinished, falling short of that instantiation of the ultimate values of truth, beauty, and goodness that God, their ultimate source, must be seeking to achieve to bring them into harmonious relation to Godself. We have not yet become fully adapted to the ultimate, eternal "environment" of God.

It was not long after Darwin published the *Origin* that some theologians began to discern the significance of the central distinctive Christian affirmation of the Incarnation of God in the human person of Jesus the Christ as especially congruent with an evolutionary perspective. Thus, again in *Lux Mundi* in 1891, we find J.R. Illingworth boldly affirming:

> . . . [I]n scientific language, the Incarnation may be said to have introduced a new species into the world—the Divine man transcending past humanity, as humanity transcended the rest of the animal creation, and communicating His vital energy by a spiritual process to subsequent generations. . . .[36]

Jesus' resurrection convinced the disciples, including Paul, that it is the union with God of *his* kind of life that is not broken by death and capable of being taken into God. For Jesus manifested the kind of human life which, it was believed, can become fully life with God, not only here and now, but eternally beyond the threshold of death. Hence his imperative "Follow me" constitutes a call for the transformation of humanity into a new kind of human being and becoming. What happened to Jesus, it was thought, could happen to all.

In this perspective, Jesus the Christ (the whole Christ event) has, I would suggest, shown us what is possible for humanity. The actualization of this potentiality can properly be regarded as the consummation of the purposes of God already manifested incompletely in evolving humanity. In Jesus there was a *divine* act of new creation because Christians may now say the initiative was *from God*, within human history, within the responsive human will of Jesus inspired by that outreach of God into humanity designated as God the Holy Spirit. Jesus the Christ is thereby seen, in the context of the whole complex of events in which he participated as the paradigm of what God intends for all human beings, now revealed as having the potentiality of responding to, of being open to, of becoming united with God. In this perspective, he represents the consummation of the evolutionary creative process that God has been effecting in and through the world.

In this perspective, the ever-present, self-expression in all-that-is of God as Word or *Logos* attains its most explicit, personal revelation in Jesus the Christ. But because it is (albeit unique for Christians) a manifestation of this eternal and perennial mode of God's interaction in, with, and under the created order, what was revealed in Jesus the Christ could also, in principle, be manifest both in other human beings and indeed also on other planets, in any sentient, self-conscious, *nonhuman* persons (whatever their physical form) inhabiting them that are capable of relating to God. This vision of a universe permeated by the ever-acting, ever-working, and potentially explicit self-expression of the divine Word/*Logos* was never better expressed than in a poem of Alice Meynell (1847–1922):

> *Christ in the Universe*
> With this ambiguous earth
> His dealings have been told us. These abide:
> The signal to a maid, the human birth,
> the lesson and the young Man crucified.
>
>   But not a star of all
> The innumerable host of stars has heard
> How he administered this terrestrial ball.
> Our race have kept their Lord's entrusted Word . . .
>
>   No planet knows that this
> Our wayside planet, carrying land and wave,
> Love and life multiplied, and pain and bliss,
> Bears, as chief treasure, one forsaken grave.

Nor, in our little day,
May his devices with the heavens he guessed,
His pilgrimage to thread the Milky Way,
Or his bestowals there be manifest.

But, in the eternities,
Doubtless we shall compare together, hear
A million alien Gospels, in what guise
He trod the Pleiades, the Lyre, the Bear.[37]

For on Earth the epic of evolution is consummated in the Incarnation in a human person of the cosmic self-expression of God, God's Word—and in the hope this gives to all self-conscious persons of being united with the Source of all Being and Becoming that is the "Love that moves the heavens and the other stars."

May I suggest that, in the second century, Irenaeus said it all, in inviting us to contemplate:

The Word of God, our Lord Jesus Christ
Who of his boundless love
became what we are
to make us what even he himself is. (*Adv. Haer.*, V praef.)

NOTES

1. T. Dobzhansky, *American Biology Teacher* (1973).
2. Genesis 2:10.
3. Genesis 3:19.
4. M. Eigen, "The Self-Organisation of Matter and the Evolution of Biological Macromolecules," *Naturwissenschaffen*, 58 (1971), 465–523. See also R. Winkler and M. Eigen, *Das Spiel* (Munich and Zurich: R. Piper and Co. Verlag, 1975). For Prigogene's work, see I. Prigogene and I. Stengers, *Order Out of Chaos* (London: Heinemann, 1984).
5. I long ago learned this device from Professor David Nichols of the University of Exeter (see A.R. Peacocke, *Science and the Christian Experiment* [London: Oxford University Press, 1971] 72, n. 1).
6. Genesis 1:31 (NRSV).
7. C. Darwin, *The Origin of Species by Means of Natural Selection*, 6th ed., chap. iii (London: Thinkers Library Ed., Watts and Co.), 97–98.
8. G.G. Simpson, *The Meaning of Evolution* (New York: Bantam Press; New Haven: Yale University Press, 1971), 20.
9. Romans, 6:23 (A.V.)
10. See K.J. Narr, "Cultural Achievements of Early Man" in G. Altner, ed., *The Human Creature* (New York: Anchor Books, Doubleday, 1974), 115–116: ". . . A

marked evolutionary expansion manifests itself after around 30,000 B.C. at the beginning of the upper Palaeolithic. The new picture that emerges can be characterised by such terms as accumulation, differentiation and specialization. There is an increase and concentration of cultural goods, a more refined technology with greater variety in the forms of weapons and tools produced and corresponding specialisation of their respective functions, more pronounced economic and general cultural differentiation of individual groups."

11. See the article by A. Richardson on Adam in A. Richardson, ed., *A Theological Word Book of the Bible* (London: SCM Press, 1957), 14.

12. D.T. Campbell "On the Conflicts Between Biological and Social Evolution and Between Psychology and Moral Tradition," Zygon, 11 (1976), 192.

13. T. Chalmers, "On the Power, Wisdom and Goodness of God as Manifested in the Adaptation of External Nature to the Moral and Intellectual Constitution of Man," *The First Bridgewater Treatise*, 1832, 308.

14. Augustine, *Confessions*, Book I [1], 1.

15. K.R. Popper, *A World of Propensities* (Bristol: Thoemmes, 1996), 12, 17

16. S.J. Gould, *Wonderful Life: The Burgess Shale and the Nature of History* (London: Pengiun Books, 1989), 306, citing D.M. Kaup.

17. R.C. Morris, *The Crucible of Creation: The Burgess Shale and the Rise of Animals* (Oxford: Oxford University Press, 1998).

18. Ibid., 201 ff.

19. Ibid., 202.

20. Ibid., 14, 22.

21. The judgment of C. de Duve, a participant in this symposium, Nobel laureate, cell biologist, and biochemist, is relevant. "Particularly remarkable, in animal evolution, is the unswerving vertical drive—with horizontal evolution producing side branches all along the way, of course—in the direction of polyneural complexity. . . . No doubt the environment played an important role in molding the details of this pathway . . . but the overriding element, surely, is the fact that a more complex brain is an asset in almost any circumstance. Viewed in this context, the emergence of humankind or, at least, of conscious, intelligent beings, appears as much less improbable than many maintain. Contrary to what Monod stated, the biosphere *was* pregnant with man (p. 7)." C. de Duve, "Constraints on the Origin and Evolution of Life," *Proceedings of the American Philosophical Society*, 142 (1998), 1–8.

22. P.S. Fiddes, *The Creative Suffering of God* (Oxford: Clarendon Press, 1988), 3.

23. A. Moore, "The Christian Doctrine of God," in C. Gore, ed., *Luz Mundi*, 12th ed. (London: John Murray, 1891), 73.

24. For further exposition, see my *Theology for a Scientific World* (TSA), 2nd enlarged ed. (London and Minneapolis: SCM and Fortress Press [1993]) 370–372; "A Response to Polkinghorne," *Science and Christian Belief*, 7 (1995), 109–110; P. Clayton, "The Case for Christian Panentheism," *Dialog, 37* (1998), 201–208 to which this account here is greatly indebted.

25. F.L. Cross and E.A. Livingstone, eds., *Oxford Dictionary of the Christian Church* (Oxford: Oxford University Press, 1983), 1027. See also Augustine, *Confessions*, VII 7, quoted in TSA, p. 159.

26. P. Clayton, *God in Contemporary Science* (Edinburgh: Edinburgh University Press, 1997), chaps. 2, 4.

27. Acts 17:28 (NRSV).

28. J.G. Dunn, *Christology in the Making* (London: SCM Press, 1980), 210.

29. Ibid., p. 211.

30. S. Coakley, "Feminine and the Holy Spirit?", in M. Furlong, ed., *Mirror to the Church: Reflections on Sexism* (London: SPCK, 1988), 124–135.

31. C. Deane-Drummond, "Sophia: The Feminine Face of God as Metaphor for an Ecotheology," *Feminist Theology,* 16 (1997), 11–31; "Futurenatural?: A Future of Science through the Lens of Wisdom," Heythrop J. XL (1999), 41–59 (specifically here, p. 5).

32. *CF.* John 1.

33. John 1:14.

34. W. Temple, *Nature, Man and God* (London: Macmillan, 1934), chap. 19.

35. A.R. Peacocke, "Matter in Religion and Science," in *God and the New Biology* (London: Dent, 1986; repr. Gloucester, Mass.: Peter Smith, 1994) chap. 9; "Nature as Sacrament" in *Affirming Catholicism,* Sept./Oct., 1999.

36. J.R. Illingworth, "The Incarnation in relation to Development," in C. Gore, ed., *Lux Mundi,* 12th ed. (London: John Murray, 1981), 151–152. But we cannot today use for this transformation his phrase "a new species" in any literal sense, for species is for us now a purely biological term.

37. A. Meynell, "Christ in the Universe," in Helen Gardner, ed., *The Faber Book of Religious Verse* (London: Faber and Faber, 1972), 292.

JOHN LESLIE

A philosopher with a deep interest in science and religion, **John Leslie** taught at the University of Guelph in Ontario, Canada for nearly thirty years. Born in India, he won a scholarship to Oxford University, where he majored in psychology and philosophy at Wadham College. He then worked in advertising before returning to Oxford to take his M.Litt. in philosophy in 1968. He joined the Guelph faculty as a lecturer, becoming a full professor in 1982 and professor emeritus in 1996. Professor Leslie has been a visiting professor of religious studies at the University of Calgary and of astrophysics at the University of Liège and a visiting fellow in the research department of philosophy at the Australian National University. In 1998, he was the British Academy-Royal Society of Canada Exchange Lecturer. In addition to articles in academic journals and chapters for numerous collections, he is the author of four books. His latest study is *The End of the World: The Science and Ethics of Human Extinction,* published in 1996.

Intelligent Life in Our Universe

John Leslie

NASA's claim to have found fossil life in a meteorite that came from Mars is widely rejected. If it were right, though, would that show that life arises easily in our universe? Not necessarily, as Davies has noted.[1] If tiny fossil organisms can travel from Mars to Earth aboard meteorites, so perhaps can tiny living ones, or again, these might travel from Earth to Mars aboard meteorites (or maybe on dust grains propelled by sunlight). Either way, finding life in both places would not disprove the theory that it originated in the solar system just once, through a tremendous fluke.

How Common Is Life in the Cosmos, and How Long Will Our Species Survive?

Even when life has appeared on a planet, its progress all the way to humanlike intelligence might be very improbable. John Maynard Smith has written—startlingly, but chaos theory could help to make it plausible—that moving an individual animal in the Cambrian seas two feet to its left could well have meant that not even the conquest of the land would have occurred, let alone the emergence first of mammals, then of humans.[2] High intelligence may do little to increase an organism's chances. Complex brains demand much childhood nurturing; they consume astonishingly much energy; and intelligent curiosity may lead one to investigate some dark hole where one's head gets snapped off.

Brandon Carter runs the following mathematical argument. It was a few billion years before life on our planet evolved intelligence. In only a few billion more years, the Sun will swell and destroy the Earth. Why was the total time available for intelligence to evolve "in the same ball park" as the time actually taken? Carter answers that intelligence typically would not evolve fast enough.[3] Imagine millions of convicts struggling to open their cells by random twisting of the combination locks. Average time required: a few years. Time available: two hours. Hardly any would succeed. If the combination locks had just a few dials, those who succeeded would take mostly about an hour. If that is the right analogy, then hardly any species achieve intelligence; their suns swell into red giants first. Our chances of detecting intelligent extraterrestrials are therefore low.

Enrico Fermi had a famous "Where are they?" argument for the same conclusion. If intelligence had been fated to appear many times in our galaxy, then it would be likely to have appeared on many planets earlier than on Earth—for how odd it would be if our planet had won a race against thousands of competitors! However, calculations suggest that it would take an intelligent species only a comparatively short time to spread right across its galaxy. (Figures of well under ten million years now seem plausible.) Why, then, have no extraterrestrials come to our planet? A plausible answer would be that intelligence evolves only very rarely or else destroys itself very quickly, possibly through nuclear or biological warfare.[4]

A controversial variant on this idea has been developed by Carter and independently by Richard Gott, a variant now known as "the doomsday argument." Hitting on this back in 1983, Carter has so far outlined it only in lectures and seminars, so that Gott developed his own version of it for publication without at all suspecting that he was other than its first inventor.[5] Just as we would not expect our species to be *the very first to reach intelligence among thousands*, so we should not expect to be *in the first thousandth, say, of all humans who would ever have lived*, let alone well inside the first billionth of a human race that was going to spread through its entire galaxy of roughly a hundred billion stars. In contrast, there would be nothing too startling in finding oneself alive at the same time as roughly 10 percent of all humans who would ever have lived. Well, in view of the recent population explosion, that fairly unsurprising temporal position is where you and I would have found ourselves if the human race became extinct shortly. This consideration can increase any pessimism we develop after considering nuclear bombs, biological warfare, and the like.

Here is another way of creeping up on the same point. If intelligent species existed in large numbers in our universe, and if each had a good chance of spreading through its galaxy, then could not intelligent observers greatly expect to find themselves in species *which had*? There would be so vastly many more observers in any species which had! If you are a lemming, expect to find yourself after a population explosion, not when there are hardly any lemmings around.

An objector might at this point bring forward the protest that we know for sure that we exist near the end of the twentieth century, before the human race has had a chance to start spreading through its galaxy, and we would be just as sure of it regardless of our estimate of how long humankind would survive. However, the protest would be misguided. Compare the case of arguing, "I know for sure that a black ball was the first one drawn from the urn. My confidence in this would be just as great, no matter whether I thought that the urn had contained only one black ball, in company with a thousand white; therefore I have no special reason to doubt that the urn still contains a thousand balls, all white." True, we do know our position in human population history so far. But what we are trying to estimate is how early that is, proportionately, in the total temporal spread of the human race. And here let us ask, not how likely it is that we *are actually* near the end of the twentieth century (answer: 100% likely, since we know we are there), but rather how likely we *would have been* to find ourselves there, had the human race been more or less sure to spread across its galaxy.

Whether defending or attacking the doomsday argument, we soon get involved in considerable complexities. Even the protest that we have to find ourselves alive now and not later, because *now is now*, cannot be handled in under a few paragraphs. In his book *About Time*, Paul Davies, one of the argument's defenders, may not have chosen the best way of dealing with this protest when he appeals to Einstein's view that the future is in some sense "already there."[6] The crucial question may instead be whether a long future for humankind is already assured, or virtually assured. Consider the following question about your probable temporal position. It was planned that three emeralds would be distributed in one century, and five thousand in some much later century. You find yourself the lucky recipient of an emerald. In which of the two centuries are you likely to be? If you know nothing beyond these facts, but believe *that all the emeralds were virtually sure to be distributed,* then you should bet that you are in the later century.

Taking the doomsday argument seriously, I wrote a book around it.[7] All the same, I am unhappy with Gott's version, which seems to be that our chance of being in *the first billionth* of all humans who will ever have lived *is one in a billion*, and that's that. Carter and I develop the argument differently. We take into account the "prior probability" of the human race spreading through the galaxy: the probability as estimated after considering such matters as efforts to get rid of nuclear bombs, but before considering Carter's point that one would not expect to have been born very exceptionally early. If having immense prior confidence that the human race would spread through the galaxy, then even after considering Carter's point, our confidence could remain high.

Again, it would seem that Carter's argument can run entirely smoothly only if the number of humans who will ever have lived is already fixed, like the contents of an urn already filled. But there are reasons, particularly coming from quantum physics, for thinking that many things are not yet fixed. Our universe appears to be indeterministic. The upshot, I believe, is that the doomsday argument acts very strongly only as a way of reducing great confidence in a long future for humankind: confidence that such a future "is as good as determined." The doomsday argument *cannot*, for instance, refute Freeman Dyson's view that the human race is fairly likely to spread right across the galaxy.[8] The most it could do would be to refute the view that its spreading across the galaxy was virtually certain. (Imagine that whether humans would colonize the entire galaxy depended on a coin that had yet to be tossed. What would be my estimate of their chance of colonizing the entire galaxy? Answer: one half, if how the coin was going to land depended, as it plausibly could, on events markedly sensitive to quantum effects.)

As a means of persuading us that the human race will not last long, does Fermi's *where are they?* do a better job? Not obviously, for while the reason why we have detected no extraterrestrials might be that all of them destroyed themselves shortly after developing high intelligence, it could equally well be that intelligence is extremely difficult to achieve. It might actually be that in the entire universe now visible to human telescopes, of some ten billion trillion stars, intelligence will arise only once. For utilitarians like me—people who think that, roughly speaking, a thousand happy lives add up to something a thousand times better than a single happy life—this provides a superb reason for trying to prevent nuclear and biological warfare, loss of the ozone layer, poisoning of the environment, and so forth, so that humankind can avoid extinction. The next three or four centuries probably will be the most dangerous. If our species gets through them safely, then colonizing the entire galaxy could well be comparatively easy. And, as Dyson has argued, even eternal life for our intelligent descendants might subsequently become possible. Dyson's reasoning starts from the point that in an ever-expanding, ever-cooling universe, the amount of energy required to process any given amount of information would become ever smaller.[9]

Fermi's argument does, on the other hand, give very strong reasons for thinking that intelligent extraterrestrials will be hard to find in our galaxy. Probably they have not evolved in it, or else those who did have already destroyed themselves. This appears more plausible than that they have spread right through the galaxy without our noticing it, possibly because they have declared our solar system an untouchable zoo, or that they have one and all resolved to stay at home, or that they have not yet been traveling long enough to reach us. Yet this is not to say that Jill Cornell Tarter's enthusiasm for listening for extraterrestrial signals is misplaced. The chances of detecting such signals may be fairly slim, but the benefits of doing so could be immense whereas the costs of searching are minimal: comparable, in fact, to those of producing a few movies about extraterrestrials. Again, in view of how many directions extraterrestrial signals might be coming from, and the number of frequencies on which any signal might be carried, searches to date can be seen to have been pitifully inadequate.

Suppose no signals were ever detected. Suppose we had reasons, too, for thinking that intelligent species would soon have transformed their galaxies in readily detectable ways, yet our telescopes detected nothing. Would it follow that we were alone in the universe? Not at all. Ours may be an "open" universe (not "closed" like a sphere's surface), and on the simplest models open universes contain infinitely many stars. Again, the currently most popular model presents a "closed but inflated" universe. Inflation, a burst of tremendous expansion very early after the Big Bang began, could easily have given us a universe stretching beyond our horizon (set by the distance that light could have traveled since early moments) by a factor of a trillion trillion trillion *squared*. That leaves plenty of room for producing intelligent races, even supposing pessimistically that intelligence appears only once in every trillion trillion galaxies!

FINE TUNING, MULTIPLE UNIVERSES, AND OBSERVATIONAL AND DIVINE SELECTION

A reason for accepting cosmic inflation is that it solves the "smoothness" and "flatness" problems. Why is our universe not filled with life-excluding turbulence (searing temperatures and hugely many black holes), and why is its space so nearly Euclidean? The standard analogy is to a highly inflated balloon, its surface almost flat over short distances and all its wrinkles smoothed away. However, a still better reason for accepting inflation may be that it solves the "fine-tuning problem."

Talk of fine tuning is something else for which we can thank Brandon Carter. What is meant is tuning in ways making life's appearance and prolonged evolution into real possibilities. Starting from points Carter raised in the early 1970s,[10] many people have compiled long lists of seeming evidence (for some of it, see Davies' *The Accidental Universe*,[11] Martin Rees' *Before the Beginning*,[12] Lee Smolin's *The Life of the Cosmos*,[13] and my own *Universes*[14]) that tiny changes in our universe's basic characteristics—in particular, in the strengths of physical forces such as gravity and electromagnetism, or in the masses of particles such as the proton and the electron—would have led to a situation in which life would never have evolved. Interest in this matter has been increased by Dyson's article discussing such affairs as the Sun's failure to explode. [15]

- It is thought, for instance, that if our universe's early expansion speed had been faster or slower by as little as one part in a billion, then it would either have collapsed almost at once or else would have swelled so rapidly that no stars would have formed. Also, a brief burst of inflation at early times, often pictured as producing the right expansion speed "automatically," would itself have depended on very accurate tuning.
- The nuclear strong force and the nuclear weak force, which dominate the center of the atom, apparently needed to have strengths falling inside narrow limits in order for any hydrogen to come out of the Big Bang, and for stars to burn in ways producing elements heavier than helium.
- Gravity's strength had to be in more or less exactly its actual ratio to the strength of electromagnetism, for there to be any stars like the Sun—and there are reasons to think that stars of other kinds are all unsuited for bringing warmth to life-bearing planets. Again, slight strengthening of electromagnetism would have caused protons to repel one another so vigorously that hydrogen would be the only possible element.
- The relative masses of the electron, the proton, and the neutron seemingly needed to be almost exactly what they are for chemistry and biology to be possible.

Why are anything between a dozen and a hundred factors "fine tuned for producing life"? The word "for" need not be taken as pointing to a divine designer, any more than "the heart is for pumping the blood," and in fact the fine tuning might have light thrown on it as follows. A very large universe may include many very different huge regions, or there may be many universes that are very different—the distinction between huge regions and universes being, in many cosmological models, a mere matter of verbal preference. Almost all the huge regions or universes have characteristics hostile to life of any kind. We intelligent living beings, however, have to find ourselves in one of the few places where conditions are life-permitting. Now, this approach to the fine tuning can draw a great deal of its plausibility from the hypothesis of cosmic inflation.

How? Well, if we are going to believe in universes or huge regions whose characteristics differ randomly, so that sooner or later there will be a universe or huge region suited to the evolution of life and of intelligence, then we need not only some plausible way of producing random variations in such things as force strengths and particle masses, but also some means of ensuring that matters vary only from one gigantic domain to another, instead of from one cubic millimeter to the next. We need to explain why all is "tuned" in the same one fashion right out to our present cosmic horizon, at a distance of roughly ten billion light years. Well, the best way to produce the random variations could be as follows. As the Big Bang cooled, one or more scalar fields appeared. Scalar fields have intensity but no direction, so cannot be detected by anything like a compass needle. However, physicists typically introduce one or more such fields to explain why particles are not all "massless" (i.e., without rest mass, like the photon) and why forces such as electromagnetism and the weak nuclear force have different strengths. Now, as Andrei Linde has insisted, scalar fields of different intensities could well have much the same potential energies—potential energies being what physical systems try to minimize, in the sense in which a ball can "try" to get to a valley bottom. This would mean that the scalar field or fields could have taken any of very many different intensities, with more or less equal ease. Force strengths and particle masses could have been randomized by this, so that the difference between, say, the masses of the proton and the electron varied greatly from one tiny region to the next. But why, in that case, are these masses the same (as spectroscopic evidence reveals) all the way out to our cosmic horizon? The answer is that inflation took a tiny region and expanded it so greatly that it stretches beyond that horizon.[16]

Some think that such efforts to throw light on fine tuning show a lack of imagination. Yes, they say, it may well be that life based on chemistry is possible only thanks to accurate tuning, but who needs chemistry? Not the beings whose habitat is neutron stars, beings who rely on the strong nuclear force rather than on the electromagnetism that underlies chemistry! Not the plasma beings inside the Sun! Not the beings who are crystalline patterns in frozen hydrogen! But to this we could well reply, first, that there are reasons for not taking such exotic beings very seriously, and second, that one needs much fine tuning even to get neutron stars or suns or frozen hydrogen. The average universe (or huge cosmic region) would probably be almost nothing but light rays and black holes, or composed of gas immensely cold and dilute, or lasting for under a million years.

Perhaps, though, God did the work that otherwise would have to be attributed to random variations between universes or cosmic regions, plus *observational selection* (nowadays called "anthropic," following Carter's seminal work) of those universes or regions whose characteristics chanced to favor the evolution of observers. Fine tuning might be a matter of divine design, divine selection of our universe's properties.

GOD, NEOPLATONISM, PANTHEISM, AND THE RISK OF HUMAN EXTINCTION

I take the God hypothesis seriously. God does not have to be a reasonlessly existing person, possessed of utterly inexplicable powers and of a mind that just happens to be orderly so that it can set about designing an orderly universe. Among philosophers, I am notorious for defending a Platonic or Neoplatonic theory about God. Summarizing a British Academy lecture of November 5, 1998, plus material from many earlier years,[17] the theory's main elements are as follows:

- It would be impossible to get rid of all realities, since some are Platonic realities. They include such facts as that two groups of two apples, if there ever existed such groups, would include four apples in total. Also such ethical facts, perhaps, as that the absence of a world consisting solely of people in torment would be fortunate, ethically needful, ethically required, whether or not there existed anyone to think about this or to have moral duties with respect to it, such as the duty of keeping such a world out of existence.
- Similarly, the existence of various things could be good, ethically required, whether or not anybody ever thought about this or had duties regarding it. The ethical need for the existence of a good world, perhaps, or perhaps of a good deity, could be absolute

and eternal. Of course only people's actions are required *morally.* If all people were absent, there would be no moral requirements. But ethical realities, facts of goodness and of badness, can go beyond moral realities.

- No study of concepts can yield a logical proof that whatever is ethically required must actually be the case, much as bachelors must lack wives. For one thing, ethical requirements might often enter into conflict with one another, so that many of them *could not* be fulfilled. Still, there is no conceptual confusion in the idea, met with in Book Six of Plato's *Republic,* that an ethical requirement could sometimes *by itself* carry responsibility for the actual existence of something. (Plato comments that The Good is itself not existence but far beyond existence in dignity, for it is what bestows existence upon things.) It might even carry this responsibility necessarily. It could be wrong to ask what "gave" such a requirement its creative power, for the Platonic theory just is that nothing would. We might almost as well ask what "gives" to the experience of the color red its power to be more like the experience of orange than like that of yellow.

    Note that some matters can be completely necessary without the necessity's being logical, where "logical" means provable by one or more appeals to the definitions of words. It is not through anybody's arbitrarily choosing to define the word "orange" with the words "reddish yellow" that those color experiences stand in the order in which they do. Instead, it is the fact that they simply do stand in this order, and must do so even for cavemen without a language, that makes "reddish yellow" another way of saying "orange" here.

- The existence of a perfect divine being might be an eternal consequence of such a being's ethical requiredness. This was suggested by A.C. Ewing, perhaps the greatest idealist philosopher of the past hundred years,[18] and also by the physicist-turned-theologian John Polkinghorne in his recent Gifford Lectures.[19] (Making no attempt to picture such an eternal consequence as a logical consequence, Ewing and Polkinghorne avoid the absurd ontological proof of God's existence, which tries to show that anyone defining God as "a perfect being" ought to agree that God exists.)

- Alternatively, we might understand the word "God" in the way favored by the long Neoplatonic tradition stretching back to

Plotinus. God is then the fact that the cosmos *has an ethical re-quiredness that is creatively sufficient.* The cosmos exists because, as a matter of eternal Platonic reality, it is better that the cosmos exist. (Those who agree with Einstein's statement that the world has "a four-dimensional existence"[20] can accept an ethical need that is creatively sufficient *as a matter of eternal Platonic fact* while at the same time recognizing that only a few billion years separate us from the Big Bang. "Change" and "the passage of the years," so long as these mean only that different cross-sections of the four-dimensionally existing whole do differ in their character-istics, are fully compatible with the inalterable four-dimensional existence of the whole itself.)

- A compromise between the two pictures of God, as a divine mind and as the world's creative ethical requiredness, is sug-gested by Spinoza. Existing because of its supreme goodness, Spinoza's divine mind contemplates everything worth knowing, including every detail of what a universe must be like if obeying laws such as ours does, and precisely how it must feel to be each of the conscious beings in such a universe—beings like you and me. Now, says Spinoza, the divine mind's contemplation of all this *just is* the reality of our universe, and of the conscious lives of you and me. In the regions of it which are the conscious lives of you and me, the divine mind is of course ignorant of many things: for instance, of how many life-bearing planets there are in our galaxy, and of whether Spinoza's world picture is right.

- Believers in God need not deny that living beings sometimes suffer disasters, through their own foolishness or otherwise. (In Spinoza's system, for example, the divine mind contemplates what a world would have to be like if people in it, making choices in accordance with the natural laws to which their minds conformed, chose in calamitous ways. The divine mind's con-templation of the resulting calamities would *be* those calamities.) Suppose you accept that our universe, a collection of such and such things formed into an orderly whole through such and such laws of interaction, is a universe that exists *in answer to an ethical requirement*: perhaps a requirement recognized and put into ef-fect by an all-creating person called "God," or perhaps one that is itself creatively effective, as various Neoplatonists think. Must you therefore fancy that ethical factors *repeatedly interfere with* those laws of interaction? Must you believe that a fleet with noble purposes meets always with a fair wind, or that good men never go hungry, or that intelligent life can spring into existence during the fury of a Big Bang? Why ever should you? You could even doubt that the continued existence of the human race will be guaranteed, regardless of how foolishly humans behave.

In this connection, consider an intriguing point about the scalar field or fields that I mentioned previously. One apparent possibility is that any such field is now like a ball caught in a hollow. It might be disturbed by a violent enough shove, then falling to lower values. Experiments at ultrahigh energies might provide the violent shove. Things would at first go wrong only inside a minuscule bubble, but this would at once expand at almost the velocity of light, destroying the entire galaxy and then the next galaxy, and so on.[21] People sometimes declare that we are safe from this, pointing to an article by Martin Rees and Piet Hut that suggests no danger could arise until physicists exceeded the energies released by cosmic rays colliding "inside our past light-cone" (i.e., in the region whose events have so far had any chance of affecting us).[22] Yet in his *Dreams of a Final Theory,* Steven Weinberg speculated that, through the use of laser beams to accelerate charged particles, even Planck-scale energies—many orders of magnitude above those of cosmic ray collisions—could be achieved.[23] In *Before the Beginning,* Rees warns us that "caution should surely be urged (if not enforced) on experiments that create energy concentrations that may never have occurred naturally."[24] Believers in God need not think that Rees is mistaken.

Dawkins has doubted whether it could make any sense to try to explain the world's existence with the aid of "so piffling a concept as *goodness.*" Would not "*Chanel Number Fiveness*" be exactly as helpful? Well, perhaps he was overlooking three main points.

1. Goodness is not a quality added to others like an extra coat of paint, or like the perfume Chanel Number Five. A thing's being good means it has qualities that make its existence required in an ethical way, a way that is importantly nonrelative (though it can be in another way relative, certainly, for whereas some things are little better than nothing, others are very good, very strongly required). While I happily accept that my own beliefs about good and bad are almost all products of evolutionary forces and social pressures, this does not force me to say that nothing ever is truly better than anything else—or, which

seems to amount to the same thing, that nothing is ever better in itself, out there in reality, much as Australia is genuinely larger than Ireland. I even think it perverse to imagine that in a blank, a situation empty of all existing things, it could not possibly be a fact, true, something that was the case, *that the absence of a world of torment was something good,* something ethically fortunate. Sure enough, evolutionary forces and social pressures could not have left their marks on the blank. And perhaps such forces and pressures would never have acted anyway, for perhaps the blank would not have replaced some previous world of things. All this, however, seems to show only that the goodness and badness in which I believe are not themselves mere matters *of how I or other people come to view things, thanks to evolutionary forces and social pressures.* What is more, there is nothing odd in saying that it would be a fact, true, something actually the case, that even in the blank, an absence of all *things,* there could be a real ethical requirement for the coming to exist of a good world, or of a good divine mind or person. Yet if so, then here would be a reality of a kind that can be found nowhere else. Here would be *an unconditionally real requirement for the actual existence of something.* (Logical requirements, in contrast, and ordinary causal requirements, are all "ify-theny." If something is round, then it is not square, and if a hammer hits a nail, then the nail must move, but the existence of moving nails and nonsquare objects is not required in any unconditional way.)

2. While we cannot point to a logical proof, intricate collection of cogwheels, or quasi-Darwinian process, that ensured that some ethical requirement (maybe for the existence of a divine being) would be "creatively powerful," i.e., itself a sufficient ground for the existence of the required object, neither can we point to any proof, mechanism, or process that made all such requirements creatively powerless. And it can be argued that both the power and the powerlessness *would be equally simple,* no pages of logical deduction or complex causal mechanisms being involved in either case. No benevolent magicians would be uttering lengthy incantations to guarantee that what started as "only" an ethical requirement "became actually able to create something." No devils would be reciting other spells to thwart "the obviously-to-be-expected tendency for the required to come to exist."

3. It can at first seem clear that ethical requirements are not in fact creatively powerful. If they were powerful, we are inclined to protest, then why would there be such limited beings as you and me, experiencing such often unsatisfactory lives? *Why not simply have infinite di-*

vine thinking, knowledge of everything worth knowing? However, any such objection could be utterly question-begging. For Spinoza, at least as I read him, there exists nothing but infinite divine thinking, knowledge of everything worth knowing. Your life and mine are just elements in that thinking. They may be very inferior elements, compared with many others, but the divine knowledge would be less complete and less good if God were ignorant of just how people like you and me must feel when living in a world like ours. And God presumably could not know this—God could not know how it felt, *exactly*—in any parts of his thought that were not filled with the conviction *of actually being you and me*. Furthermore, any such conviction would be a correct conviction; for according to Spinoza, parts of the divine thought are what you and I truly are.

None of this rejects the world that scientists describe. No attempt is being made to convince people that the laws of physics are illusions, or that Darwinian forces and social pressures are anything but what scientists like Dawkins say they are. Questions of why the world exists, and of why it obeys causal laws, are simply not the same as questions about what the world's basic laws are, and how they make possible the evolution of intelligent life. Questions about what the world's patterns are differ from Spinoza's question of whether what carries those patterns—the pattern of the stars; the pattern of the Earth and of its oceans, mountains, and trees; the pattern of the quarks and leptons inside each atom; the pattern of your thoughts and mine; and the patterns of countless universes beyond the one we live in—is an infinite divine mind, a mind whose complexly structured thought extends to every fact worth knowing.

NOTES

1. P. Davies, *The Fifth Miracle* (London: Penguin Press, 1998), 188–201.
2. J. Maynard Smith, "Taking a Chance on Evolution," *New York Review of Books*, 14 May 1992, 34–36.
3. B. Carter, "The Anthropic Principle and its Implications for Biological Evolution," *Philosophical Transactions of the Royal Society of London,* A 310, 346–363.
4. See pages 241–242 of W. Sullivan, *We Are Not Alone,* rev. ed. (New York: Penguin Books, 1993). For a fine review of suggested answers to Fermi's problem, consult G.D. Brin, "The 'Great Silence': The Controversy Concerning Extraterrestrial Intelligent Life," *Quarterly Journal of the Royal Astronomical Society,* 24 (1983), 283–309.
5. J.R. Gott, "Implications of the Copernican Principle for our Future Prospects," *Nature,* 363 (1993), 315–319.

6. P. Davies, *About Time* (London: Penguin Books, 1995), 258–264.

7. J. Leslie, *The End of the World: The Science and Ethics of Human Extinction* (London and New York: Routledge, 1996; ppb., rev., 1998). Despite its potentially alarming title and its discussion of scores of different risks, the book argues that the human race stands a good chance of surviving the period of greatest danger, which is the next few hundred years. See also these other writings of mine: "Time and the Anthropic Principle," *Mind,* 101 (1992), 521–540; "The Doomsday Argument," *The Mathematical Intelligencer,* 11 (1992), 48–51; "Testing the Doomsday Argument," *Journal of Applied Philosophy,* 11 (1994), 31–44.

8. F. Dyson, *Imagined Worlds* (Cambridge, Mass.: Harvard University Press, 1997). See chapter 4 in particular.

9. F. Dyson, "Time without End: Physics and Biology in an Open Universe," *Reviews of Modern Physics,* 51, (1979), 447–460.

10. See particularly B. Carter's "Large Number Coincidences and the Anthropic Principle in Cosmology," in J. Leslie, ed., *Modern Cosmology and Philosophy* (Amherst, N.Y.: Prometheus Books, 1998), 131–139.

11. P. Davies, *The Accidental Universe* (Cambridge: Cambridge University Press, 1982).

12. M. Rees, *Before the Beginning* (Reading, Mass.: Addison-Wesley, 1997).

13. L. Smolin, *The Life of the Cosmos* (London: Weidenfeld and Nicolson, 1997).

14. J. Leslie, *Universes* (London and New York: Routledge, 1989; rev. 1996).

15. F. Dyson, "Energy in the Universe," *Scientific American* (September 1971), 51–59.

16. A. Linde, "The Universe: Inflation out of Chaos," in J. Leslie, ed., *Modern Cosmology and Philosophy* (Amherst, N.Y.: Prometheus Books, 1998), 245–253.

17. See, for example, these writings of mine: "Efforts to Explain All Existence," *Mind,* 87 (1978), 181–194; *Value and Existence* (Oxford: Blackwell, 1979); "The World's Necessary Existence," *International Journal for Philosophy of Religion,* 11 (1980), 207–223; "Mackie on Neoplatonism's 'Replacement for God,'" *Religious Studies,* 22 (1986), 325–342; chapter eight of *Universes* (London and New York: Routledge, 1989, rev. 1996); "A Spinozistic Vision of God," *Religious Studies,* 29 (1993), 277–286; "A Neoplatonist's Pantheism," *The Monist,* 80 (1997), 218–231; and "Cosmology and Theology," 1998, in the all-electronic *Stanford Encyclopedia of Philosophy* at http://plato.stanford.edu/info.html (or go to http://plato.stanford.edu.entries/cosmology-theology/ for the article itself).

18. A.C. Ewing, *Value and Reality* (London: Allen and Unwin, 1973); see especially chapter 7.

19. J. Polkinghorne, *The Faith of a Physicist* (Princeton: Princeton University Press, 1994). See especially page 58.

20. The words are from Appendix Five to the fifteenth edition of Einstein's *Relativity: The Special and the General Theory* (London: Methuen, 1920).

21. S. Coleman, and F. De Luccia. "Gravitational Effects on and of Vacuum Decay," *Physical Review D,* 21 (1980), 3305–3315.

22. P. Hut and M. Rees "How Stable is Our Vacuum?" *Nature,* 302 (1983), 508–509.

23. S. Weinberg, *Dreams of a Final Theory* (London: Hutchinson, 1993), 187–188.

24. Rees, *Before the Beginning,* 205–207. The risk of our upsetting the vacuum is discussed in detail on pages 108–122 of my *The End of the World* (London and New York: Routledge, 1996 and 1998).

PART III
EXTRATERRESTRIAL LIFE AND OUR WORLD VIEW

The English-born American physicist **Freeman J. Dyson** is widely recognized for his contributions to quantum electrodynamics and the theory of interacting electrons and photons—and perhaps even better known for his creative speculations on subjects ranging from space travel to extraterrestrial civilizations. He went to Cambridge University from Winchester College, and after civilian service doing operations research at the headquarters of the RAF Bomber Command during World War II, he took his B.A. in mathematics at Cambridge in 1945. A fellow at Trinity College, Cambridge, in 1946–1947, he was a Commonwealth Fellow at Cornell University and the Institute for Advanced Study in Princeton for the next two years. After another two years as a research fellow at the University of Birmingham, he became a professor of physics at Cornell in 1951. Two years later, he returned to the Institute for Advanced Study where he was a professor of physics until 1994 when he became professor emeritus. He has been a visiting professor at Yeshiva University and the Max Planck Institute for Physics and Astrophysics. During the late 1950s, Dr. Dyson helped design the nuclear reactor, Triga, and the Orion space ship at General Atomic Laboratories in San Diego, California. The recipient of honorary degrees from seventeen American and European colleges and universities, including Princeton, Oxford, and the Federal Institute of Technology (ETH) in Zurich, he is a Fellow of the Royal Society and a member of the U.S. National Academy of Sciences, as well as a foreign associate of the French Academy of Sciences and an honorary fellow of Trinity College, Cambridge. The author of nearly 300 scientific papers, he also has been a frequent contributor to *The New Yorker, The Atlantic Monthly,* and *The New York Review of Books.* His latest book is *Imagined Worlds* (Harvard University Press, 1997).

The Many Worlds of Neurology

Freeman J. Dyson

We have known for hundreds of years that the universe has room in it for other intelligent inhabitants besides ourselves. If our ongoing attempts to detect their existence should be successful, this will be a big triumph for science but will not be in any sense a setback for theology. Since the time of Giordano Bruno, the multiplicity of worlds has been a subject for theological speculation. Isaac Newton himself remarked in one of his theological manuscripts: "And as Christ after some stay in or near the regions of this earth ascended into heaven, so after the resurrection of the dead it may be in their power to leave this earth at pleasure and accompany him into any part of the heavens, that no region in the whole Universe may want its inhabitants." God may be portrayed in a million different shapes in a million inhabited worlds, without any diminution of his greatness.

Likewise, the transition from a Newtonian cosmology of infinite space and absolute time to an Einsteinian cosmology of relativistic space-time has not changed the age-old mystery of God's relation to the physical universe. I see no reason why God should be inconvenienced if it should turn out that our universe started with an unpredictable quantum fluctuation giving rise to an inflationary expansion, or if it should turn out that we live in one of a multitude of universes. My conception of God is not obscured by my not knowing whether the physical universe is open or closed, finite or infinite, simple or multiple. God for me is a mystery, and will remain a mystery after we know the answers to these questions. All that we know about him is that he works on a scale far beyond the limits of our understanding. I cannot imagine that he is greatly impressed by our juvenile efforts to read his mind. As the Hebrew psalmist said long ago (Ps. 147), "He hath no pleasure in the strength of an horse, neither delighteth He in any man's legs." Translating the psalmist's verse into modern polysyllabic idiom, we might say, "He hath no pleasure in the teraflops of a supercomputer, neither delighteth He in any cosmologist's calculations."

Instead of discussing the new universes of astronomy and cosmology, I will discuss the new universes of neurology. Neurology comes closer than cosmology to the questions that are at the heart of theology. Neurology gives us evidence of the way human perceptions and human beliefs come into being. By studying the perceptions and beliefs of people who live in universes different from ours, we may better understand our own. I am a physicist with no pretensions to be an expert in neurology. When I write about neurology, I write as a layman. My knowledge of neurology is largely derived, not from the technical literature, nor even from the nontechnical literature, but from television programs addressed to the general public. I watched four one-hour programs, with the neurologist Oliver Sacks as guide. These depict in vivid fashion the four different universes inhabited by four groups of people with different kinds of neurological impairment. They have certain features in common. Each of the four neurological impairments is congenital, each deprives the affected people of an important human faculty, and each of them is ameliorated by the amazing ability of the human brain to work around obstacles.

The simplest of the four syndromes is achromatopsia, the severe form of color-blindness in which the color-sensing cones in the retina are missing and only the rods remain. People with achromatopsia have excellent night vision but are almost blind in direct sunlight. Many of them adapt to their disability by learning to live like nocturnal animals. Sacks showed us a community with a high incidence of achromatopsia, living on a South Pacific island. There the achromatopes specialize in night fishing, a productive occupation for which their disability turns into an advantage.

Far greater obstacles are faced by people with Usher's syndrome, who are born totally deaf and then in middle age become gradually blind. They too can adapt to their disability if they live in a supportive community. As children they become fluent in sign language. They are able to communicate with one another and to absorb an education as readily as other deaf children. Then as adults, when their sight begins to fade, they can continue to communicate by sign language, the listener touching the hands of the speaker to feel the signs. They can continue to read and write by transferring their skills from print to Braille. Within the community of the deaf-blind, they are not isolated by their double disability and can maintain the social contacts that give meaning to their lives.

The third of the four disabilities is Williams' syndrome, a genetic defect with consequences less easily described but more profound than Usher's syndrome. People with Williams' syndrome have all their five senses but lack the ability to integrate their sensory universe into a quantitative framework. They do not live in the solid three-dimensional world that normal people take for granted. They have great difficulty in forming concepts of shape, size, and number. They cannot draw pictures of things, and their world contains no mathematics. They have a characteristic facial appearance that marks them as different from other people. To compensate for these disabilities, many of them are verbally and musically gifted. Also socially gifted, they have childlike spontaneity and cheerful temperaments that enable them to make friends easily.

The fourth and most mysterious disability is autism. Autistic people have their senses unimpaired and have no difficulty with abstract concepts of shape and number. Their disability lies at a deeper level. They are born without the normal human ability to attach meaning to things that they see, hear, and feel. They have great difficulty learning to talk, and many of them remain speechless all their lives. It happens that the leading character in the autism section of Sacks's program is Jessica Park, a lady whose family I have known since before she was born forty years ago. Her mother, Clara Park, has described her agonizingly slow development in *The Siege,* a classic book in the history of autism. Jessica was, as her mother wrote, "Faced with a world in which an unreadable welter of impressions obscures even the distinction between objects and human beings." Like other autistic children who learn to speak, Jessica for many years used the pronouns "I" and "you" interchangeably. She had no concept of her own identity or of the identities of other people. Her mother recorded the fact that she used the word "heptagon" correctly before she used the word "yes." Through the patient and devoted efforts of her parents and teachers, Jessica has continued for forty years to learn new social skills and to increase her command of spoken language. Her intellectual growth has never stopped. Every year she becomes more independent and more capable of managing her own affairs. Through her paintings she is able to communicate glimpses of her inner world that cannot be communicated in words. Her paintings are exhibited and sold and bring her a modest income. In the television program we see her as she is today, after forty years of adapting to a world that is still largely beyond her comprehension. She speaks to a public audience and responds to questions. She is proud and happy because her gifts as an artist have been recognized, and she talks about her paintings. Her speech sounds unnatural but is loud and clear.

What have these four disabilities to do with theology? Each of the four groups of people I described lives in a different universe, and we normal people live in a fifth universe different from theirs. Since we are the majority and have organized our universe to suit our needs, they have been forced to adapt their ways of living to fit into our society as best they can. On the whole, they have adapted well to our universe, but they still do not belong to it. They are aliens living here as guests. I find it illuminating to imagine the situations that would arise if the people with any one of the four disabilities were the majority and we were the minority. H.G. Wells already explored such a situation in his story, "The Country of the Blind," a hundred years ago. If the majority were suffering either from achromatopsia or from Usher's syndrome, we would be in a situation similar to Wells' story. The gifts of color-vision and hearing that seem to us so precious would have little value in the universes of the achromatopes or of Usher's syndrome. In the Usher's universe, our spoken language would be for our private use only. We would be forced to think in sign language to fit into the prevailing culture. But these first two disabilities are superficial compared with the third and fourth. The universes of Williams' syndrome and autism differ from ours profoundly enough to require a different theology.

In the Williams universe, there is no mathematics and no science. Music and language flourish, but there is no concept of size or distance. The glories of the natural world are enjoyed but not analyzed. Nature is described in the language of art and poetry, not in the language of science. What kind of a theology can arise in the Williams universe? We can imagine many possibilities for a Williams theology, all of them different from our own. Our Judeo-Christian theology begins with the first chapter of Genesis, with days that are numbered and counted. "And the evening and the morning were the first day," and the second day, and so on up to the sixth day. Our conceptions of God, like our conceptions of the universe, are rooted in an exact awareness of the passage of time. These conceptions are alien to the Williams universe. A Williams theology would more likely resemble the theogony of the ancient Greeks, with gods riding in chariots across the sky and demigods hiding in bushes and caves on the earth.

In the autistic universe there is no sin. Jessica Park's mother remarks on the fact that her word is absolutely trustworthy. Jessica cannot tell a deliberate lie because she has no concept of deceit. She cannot conceive of other people's thoughts and feelings, and so the idea of deceit cannot arise. There is no way for her to imagine doing deliberate harm to other people. When she hurts people, by losing her temper or throwing a tantrum, the hurt results from impatience and incomprehension, not from malice. If sin means deliberate malice, then Jessica is incapable of sin. When Jessica's father was asked whether she loves her family, he answered, "She loves us as much as she can." That is a precise statement of Jessica's condition. In the autistic universe, humans love each other without understanding each other and are incapable of hate. The theology of the autistic universe must be radically different from Judeo-Christian theology. Since there is no sin, there can be no fall from grace and no redemption. Since other people's sufferings are unimaginable, the suffering of an incarnate God is also unimaginable. The autistic theology will be like Jessica's character, simple and transparent, concerned only with innocent joys and sorrows. The strongest link between Jessica's universe and ours is that we share a common sense of humor and can laugh at each other's jokes.

The most important lesson for us to learn from imagining these alternative universes is humility. In each of the four universes, humans are well adapted to their situation and are totally unaware of what we consider to be their disabilities. They believe that they are well informed and aware of everything that is going on in the world around them. In the Williams and autistic universes, I imagine them building a religion and a theology to explain their universe and their place in it. We know, of course, that they are unaware of huge and essential parts of their environment and are incapable of understanding what they cannot imagine. We know that their religion and theology are deeply flawed because they are based on a partial view of reality. If we are honest, we must ask ourselves some hard questions. Why should we believe that we are different? Why should we believe that our view of reality is not also partial, that our religion and theology are not equally flawed? How do we know that there are not huge and essential features of our universe and of our own nature of which we are equally unaware? Why should we believe that the processes of natural selection, which shaped our brains to allow us to survive the hazards of living in a world of fierce predators and harsh climates, should have automatically given us a complete grasp of the universe in which we live? These are the questions that neurology raises. As we struggle to answer them, neurology will be more helpful than cosmology. Oliver Sacks has shown us glimpses of alien universes. These glimpses are powerful arguments for the thesis that there may be more things in heaven and earth than we are capable of understanding.

JILL CORNELL TARTER

A patient and dauntless explorer seeking signs of intelligent life on other planets, astronomer **Jill Cornell Tarter** is the founding director of Project Phoenix, the SETI Institute's privately-funded continuation of a targeted search for extraterrestrial intelligence. Her work is listening for radio signals that would provide evidence of another distant technology. With an undergraduate degree in engineering physics from Cornell University (named after her distant relative Ezra), where she was the only woman in her engineering class, and the first to hold the Procter & Gamble Scholarship, in the university's College of Engineering, Dr. Tarter began her study of astronomy at her alma mater and went on to concentrate in high-energy astrophysics at the University of California, Berkeley, where she completed a Ph.D. in 1975. In 1977, Dr. Tarter was appointed an assistant research astronomer at Berkeley's Space Science Laboratory; from there she initiated a cooperative agreement with NASA to manage a SETI observational program. Named associate research astronomer in 1983, she was made project director of the NASA/SETI High Resolution Microwave Survey in 1989. When Congress abruptly terminated the program in 1993 and the search project went private, Dr. Tarter and her associates began roving from telescope to telescope to carry on their research. In 1997, she became the first holder of the Bernard M. Oliver Chair at SETI. She also became the role model for Ellie, the heroine of the 1997 movie *Contact,* based on Carl Sagan's novel. Dr. Tarter lectures widely and is the author of more than 100 scientific articles. A former president of the International Astronomical Union's Commission 51, she is chair of the International Academy of Astronautics SETI Committee.

SETI AND THE RELIGIONS OF THE UNIVERSE

JILL CORNELL TARTER

Extraterrestrial intelligence exists, or it doesn't. Even if extraterrestrial intelligence exists, we may be unable to find credible evidence thereof; some people say we already have enough evidence. God exists, or she doesn't. Even if God exists, we may be unable to find credible evidence thereof; some people say we already have enough evidence.

Most people accept with equanimity the first statements referring to extraterrestrial intelligence (ETI), but the parallel construct relating to God arouse visceral, belief-based reactions. Both subjects, ETI and God, are appropriately described by Martin Rees' assertion, "Absence of evidence is not evidence of absence."[1] In our current state of ignorance, we are free to continue believing in either, neither, or both. Why is one subject so much more emotionally charged? Both concepts have long histories;[2] humanity has long puzzled over each. Only a few scientists (considered by their peers to be on the fringe), and the odd science fiction writer, subscribe to the thesis that ETI has created humans or defined their purpose, although that is within the realm of possibilities (e.g., directed panspermia).[3] Therefore, the existence or nonexistence of ETI is of little practical consequence to most humans, with such tragic exceptions as the Heaven's Gate cultists and individuals whose lives have been disrupted by what they believe has been an actual alien encounter. But God is believed to be responsible for our existence and thus is taken personally, on a daily basis, by the faithful. Is the difference in emotional response to these two questions of existence perhaps because religious belief is an unintended consequence of the evolutionary structure of our own brains,[4] with God being a uniquely human creation, while the existence of ETI (or lack thereof) is determined by the universe without human consent?

The world's religions differ in their description of God, and even in the number of Gods, although some claim to have empirical data on the subject. By their very nature, these nonreproducible miracles do little to settle the controversy. They are selective in their impact, encompassing only one set of believers at a time, and do not tend to be mirrored by analogous events elsewhere. While some religions find the current body of cosmological knowledge fully consistent with their beliefs, others, for which there is a special relationship between humans and their God, have been uncomfortable since Copernicus first moved the Earth from center stage.[5] Although usually not phrased in those terms, centuries of ecclesiastical and philosophical debate have revolved about whether the principle of mediocrity[6] might not require a large (but finite) number of Sons of God and a like number of resurrections. How might the detection of extraterrestrial intelligence inform, disrupt, or consolidate religious belief systems?

First, a few comments on what is plausible, or even possible. We are a very young technology in a very old galaxy (one hundred years vs. ten billion years). We live in the first generation that is capable of attempting to try to answer the age-old question, Are we alone? by doing an experiment. There is no experiment we can conceive at the present time that directly detects the existence of extraterrestrial *intelligence*. Intelligence is difficult to define precisely and impossible to detect at distance. What we can attempt to do is detect the manifestation of an extraterrestrial technology, and having done so, infer the existence of intelligent extraterrestrial technologists. So what is the right experiment? Wait for them to land on the lawn of the White House; debrief "abductees" about the nature of their abductors, in search of some otherwise unknowable fact; enumerate all unexplained observational phenomena, seeking those that might be consistent with an extraterrestrial, technological explanation; explore our local solar neighborhood for alien artifacts; attempt to sense remotely the existence of another technology (in the vicinity of nearby stars or at random on the celestial sphere)? Of these experiments, only the last one permits the construction of a protocol that could, even in theory, produce a significant negative result. This concept of a significant negative result is very important and is ultimately why most searches for extraterrestrial technology today focus on the detection of artificial radio signals. By recognizing that the current electromagnetic signature of the Earth, at certain radio frequencies, outshines the emission from our host Sun by factors of billions, it is possible to design a hypothetical experiment that would be sensitive enough to detect a radio analog of the twentieth-century Earth, if it exists, anywhere within the Milky Way galaxy. By requiring no more of an extraterrestrial technological civilization than what we ourselves are capable of, we can calibrate the required sensitivity of our experiment. Having said this much, we hastily admit that such an exhaustive search is far beyond our current capabilities. Our own technology is primitive; just barely capable of searching our own neighborhood. Therefore, any other technology that we detect in the near future will be more advanced, simply because we could not detect any technology more primitive than our own, and the probability that their technology would be exactly at our stage of development is vanishingly small.

Furthermore, for any of the experiments currently being conducted to be successful, extraterrestrial technologies must not only exist, but on the average they must be long lived. The degenerate form of the Drake equation[7] can be written $N \leq L$, where N is the number of technological civilizations currently within our Milky Way galaxy, and L is the longevity of that detectable technology (in years). Bearing in mind that the inequality may be extreme, this equation is sufficient to inform us that technological civilizations will not be spatially and temporally coincident unless L is very large. Statistically, a technological civilization will only be located nearby if N (and therefore L) is very large.

From these arguments, we know (even without the exchange of any information) that the extraterrestrial technology detected by our primitive technology necessarily will be far older than we are. Let us quantify far older. A strong signal detected from a long distance requires the development time for their technology to produce that strong signal, and transmission for a long time (in terms of stellar lifetimes) so that when our own technology evolves, and we look in the correct direction, the signal will be there. Similar longevity is deduced from the detection of a nearby signal. For one of the nearest 1,000 solar-type stars in our galaxy to host another technology, the average longevity L must be measured in tens of millions of years. The important point here is that if the technologists are as long-lived as their technology, then they will have had to develop a more stable form of social structure than that which currently characterizes the planet Earth. At a minimum, this inferred result (their longevity) is likely to have a great deal to say about religions throughout the universe. In my opinion, it will mean that the detected, long-lived extraterrestrials either never had, or have outgrown, organized religion.

Organized religions ultimately derive their identities from some God or Gods in whom are vested ultimate knowledge and understanding (I am a scientist and not a student of religions, and thus uncomfortable making such generalizations, but I believe that this minimal statement has wide applicability and may even be inclusive.) In many cases, this has led to a doctrine of divine right, under which the most inhumane practices have been justified. While it is comforting to think of organized religion as an agent for stability and tolerance, in fact, religious wars have been some of the most destabilizing of any human activities. From the ancient Crusades to modern conflicts in Northern Ireland, Bosnia, the West Bank, and Iran/Iraq, religious disputes have proved the most difficult to extinguish. They smolder beneath the terms of secular settlements, only to erupt generations later. Based on our poor human example with religious intolerance, the existence of an old (tens of millions of years!), stable, technological civilization therefore implies a single religion, devoid of factions and disputes, or no religion at all.

If God(s) exists, then a single, universal religion is the obvious possibility. For old technologies to exist, this universal religion would have to be compatible with scientific inquiry. Given the historical terrestrial conflicts between many religions and science, and the current resurgence of attacks by fundamentalist religions on those sciences related to the origin of life and a cosmic context for humans, it is hard to reconcile the existence of an old technology with organized religion. Or at least it is hard to reconcile with the terrestrial examples thereof, which emphasize the individual differences in human beliefs and traditions, rather than the commonality of humanity.

Nevertheless, let us suppose that elsewhere there is a universal religion that accurately reflects the existence of God or Gods; one that also permits a long-lived, stable, technological civilization that utilizes some technology we are capable of remotely sensing. What might we expect to hear from them? If the detected technology is information-bearing, rather than an accidental proof of existence, we can expect to learn about their God(s) and themselves, as well as their view of the universe and its other inhabitants. Because new information about the universe is verifiable observationally (once it has been comprehended) skeptics and true believers[8] alike will be converted to the revealed, superior religion; even if its practices are at first repugnant.[9] Would our collection of diverse, terrestrial religions and the currently nonreligious really convert so readily? I think it would be very hard to prevent. The message (assumed to have been decoded, without ambiguity) will be a missionary campaign without precedent in terrestrial history. Although it probably will not contain any overt proof of the existence of God(s), it will contain much information about the universe that appears Godlike. Unlike previous revelations, this new information would be something that science and engineering will, in time, be able to digest, verify, and reproduce. This will happen everywhere, for all people, assuming (as I do) that the information will be widely distributed, because it will be impossible to systematically suppress it over time. The information will change our lives and our world view, and we will not be able to put the genie back in the bottle. We have a history of old religions being abandoned when confronted with the superior technologies of terrestrial missionaries. In the face of a demonstrably stable social organization, and superior understanding of the nature of the universe, it will be hard for humanity to resist the appeal of this universal religion and its God(s). The only real possibility for less than total conversion arises from any ambiguities in the message and its decoding, leading perhaps to multiple sects. But here, too, the necessary longevity of the extraterrestrial technology argues against this possibility. Large L (and N), plus our late arrival on the galactic scene, dictate that ours will not be the first encounter of a superior technology with an emergent one. The information-bearing message we have postulated will be crafted for unambiguous transmission of that information.

And if God(s) does not exist? We can imagine that elsewhere long-lived technologies may have been developed by intelligent creatures who never had the need to invent God(s) or religions, or who did so in their youth, but later replaced them with a more scientific world view. An information-rich message from these extraterrestrials will, over time, undermine our own world's religions. As in the previous example, skeptics will quickly be persuaded by those new pieces of information about the universe that are verifiable. For them, the absence of any information about God(s) will be conspicuous in the extreme. However, for true believers, it will be impossible to prove the negative; their belief in the existence of God(s) is beyond proof. But subsequent generations of humans, who mature with the knowledge of the existence of other technologies having long histories and no apparent need for religion, will find it harder and harder to subscribe to the unique terrestrial beliefs.

It is however possible that we shall some day detect evidence of an extraterrestrial technology, without the ability to learn anything about the technologists or their theology. They exist; we are not alone. But what happens next? All the inferential information about longevity still applies, but it will have a slower impact when it arrives without new, world-altering information. Those terrestrial religions that claim the most favored relationship between God(s) and humans will either have to adapt, or if they cling to their "chosen" status, the extraterrestrials will be defined as the newest infidels. Removing the "enemy" to celestial distances might defuse terrestrial conflicts. In contrast, those religions with the most catholic of doctrines will begin to adopt a more cosmic perspective. As they stretch to accommodate the actual fact of the existence of other intelligent beings, rather than the mere possibility, they may also stretch enough to accommodate other human religious traditions. It is possible to imagine the amalgamation of currently discrete religious organizations and the evolution of a doctrine that encompasses at least all the faithful inhabitants of this planet. It is also possible to imagine that the first organized religion to incorporate the existence of extraterrestrials might find even more fertile grounds for conflict with more traditional religions.

Of the two contact scenarios, the information-rich model is to be preferred. As mentioned, the longevity/stability requirements that underlie this entire construct imply that this will not be the first contact between an old and a young technology. Assuming that their own continued longevity/stability does not demand the elimination of the emerging technology, it is likely that they will act in our best interests, as reflected by the information content of the message. This is not an appeal for extraterrestrial salvation, but an acknowledgment that a mediated paradigm shift is less likely to have negative consequences than if it is left in our inexperienced human hands. While the outcome of either contact scenario will probably be satisfactory for skeptics, because the requisite proofs will be there, providing the compelling motivation to shift their religious beliefs if necessary, the same cannot be said for the true believers. The major religions of the world may be able to accommodate the *idea* of extraterrestrials into their current dogma,[10] but some of them may be quite discomforted by the information revealed by the *fact* of extraterrestrial technologies.

NOTES

1. M. Rees quoted in *Project Cyclops* (NASA publication CR 114445, Moffett Field, Calif. 1971), 3

2. S. Dick, *Plurality of Worlds: The Origins of the Extraterrestrial Life Debate from Democritus to Kant* (Cambridge: Cambridge University Press, 1982).

3. F. Hoyle and C. Wickramasinghe, *Lifecloud: The Origin of Life in the Universe* (New York: Harper & Row, 1978); F. Crick, *Life Itself: Its Origin and Nature* (New York: Simon & Schuster, 1981).

4. S. Shostak, *Mercury*, May-June 1998, 31.

5. While T. Peters (*The Center for Theology and the Natural Sciences Bulletin*, 14(3) 1994) argues cogently that certain Christian religious scholars found no contradictions with the Ptolemaic world view, the necessity for a twentieth-century Galileo Commission demonstrates the discord between religious and scientific doctrines and the power struggle over which world view was to take precedence.

6. A useful scientific construct that postulates that we do not exist in any favored position in time and space, therefore what we measure or experience here and now must be typical of the universe as a whole.

7. F. Drake and D. Sobel, *Is Anyone Out There?* (New York: Delacorte Press, 1991), 52.

8. C. Raymo, *Skeptics and True Believers: The Exhilarating Connection Between Science and Religion* (New York: Walker and Co., 1998).

9. S. Shostak, 31.

10. M. Ashkenazi, "Not the Sons of Adam: Religious Responses to ETI." Paper presented at the 42nd Congress of the International Astronautical Federation, Montreal, Canada, October 7–11, 1991; T. Peters, *Center for Theology and the Natural Sciences Bulletin*.

ERNAN MCMULLIN

The O'Hara Professor of Philosophy Emeritus at the University of Notre Dame, **Ernan McMullin** is an internationally respected philosopher of science who has written and lectured extensively on subjects ranging from the relationship between cosmology and theology, to the role of values in understanding science, to the impact of Darwinism on Western religious thought. A graduate of Maynooth College in Ireland, where he received an undergraduate degree in physics and a bachelor of divinity degree in theology, he went on to study theoretical physics at the Dublin Institute for Advanced Studies and earned a Ph.D. in philosophy at the University of Louvain in 1954. Joining the Notre Dame faculty as an assistant professor of philosophy that same year, he was named to the John Cardinal O'Hara Chair in 1984 and chaired the department from 1965 to 1972. He has been a visiting professor at the University of Minnesota, the University of Cape Town, the University of California at Los Angeles, Princeton, and Yale, a Phi Beta Kappa National Lecturer, and a Cardinal Mercier Lecturer at the (Flemish) University of Leuven. In addition, he has served as president of the American Catholic Philosophical Association, the Metaphysical Society of America, the Philosophy of Science Association, and the Western Division of the American Philosophical Association, as chair of the History and Philosophy of Science Section of the American Association for the Advancement of Science, as a member of the executive committees of the History of Science Society, the Council for Philosophical Studies, and the Society of Christian Philosophers, and as a member of numerous scholarly and scientific committees, congresses, and panels. A fellow of the American Academy of Arts and Sciences, the International Academy of the History of Science, and the American Association for the Advancement of Science, he holds honorary degrees from Maynooth, the National University of Ireland, and Loyola University (Chicago). A member of many editorial boards, Dr. McMullin is the author of numerous scholarly articles and nine major books and the editor of a series of monographs on logic. His latest volume is *The Inference That Makes Science*, published in 1992. He is working on a study of rationality, realism, and the growth of knowledge.

Life and Intelligence Far from Earth: Formulating Theological Issues

Ernan McMullin

Two searches are currently being conducted that bear on the issue of the uniqueness or otherwise of the development of life and intelligence here on Earth. Their aims, the technological resources they employ, and the conceptual problems they face are altogether different. The more venturesome of the two, SETI, looks for clues to the work of distant intelligences in the torrent of electromagnetic radiation that pours down constantly on our planet. Terrestrial technological developments of the past century have shown how such radiation can be modified by the deliberate intervention of intelligent agents. Already the electromagnetic radiation emanating from Earth over the past three-quarters of a century carries the distinctive mark of such an agency. The presence of such a mark could be determined by agents of equivalent or greater technological ability as far from Earth as the radiation itself can effectively carry. And the reverse is also true and is the basis of the SETI enterprise: we might be able to discern such an imprint in the radiation falling on Earth, if such is present.

The second search, the search for extraterrestrial life (SETL), is both broader and narrower than SETI in key respects. It is broader because it seeks physical traces beyond Earth of life at any stage of development; it is not limited to intelligent life. It is narrower because it is restricted, as I define it, to our own planetary system, including the asteroids that circle it and the meteoritic fragments that constantly penetrate the Earth's atmosphere. It relies on physical evidence other than radiation-modification, evidence that a form of life exists, or in the past existed, at some locus in our solar neighborhood outside our own planet. Such evidence can, in practice, be retrieved only from sources within the solar system; interstellar distances are too great for any form of communication other than by means of radiation.

SETI, on the other hand, has long abandoned the solar system. There is no longer any reasonable expectation of finding intelligent life anywhere in the solar neighborhood other than on Earth. Instead, the focus of SETI is on the planets of distant suns in our galaxy, from which electromagnetic signals or the distinctive "noise" caused by radio or television broadcasting could reach us. Perhaps one might also look in the electromagnetic spectrum for clues to the presence of chemical processes indicative of life. But the mission of SETI is with the clues to its presence that *intelligent* agency can, deliberately or indeliberately, bring about. SETI and SETL thus look for different things in different regions, using different means.

The U.S. Congress has apparently decided that SETI is too speculative, too "far out," to merit taxpayer support. On the other hand, it is enthusiastic about SETL. Financial appropriations for NASA are obviously influenced to a quite striking degree by the hopes of finding direct evidence of life, past or present, elsewhere in our own planetary system. And NASA has adjusted its sights accordingly. The immense fuss recently over the alleged traces of rudimentary life left in a meteorite likely to have come to Earth from Mars bears eloquent witness to the importance in political, as well as intellectual, terms that SETL has come to possess. My concern is with the potential philosophical and more especially the theological implications of these searches. Were they to be successful, what difference would it make, in philosophical or in theological terms?

ETL: ALTERING THE PROBABILITIES

Let us begin with SETL, the simpler case. Suppose we *do* find unequivocal traces of life, present or past, somewhere else in our solar neighborhood. Suppose further, and this supposition could raise some difficult issues, that it could be shown that this ETL did not, in fact, originate on Earth at some point in the past, that in other words it descends from an independent evolutionary lineage. What would be the consequences of such a discovery?

The most obvious one would be for science and more broadly for philosophy. There has been a vigorous debate in recent years over the likelihood of the occurrence of the complex series of processes, whatever these may be, that would give rise to living cells. The exuberance that greeted Stanley Miller's production in the 1950s of amino acids by simple mixing processes operating in conditions that supposedly mimicked early conditions on Earth has given way to a sober realization of just how complex even the simplest cell is and how difficult it is to reconstruct a pathway that might plausibly lead to its first realization. Although progress has been made in that direction, suggesting for example an "RNA world" as an intermediate stage, it seems fair to say that as biochemists and molecular biologists discover more and more intricate levels of interdependence in cellular structure, the pathway to first life appears to lengthen as well as to narrow.[1]

It is not surprising, then, that estimates of the likelihood of occurrence of a pathway having such an outcome would vary so wildly, some seeing such a pathway as a string of improbable events whose cumulative probability is as near zero as makes no difference,[2] others arguing that it is an "obligatory manifestation" of matter bound to arise when conditions are appropriate.[3] The problem, of course, is to discover what these conditions are and how likely it is that each will be realized at the proper moment. Necessary conditions affecting a lengthy historical process, necessary, if the process is to lead to a designated outcome, are notoriously hard to deal with. Stephen Gould has made much of this point in discussing the historical contingency of the evolutionary line leading to the human.[4] It is tempting to think of the origin of life, by contrast, in simpler terms of deterministic chemical processes. But this may ignore the troublesome possibility of an environmental condition, a "without which not," that happened to be just right at just the right time. At this point, we simply do not know enough to adjudicate between the vastly different theoretical probability estimates presently on offer.

When estimating the probability that a process will lead to a particular outcome, two very different kinds of evidence can be advanced. One is based on an understanding of the process itself. For example, one might estimate the probability of a dice coming up a 6 as 1/6, based on the physics of dice-throwing. This may be called a "theoretical" probability because it relies on a theoretical grasp of the process itself. On the other hand, one might simply throw the dice a number of times and take the ratio of 6s to determine the empirical probability. The assumption, of course, is that the larger the number of throws and the more accurate the theory of the process, the more likely it is that the two sorts of probability will converge. Sometimes only one of the two sorts of evidence is available. In epidemiology, for example, it is usually the empirical probability of a particular correlation, of lung cancer and heavy smoking say, that initially comes to notice, often in the absence of any sort of understanding of the processes involved. On the other hand, when one asks about the likelihood that a particular sort of process known to have occurred once on Earth might also occur elsewhere in the universe, one is clearly asking for a theoretical probability. And where the theory is still tentative, full of phrases like "it is theoretically possible that . . . ," the answer to the request for a probability estimate has to be even more tentative.

That is why even the beginnings of an empirical probability are so important. Finding an independent evolutionary origin of living matter somewhere else in our solar system would, at the very least, discredit the hypothesis that life is an extremely rare cosmic phenomenon, so rare that we have to take seriously the possibility of its having been "seeded" on Earth from a chance meteor impact.[5] Early in the century, the most widely accepted theory of planetary formation linked it to tides caused by the near approach of one star to another, a very rare occurrence in our thinly spread galaxy. So the theoretical probability of a star's possessing a planetary system was thought to be quite low. But, of course, now that we have more or less established the presence of planetary companions close to a growing number of nearby stars, frequency probability has come into play in support of a very different theoretical account of planetary formation, and the combined evidence of the two sorts have made it seem possible that planetary systems may be the norm rather than the exception. Finding traces of a single independent locus of life elsewhere in our solar system would affect probabilities just as much, possibly even more so. The process by which the first cells come to be are almost immeasurably more complex than that by which planets form, and a satisfactory theoretical account is accordingly far more difficult to arrive at in the former case than in the latter. Discovering that a life-producing sequence had occurred elsewhere in the neighborhood of our own star would leave the theoretical questions still to be answered but would drastically alter our estimates of how likely or unlikely the origin of life is, in cosmic terms.

ETL AND CHRISTIAN THEOLOGY

Now, to a very different question. How would such a discovery affect theology? I have to specify the question further since a good deal depends on *which* theology is meant: whether, it is the theology of one of the three great Abrahamic faiths of the West or that of Hinduism, say, with its very different perspective on time and on transformation. I will limit this essay to the tradition I know best, Christianity. And I argue that the discovery of life-traces elsewhere in the solar system should be of major significance to the Christian theologian.

Let us go back to the early centuries of Christian church history. The question of origins was of great concern to theologians of that day. The opening chapters of the Bible recounted in majestic detail how God had brought the universe to be and in a period of six days had populated it, in a series of separate Divine actions, with the diversity of creatures that we now see around us. The first origin of life, as of stars, planets, seas, and all else, lay in a creative action on God's part, bringing each material kind to be suddenly, with no need for a period of gradual preparation. It was a simple picture. And it was plausible, given the powers attributed to the Creator and the almost complete absence of any other account of how the complexities of the natural world, particularly the living world, could first have come to be.

But as early as the fourth and fifth centuries, a very different way of understanding the work of Creation began to find favor among Christian theologians. They were struck, for example, by the way in which the Genesis text spoke of earth and waters as "bringing forth" living creatures. It seemed as though pre-existing materials had played a crucial part in the coming to be of the first living things. Gregory of Nyssa, for one, took this to mean that the potencies were already somehow present, only waiting the appropriate moment to be activated by the Creator.

It was Augustine, however, the greatest theologian of the early Church, who brought this alternative to the literalist reading of Genesis into clear focus.[6] He noted, as others had done, that the "days" of the Genesis account could not possibly be taken literally, since, for one thing, the Sun was not created until the fourth "day." More important, Augustine was developing and deepening the notion of Divine creation itself. It was no longer to be just the imposition of form on, or the communication of motion to, pre-existent matter, as it had been for Plato or Aristotle. It was to be a radical bringing to be, without material antecedents. Since time is a measure of material change, time must itself be created, brought to be in a single creative act that encompasses past, present, and future, these last being limitations that confine the creature but not the Creator. In such a perspective, Augustine argued, it was necessary to read the Genesis account as metaphor, to be read literally only where this was theologically indicated.

How, then, did the variety of material kinds originate? Augustine proposed that the Creator implanted the "seeds" or potencies of each separate kind in the created universe from the first moment of its existence: "He made all things together, disposing them in an order based not on intervals of time but on causal connections" (*De Genesi ad litteram*, V, 5). Thus, "there was invisibly present all that would later develop . . . not only sun, moon, and stars . . . but also the beings which water and earth produced, in potency and in their causes before they came forth in the course of time" (V, 23). The capacity of bringing each living kind to its first appearance was present in the universe from its very beginning; they would appear, each in its time, when the conditions of water and earth were right. And Augustine would set no limits on how long that might take. This is not an evolutionary account, as we understand that label today, since each species has a separate origin from its own "seed." But it *is* developmental; it allows for the first appearance of the different kinds at different times, in a sequence determined by their needs. Augustine remarks that the processes of development that his account entails are "hidden from the eyes" but "not from the mind." And he adds, cautiously: "Whether such development must necessarily come about is completely unknown to us" (VI, 16).

Here, then, were two very different accounts of origins, one relying on a literal reading of Genesis, the other on a theological development of the consequences of the Christian doctrine of creation. If God is truly the omnipotent Creator we take God to be, Augustine seems to be saying, it is more appropriate to suppose that all that the created universe needs is there from the beginning, with no need for later miraculous supplementation on the Creator's part. The only exception Augustine allows is the human soul (his Neoplatonic understanding of the gulf between soul and body forbade him to suppose that soul might come from matter).

There is no room here to discuss the later fortunes of these two contrasting accounts of how the Creator brought our universe to be. In the Middle Ages, Aquinas allowed that either was possible, although he leant rather more to the literalist one, not least perhaps because as a good Aristotelian, he could hardly have admitted a warrant in natural philosophy for the existence of Augustine's "seeds." But with the break-up of Christendom into warring camps in the sixteenth century, with theological division hinging on the exact reading to be given to specific passages in Scripture, literalism in hermeneutics came to be more and more the norm. And the adaptation of means to end in the structure and behavior of all living things seemed to point to the need of a Creator capable of grasping that adaptation and fashioning the living kinds, one by one, accordingly.

No need to carry the story further. Were traces of life to be discovered elsewhere in our solar system today, it would favor the Augustinian idea that the "seeds" of life were implanted in matter from its first appearance. Such seeds could presumably come to fruition anywhere where "water and earth" provided the right environment. On the other hand, such a discovery would challenge the belief that the origin of life on Earth required a miraculous intervention on God's part. It would do so for two reasons. First, as we have seen, the discovery would strengthen the case for an evolutionary origin of the first life as a consequence of the ordinary processes of nature. Second, those Christians who believe that the first terrestrial life must have had a miraculous origin would be likely to link that life to the economy of earth, to human well-being. Why, in that perspective, would God causally intervene to place simpler forms of life elsewhere?

To many, probably most, scientists, the "special" creation of life by God has little credibility to begin with, and thus hardly needs further challenge. But two things should be kept in mind. One is the strong support enjoyed by "creation science" in some quarters in the U.S., for reasons that range back to immigration patterns in the formative years of the new republic and forward to the effects of stringent church-state separation on American public education. (The recent appropriation by the media of the label "creationist" for the proponents of so-called creation science has been both unfortunate and confusing, since nearly all Christians believe in God as Creator, but relatively few adopt the literalist reading of the first chapters of Genesis that undergirds creation science.)

Those who defend creation science, particularly in the version that restricts the history of Earth to the matter of a few thousand years, are not likely to be moved by one additional reason to accept the evolutionary origin of life. But there are Christians, including some serious philosophers of religion, who, though willing to allow broad scope to evolution, argue that in view of the lack of any satisfactory theoretical account of such key transitions as the origin of the first cell, it is more likely in the Christian perspective to suppose that the Creator in such cases may have intervened to bridge what might otherwise be an unbridgeable gap.[7]

I disagree with this approach for reasons that might be broadly characterized as Augustinian.[8] But I think it has to be taken seriously.

What prompts it is a reaction to the supposition on the part of many spokesmen for evolution that an evolutionary origin is the only *possible* way for life to begin, excluding implicitly therefore even the *possibility* of a Divine intervention. Critics of this line of argument do not necessarily deny that evolution has occurred. Nor do they need to deny that in the long run the gaps they perceive in the current evolutionary arguments may close. But in the interim, they claim that a Christian has more reason to believe in the possibility of a miraculous supplementation to cosmic development on God's part where such supplementation seems to be needed, as it does where the origin of life is concerned.

The discovery of an independent development of life elsewhere in our planetary system would pose a serious challenge to this view. It would tend to close the gap, not by filling out the requisite theoretical reconstruction of how the process of origin actually took place, but by suggesting that because the process has occurred twice in close proximity in cosmic terms, it seems overwhelmingly likely that the gap ultimately *can* be closed. Further, as before, proponents of this view would have to ask themselves why, in their perspective, God would act in this "special" way in reaches of space where more complex forms of life quite evidently do not and could not exist.

The discovery of intelligent agency elsewhere in our galaxy would raise a further, and potentially much more challenging, set of philosophical and theological questions. Knowing that life had evolved elsewhere than on Earth, and relatively nearby at that, would *already* carry with it significant implications. But knowing that *intelligent* life is not confined to Earth would cut a good deal deeper. No wonder that the ETI search seems to inspire so much more passion than does the more workaday search for ETL!

THE SEARCH FOR ETI

Investigation of incoming radiation patterns, likely to remain our only possible source of ETI information, could yield two very different sorts of positive outcome, one much more dramatic (and problematic) than the other. The pattern might do no more than indicate that intelligent agency must have been involved in its production. It could do that in at least two different ways. The pattern might constitute a deliberate signal, one that could not plausibly be generated by a natural process alone, like a series of "pips" counting out the series of small prime numbers, for example. Or the pattern could be a byproduct of intelligent agency, such as the radiation "noise" generated by the radio and TV signals of a technological civilization like our own. Either type of pattern would warrant our concluding that intelligent agents were active at that distant location at the time the radiation was emitted. It would, however, tell us little more about those agents than their presence and their technical capabilities.

The radiation pattern might, however, be something potentially a good deal more significant: an actual message, a linguistic communication of some sort that could be decoded. The implications of such an extraterrestrial communication are, to all intents and purposes, impossible to assess without knowing what the message contains. Science fiction writers have explored many possible ramifications of different sorts of message. But I doubt whether even the most fertile imagination could encompass the range of challenges that a communication with another advanced civilization could offer. I am skeptical, however, about an indispensable premise to this scenario: the ability to decode such a radiation pattern in the absence of any other information about the organisms responsible for its transmission.

It might be best, then, to limit our inquiry to a more manageable, but still intriguing, possibility: not the interpreting of an extraterrestrial message but simply the discovery that intelligent agents of some sort *do* exist out there somewhere. What difference would such a discovery make? It would, of course, confirm the strongly held belief of many evolutionary thinkers that in a universe as vast as ours, with an uncountable number of niches where life might develop, it would be altogether extraordinary if in some of those niches continued evolution would not result in the appearance of advanced intelligence. On the other hand, it might also serve to quiet the doubts regarding ETI expressed by others in the evolutionary tradition who tend to regard the terrestrial evolutionary sequence leading to intelligence as full of contingencies, of numerous junctions at any one of which the progression toward intelligence could have been halted. Determining that there is at least one other center of intelligence besides Earth would not, of course, go very far in helping to decide just how likely it is that long-continued evolution of different life forms would eventually yield intelligent agents, or for that matter to decide on the prior issue of how likely biological evolution itself is at locations other than Earth. But it would, at least, refute the assumption of the uniqueness of the human mind and might raise new issues for philosophers, particularly those in the idealist tradition whose emphasis is on the shaping powers of mind.

There has always been a question about the extent to which our own minds have been themselves shaped by the contingencies of our evolutionary history. Much of the philosophical writing about mind has taken for granted a universalist notion of mind that implicitly assumes that mind will be the same no matter where and in what historical circumstances it is found. Recent work by anthropologists, psychologists, and others, would tend to call this assumption into question. Discovering that ETI indeed exists would not of itself settle this issue, but it would surely raise it in a new and more urgent way.

Such a discovery would seem likely to have an even more dramatic effect in the domain of theology. So it is to speculate on this effect that I turn in the remainder of my essay. And I lay emphasis on the Christian tradition, particularly in the final sections, where it will appear that this tradition would face a more insistent challenge from the discovery of ETI than would other major Western religious traditions.

THE THEOLOGICAL ISSUE OF PARTICULARITY

The story of the Creation from which the sacred books of all three of the major Western faiths begin is shaped, in part at least, by the Earth-centered cosmology of the people for whom those writings were intended. The fashioning of the Earth and its contents culminates in the breathing of life into the dust of Earth to make the first humans. The heavenly bodies enter only as accessories, the two principal ones serving terrestrial needs, the remainder appearing only as distant and mysterious decoration. Humans are gifted with powers of understanding and free choice that lead them to be described as made in the image of God. Yet this same combination of powers leads them to fall short of the ideal that God had set for them. There is a rupture between creature and Creator; humans now find themselves in a different and more difficult world.

After the great flood, Noah's progeny disperse across the face of the Earth to repopulate distant lands; they give rise to new peoples whose names soon vanish from the main story. The focus of that story abruptly narrows to a single individual, Abraham, a man whose obedience to God (unlike that of Adam) survives the most severe test. With that man, God makes a covenant that extends to Abraham's descendants; they are the chosen ones, raised up above all others and yet also bound to respect their own demanding side of the covenant. When they are enslaved in Egypt, their Protector raises up for them a charismatic leader, Moses, who guides them toward a promised land whose inhabitants will be cleared to make way for them.

The particularity of this account is striking. No longer is God dealing with the nations, with all those who are made in the Divine image. God's concern appears now to be with a single people bound together into one in the first place by genetic descent. What is at stake for the people of Israel is God's special favor. Distant peoples fade from view, their status in the eyes of God uncertain. Nearby peoples come into view only when their fortunes intersect with those of the people of Israel; when that happens, the Israelites may, if necessary, call on their Protector to smite these others as enemies. The tension in this complex narrative between the more and more explicit affirmation of the God of Israel as the Creator of all that is and the expectation that this same Creator will favor one particular people over all others in war and in peace leaps from the page.

The Christian Gospels draw the boundaries quite differently and less sharply, but boundaries there still are. Baptism, not genetic descent and obedience to the law, is the mark of the new Christian. Baptism is open, however, to people of any race who choose to be followers of Christ. A newly expanded doctrine of original sin asserts that human beings lost favor with God through the disobedience of the first humans; although the life and death of Christ has made it possible for human beings to regain that favor, the enduring effect of that first sin can (it seems) be wiped away only by the grace of baptism. The stakes are now much higher. More clearly than before, God's favor is seen not as bringing advantage to this earthly life but as prelude to an afterlife of union with God, beyond the ravages of time. Only fidelity to Christ's word can prepare for and ensure such a union; and its loss is terrible beyond imagining.

Independently, then, of the questions raised by ETI, the religions of the Book have always had to face the difficult issue of particularity. It was inherent in the very idea of God's choosing particular individuals through whom to communicate and a content of that communication that would mark off one human group in a way that seemed to privilege it in God's sight. Is salvation possible outside the chosen group? What of those who have never heard of Moses, of Christ, of Mohammed? If they too are eligible for salvation, what then was the function of the Book? Theologians of all three faiths have struggled with this knot of questions for centuries, softening the harshness of exclusions in a variety of ways, interpreting fidelity to the Book as indispensable witness, for example, instead of as some sort of inside track.

The discovery of ETI would not, from this perspective at least, raise an entirely new issue for Western theologies. Coping with the reality of the Stranger has always been a challenge for the theologians of the Book; the challenge of ETI would, in that regard at least, be no different than that of the peoples of Mesoamerica for the questing Europeans of the sixteenth century. But the proven reality of ETI might even more effectively encourage a broadening among the theologians and religious believers generally of the realization that the Creator of a galactic universe may well choose to relate to creatures made in the Creator's own image in ways and on grounds as diverse as those creatures themselves.

PLURALITY OF WORLDS

In popular discussions of extraterrestrial intelligence, it tends to be assumed that the discovery of such intelligence would pose new problems, new challenges, for religious believers. But as historians of science have recently reminded us, the notion that we should expect to find such intelligence came, in significant part, from Christian theologians in the first place.[9] The revival of Aristotelian natural philosophy in the Latin West in the thirteenth century led to a rupture of serious proportions between Aristotelian philosophers (many of them also theologians) and theologians of a more traditional persuasion. One of the main issues that divided them was the status of propositions in natural philosophy. According to Aristotle, scientific demonstration should proceed deductively from propositions perceived to be true, indeed necessarily true, in their own right, after the manner of geometrical axioms. Theologians were quick to point out that if Aristotle's cosmology be allowed this status, it would imply that the general structure of the world could not be other than it is, thus compromising the key Christian doctrine of Divine freedom. The theology of creation deriving from Augustine maintained that the Creator was in no way constrained in fashioning the sort of universe in which we find ourselves.

One of the test cases between the two sides of this debate was whether there could be a plurality of worlds. For the Aristotelians, this was impossible. Were there to be another world, it would still have to be of the same general sort as this one; a simple analysis of natural motion would then show (as Aristotle argues in two dense chapters of his *De Caelo*, I, 8–9) that it would reduce necessarily to the world we already have. To many theologians of that day, this seemed an implicit denial of Divine omnipotence. And so the possibility of a plurality of worlds became a rallying point for those who were alarmed at the necessitarian tendencies of the new natural philosophy. Despite the efforts of Thomas Aquinas to mediate the quarrel, the Aristotelian position was condemned in 1277 by a council of the bishops of France, thus giving an official status to the doctrine of the possible plurality of worlds.

What the defenders of this doctrine maintained was no more than the *possibility* of other worlds, that is, God's freedom to create such worlds if God desired to do so. They did not argue that God has, in fact, done so; they would have seen no reason to suppose that a plurality of worlds actually existed. But they had not only opened the way to such a supposition, they had given it broad theological sanction.

With the revival of Neoplatonic ideas in the Renaissance, a further step was taken, the introduction of what later writers would call a "principle of plenitude." The principle was of philosophical, rather than of specifically biblical, origin. But it rested on a particular view of the nature of God, one that had some resonance with the traditional Augustinian doctrine of the omnipotence of the Creator, so it might also be called theological in a somewhat broader sense. The principle lays down that a Creator such as is envisioned in the Christian tradition must bring to be all that is possible, out of the fullness of the Divine power and goodness. It is the presumed nature of God that leads to the expectation that a plurality of inhabited worlds is not only possible, but in some sense necessary.[10]

Developments in astronomy in the seventeenth century gave fresh impetus to these ideas, not only of an actual plurality of worlds, but of worlds inhabited perhaps by living and even intelligent agents. As historians have shown in some detail, the likelihood of ETI became almost a commonplace in western Europe in the eighteenth and nineteenth centuries.[11] What is especially striking about this development is the support that this idea of ETI received among Christian thinkers of that time. They were aware of the difficult questions that the reality of ETI would pose for Christians. But for most of them, this potential negative was evidently overcome by their conviction that the presence of ETI in many parts of the universe was what one should expect from an omnipotent Creator, whose power and goodness would in this way be made manifest. As telescopic evidence for the vast scale of the universe mounted, it seemed more and more likely (it was argued) that the Creator would not have left these vast spaces empty of the only sort of life that could freely offer homage to the One on whom this mighty frame depends for its very being.

When Christians are asked today what response religious believers ought to make to the growing conviction that the operations of evolution on a cosmic scale would almost necessarily eventuate in life and intelligence in a great number of locations, their first answer might well be that such a plenitude is just what one *should* have expected, given the premium that the Genesis account of origins already sets on the gifts that allow human beings to be regarded as somehow imaging their Creator. It is in these gifts and their possessors that the story of the Creation in Genesis seems to find its deepest meaning. Would it not seem, then, that as the dimensions of the Creation prove incomparably greater than those of the central Earth of early tradition, the bestowal of that image could hardly be restricted to that single locus?

Not everyone saw it in that way. Indeed, some critics turned matters around to make the plurality of worlds an argument *against* Christianity. Notable among these was Thomas Paine who in *The Age of Reason* (1793) argued that "the two beliefs cannot be held together in the same mind; and he who thinks that he believes in both has thought but little of either."[12] Paine took for granted that the astronomical science of his day had already established the plurality of worlds. Telescopes showed a vast number of fixed stars; "the probability therefore is that each of those fixed stars is also a sun, round which another system of worlds or planets, though too remote from us to discover, performs its revolutions. . . . "[13] And so: "the solitary idea of a solitary world . . . in the immense ocean of space, gives place to the cheerful idea of a society of worlds, so happily contrived as to administer, even by their motion, instruction to man."[14] And since the Creator has filled our own world with life at every level of size and complexity, we should expect that the same would be true of that vaster universe; the immensity of space cannot simply be "a naked void lying in eternal waste."[15] Although there are overtones here of the principle of plenitude, Paine's argument hinges not so much on the nature of God as on the belief that the Creator "organized the structure of the universe in the most advantageous manner for the benefit of man" as well as for the humanlike inhabitants of the multitude of other words.[16]

Paine goes on to assail Christian belief, to a deist like himself a lamentable aberration. Christians, he says, are faced with a dilemma:

they must either believe that "the Almighty, who had millions of worlds equally dependent on his protection, should quit the care of all the rest and come to die in our world because, they say, one man and one woman had eaten an apple," or else suppose that "every world in the boundless creation, had an Eve, an apple, a serpent, and a Redeemer." In this latter case, "the person who is irreverently called the Son of God, and sometimes God himself, would have nothing else to do than to travel from world to world, in an endless succession of death, with scarcely a momentary interval of life."[17]

Laying aside the element of conscious caricature in these passages, one can easily enough discern the sort of challenge that Paine is posing to believers in the Incarnation, that is, in God's taking on human nature in a particular individual who grew up long ago in Galilee. His objection is posed to Christians only, not to Jews or Muslims who could, without much of a stretch it would seem, allow that intelligent peoples elsewhere in our galaxy might be granted by a magnanimous Creator their own Moses, their own Mohammed. How, Paine asks, are believers in the Incarnation to adjust to a new cosmology in which the created universe no longer centers on the Earth and in which humanity is scattered across myriad planets? It was easier to accept the idea of God's becoming man when humans and their abode both held a unique place in the universe. But is it any longer credible in the light of the new questions that the plurality of inhabited worlds poses?

Paine's challenge has been repeated many times since his day, recently again by Roland Puccetti in his *Persons: A Study of Possible Moral Agents in the Universe*.[18] Puccetti draws on P. F. Strawson's influential analysis of the notion of a person[19] to argue that persons must be corporeal and hence cannot be in more than one place at the same time; they must be capable of moral agency and hence must be able to experience sensations and emotions as only corporeal beings can. This, of course, would mean that the notion of a person could not be applied to God, not at least in the traditional understanding of God as a spiritual being. (This would be ironic in light of the fact that the term "person" in its Latin version *persona* was first used, in something of its modern sense, of *God* not of corporeal beings, when theologians of the early Christian centuries attempted to illuminate the difficult doctrine of the Trinity.)

In a final chapter, Puccetti asks (somewhat illogically it might seem), But suppose we *do* apply the term "person" to Christ, what are we to make of the doctrine of the Incarnation, given that we are now certain on scientific grounds (according to him, at least) that civilizations have developed frequently elsewhere in our galaxy? (He even suggests that 10^{18} might be the best current estimate for the number of ETI sites in the known galaxies.[20]) It would be impossible even for God, he argues, to become incarnate in so many locations in the time available, given that a person cannot be present in more than one place at once. Alternatively, if defenders of Christian faith were to hold that God became incarnate on Earth only, they would be faced with the objection that the inhabitants of other planets would be unlikely ever to learn of it. How, then, would they be saved? Since the Incarnation is central to Christian belief, Puccetti concludes that the discovery of this vast plurality of inhabited worlds undermines the Christian religion decisively.

His argument rests on some shaky presuppositions.[21] The sort of linguistic fundamentalism that would prescribe necessary conditions for an ordinary-language term like "person" has been effectively challenged in recent philosophy, most notably by Wittgenstein. We have not the least idea how many ETI sites there may be in our own galaxy, let alone in the collection of all galaxies. The use of the Drake equation, with its seven (more or less) unknown quantities, to estimate, even very roughly, their actual number is inadmissible, given the state of our knowledge of the processes underlying the probabilities making up the equation.

Puccetti's argument rests on the assumption that the number of ETI sites can be known to be very great. One has to be wary here of a fallacy induced by the contemplation of large numbers. It goes like this: out of a million planets (with conditions suitable for life, where life has developed, . . .), it is surely a "conservative estimate" to suppose that 1 percent, at least, of those will (go on to develop life, will progress toward intelligent life . . .). And, lo! that gives us 10,000 candidates right away. But without a fair degree of knowledge of the necessary conditions involved in the process whose probability is being estimated, this kind of argument is logically treacherous. It is one thing to discover one or a small number of ETI sites based on the interpretation of incoming radiation. It is another thing entirely to establish, on the basis of a theoretical analysis of the multiplicity of processes involved in the appearance and survival of intelligent life, that the number of centers of such life in the universe is of a certain order or even that it is, in very general terms, extremely large. So I am making the much simpler assumption that a *single* center of ETI is discovered, not on the basis of a theoretical analysis of the component genetic processes but directly, by interpretation of radiation patterns. The consequences for Christian theology are less drastic perhaps—Puccetti's "not enough time" argument cannot get started, for example—but in essence they are quite similar.

.When people speculate about the implications for Christian theology of an ETI discovery, they tend to assume that Christian theology is a sort of given, that the main outlines of Christian belief are more or less agreed on. But of course this is not the case. Not only are there significant differences in this regard between Christian denominations, but even in a single denomination there are areas of vigorous debate, and particular doctrines can evolve over time. I turn briefly now to several interrelated Christian doctrines, each of them relevant to the ETI discussion, in order to show that the questions ETI would pose for Christian theology depend quite sensitively on how these doctrines are themselves to be formulated.

"ORIGINAL" SIN

The first of these is the doctrine of original sin that Paine evokes in the mocking dilemma he poses to the Christian believer. Are we to suppose, he asks, that God would come to die in this, out of all the inhabited worlds, just because a man and a woman ate an apple? Or alternatively that in each of those worlds there would be "an Eve, an apple, a serpent, and a Redeemer"? The Genesis story of the disobedience of Adam and Eve and its consequences carries meaning at many levels, however. It is a powerful myth, in the original sense of that term, conveying truth in multiple, although inevitably tentative, ways. The main thrust of the story is clearly to emphasize that the source of the evil we see all round us in the human world lies, not in the original creation ("And God saw that it was good . . ."), but in the human will itself.[22]

The story of Adam is scarcely mentioned in later books of the Bible until Paul in Romans 5, reflecting on the mission of Christ, compares Adam and Christ: "As by one man's disobedience many were made sinners, so by one man's obedience many will be made righteous." Christ came to redeem humankind, to restore a friendship with God that had been lost. But it was Augustine, once again, writing in the early fifth century, who gave the doctrine of original sin its most influential early formulation. Trying to steer between the extremes of Manichaeism, which took evil to be part of the Creation itself and Pelagianism, which held the human will to be neutral initially, capable of avoiding sin entirely like Adam's before the Fall, Augustine proposed that the human will has an inborn predisposition to evil and that this predisposition comes through genetic descent from a single historical couple and is linked with the concupiscence involved in human conception.

Theologians today would for the most part reject, or substantially modify, this pessimistic vision. There is an immense literature, particularly from recent decades, returning to the original Genesis story and interpreting it in a variety of ways.[23] My intention here is only to draw attention to this fluidity, not to review the literature with the care it deserves or to take sides in the debate itself. Most of these writers would question the literal interpretation that links human sinfulness to a single contingent historical act on the part of a single historical ancestral couple. Many would trace human sinfulness to a division between flesh and spirit that has deep roots in humanity's animal ancestry. Some would link it to the way in which moral character is shaped by outside influences, to the temptations of the Other (the "serpent"). Some would still suppose that there was a primal turning away from God that has some causal relation to the later human condition . . .

The discovery of an ETI site would not, so far as I can see, help to resolve this by now quite convoluted debate. But it would prompt such questions as, Ought one expect, from the Christian standpoint, some analogue of original sin at that distant location? And obviously, the answer would depend on a reasonably precise understanding of what would count as such an analog. Ought we expect an "Eve," as such science fiction classics as C.S. Lewis' *Perelandra* and Walter Miller's *Canticle for Leibowitz* suggest? Might an elsewhere-Eve choose differently and in that way preserve the innocence of her descendants? Questions like these presuppose a relatively literal reading of the original myth and the belief that the entire course of human history would have been radically altered had an original couple happened to choose a virtuous God-directed course.

Critics of this approach would argue that this sort of literalism obscures the larger and more significant meanings of the Genesis myth. They would not look for an Eve or an Adam, less still for an individual act of disobedience to an authority recognized as in some manner transcendent. Regarding ETI, they might instead ask, Do these distant agents have a divided nature like ours? What sort of balance did their evolutionary ancestry leave them between reason and passion? How far does their intelligence carry them in an understanding of the sources and sanctions of morality?

There is nothing, it would seem, about the doctrine of original sin that would make it more or less likely that there should be ETI out there in the first place. We might perhaps speculate that an omnipotent Creator would want to try more than once the fateful experiment of allowing freedom to a creature. So there may be a slight lean of the balance in the direction of ETI, indeed very many types of ETI, as more than one theologian has urged. But when it comes to the questions asked above, What manner of creature will these intelligent aliens be? How will they relate to their Creator? Will there be an analog of our very evident sinfulness? The mere realization that intelligence lies behind some radiation pattern will not, of itself, lead to any answers. But that, of course, does not make the formulation of these questions themselves any less intriguing!

SOUL AND BODY

A second matter of ETI-relevant debate both in philosophy and in theology is the question of the human soul. Ought we expect these aliens to possess souls, and if they do, will some analog of the Christian doctrine of salvation apply to them? Here two very different answers might be given, depending on how the notion of soul itself is understood.

The strong dualism of soul and body that one finds in early Christian documents owes more, historians of theology suggest, to Greek influence than to the authority of the Bible. Here, once more, Augustine is a major source. He construes soul and body, after the fashion of Plato, as two separate substances, yoked in uneasy union. In a weaker version of dualism inspired by Aristotle, Thomas Aquinas represented soul as the substantial form of a matter-form composite, and thus not a complete substance in its own right. Nevertheless, Aquinas (unlike Aristotle) argued that it could exist, although only in an incomplete manner, apart from body. In both these versions of dualism, the soul, being spiritual, is of its nature immortal. And this is held to follow directly from the nature of intellect, represented as an immaterial power independent of body.

In this view, intelligent beings, no matter where found in the universe, would be of their nature immortal, quite independently of any special relationship with God. It would be an immortality of the soul only, unless perhaps an unfallen race would be exempt from death, as Paul's account in Romans seems to imply. (Yet Paul's assertion that death came into the world through Adam's sin cannot be taken literally; death is a necessary condition for the lengthy evolutionary process leading to the appearance of the first humans.) For Aquinas, immortality of soul without body would call out for completion; it might suggest that in such a case some special action on God's part (Incarnation?) would be needed. For the Augustinian dualist, on the other hand, it is something of a puzzle why a resurrection of the body should be offered in the first place. Why should humans not be restored to God's friendship without need for the awkwardness of a reunion with body? There is a whole nest of issues here consequent on any dualistic affirmation of the natural immortality of mind. The discovery of ETI would mean that we humans are not only not the unique intelligences in the universe, but we are also not the only agents who will never cease to be.

Although soul-body dualism has been a more or less standard feature of Christian language and belief, it faces a variety of challenges from the scientific, the philosophical, and even the theological points of view.[24] Consequently, Christian theologians have cautiously begun to explore an alternative that already has found a degree of favor with both scientists and philosophers of mind.[25] It is nondualistic; it gives a unitary account of human nature, avoiding the many difficulties that dualism faces in that regard. It is nonreductive; it maintains that the language of the mental cannot be reduced to the language of physics and chemistry, thus retaining one of the key features of the dualist accounts. It can be described as a form of materialism, but because of the reductionist overtones associated with that label, some prefer to call it nonreductive physicalism. If it is labelled a materialism, two provisos would have to be made: first, that it does not exclude the category of the spiritual, and second that matter be recognized as having within it potentialities that go beyond the equations of physics and chemistry. Mind would, then, constitute the highest level of functioning in a hierarchical account of human nature, leaving open the further question whether mind always needs a material basis as its physical support.

In this perspective, mind would not naturally survive the death of body. Thus, the discovery of an ETI site would not carry with it the implication that these beings also are immortal. Further, the Christian promise of resurrection would now refer to a resurrection of the whole person, not just to a rejoining of two separated components. It would be a consequence of grace, not of nature. The Creator, so far as we can tell, would be under no obligation to extend this grace beyond Earth or even to all the intelligent agents who have been or will be part of the human ancestral line. Immortality would be detached, partially at least, from ontology. If God were to extend a similar grace to a people not of human ancestry, God also might elect to become incarnate in their nature or to interact in some other way with them. From the Christian perspective, that could depend on how this distant people responded to the challenge symbolized by the tree of good and evil in the Genesis story.

INCARNATION

Lying deeper than questions about original sin and the soul-body distinction is the issue of the Incarnation itself, the defining doctrine of the Christian tradition. Beginning with Paul in the New Testament, theologians have struggled to make sense of the belief that the Creator of the universe somehow took on mortal human nature and died an agonizing death on the Cross. Paul, as we have seen, portrayed Christ's death as redeeming humankind from the estrangement from God that resulted from Adam's sin. In this perspective, the death and resurrection of Christ are the focal points in the Incarnation narrative; Christ "was handed over to death for our sins and raised to life for our justification" (Romans 4:25). Among the Greek-speaking theologians of the early Church, the emphasis shifted and broadened: it was the Incarnation itself that brought about human salvation. By taking on human nature, God raised up that nature; the life and death of God as man revealed the depth of the Creator's love for his human creatures, errant though they are.

At the end of the eleventh century, Anselm of Canterbury painted a much bleaker picture. Adam's sin, indeed *any* sin on the part of a creature, is so great an offence that nothing humans themselves could do could expiate it. Only the death of God as man could turn away the terrible anger of God; Christ's death is thus a working out of penal justice. Duns Scotus in the late thirteenth century reformulated the contrary view that it was the simple fact of God's becoming man that restored humans to grace; Christ's life, lived in obedience as witness to God's love, was all-sufficient. The Reformers of the sixteenth century, however, turned to Paul and Augustine to warrant an even more somber vision, perhaps, than theirs: human depravity in consequence of the Fall was so deep that no creature could turn aside the Creator's anger. There was no other remedy than for the Son of God, in his mercy and love, to "take upon himself the load of awful and eternal wrath and make his own body and blood a sacrifice for the sin."[26] By way of reaction in our own day, many theologians hold that it is misguided to suppose that Jesus died to change the Father and not us. They argue that God (Father, Son, and Holy Spirit) has never ceased to love humankind and that the mission of Jesus on Earth (and indeed earlier of Israel and later of the Church) was to reveal, to bear witness, that God is actively at work to transform us and ultimately to lead us back to our Creator.[27]

These sketchy remarks are not intended to provide a serious review of the voluminous theological literature on the Incarnation. But perhaps they may be enough to make two general points. First, working from the slender and not always easily reconciled clues afforded by the Bible and the life of the Church, theologians have found very different ways of interpreting the significance of the Incarnation. Ought it be understood primarily as an expression of God's love or primarily as an expiation for human sin? And second, how do we dare, even with the help of the revelation that began with the children of Abraham, that came to a focus in Christ and his message, and that continues to unfold in the life of the Church today, how do we dare to dispute about the Creator's motives in the first place? How can we limit the ways in which the Creator of a galactic universe might relate to agents like ourselves on other distant planets?

Critics of the Christian belief in Incarnation tend to assume (as Paine and Puccetti did) that the existence of ETI faces Christians with a destructive dilemma: God becomes incarnate only on Earth or else becomes incarnate on every inhabited planet. And either way, they claim, there are problems. The argument seems simplistic, a rhetorical ploy prompted perhaps by the conviction that if people are naive enough to believe in this sort of story, then these are the naive questions they must face. At a more serious level, however, the review above of conflicting theological interpretations of the Incarnation suggests that such differences of interpretation would have definite consequences for the ETI situation.

If the Incarnation and the death of Christ be seen as the response to human sin, and if that sin itself be seen as a contingency that might well not have occurred, then the question about an ETI race might be, Did its first progenitors fall when challenged? If they did, then the Son of God might become incarnate in their nature and die to expiate their sins. If they did not (the *Perelandra* scenario), then an Incarnation there would not be called for. If it be supposed in addition, however, that Christ's death on Earth was a unique event, sufficient of itself to restore the balance disturbed even at the cosmic level by the sin of Adam, then a further Incarnation on other inhabited planets would be unnecessary: even if these peoples (or their representatives) also had disobeyed a primal command of God, the balance would be restored by the death of Christ on a distant Earth.[28]

If the Incarnation be regarded as sufficient of itself to restore on Earth the balance destroyed by sin, then once again, we have to ask of our ETI: how do (did) they stand, morally, in the sight of their Creator? Do (did) they need the sort of redemption effected by the Incarnation on Earth? A further question arises, Do these ETI share in "human" nature sufficiently to be redeemed by the redeeming action of God on Earth? Or does each race of ETI constitute a different nature, and each therefore stand alone in moral terms?[29] Finally, if the Incarnation be simply construed as a revelation of God's goodness, a contingent grace from God, then the alien people might or might not be favored in this way. They might, for a variety of reasons, need it less (or perhaps even more) than we do. The issue of a primal choice on their part would not arise.

This is all very artificial. But it does bring out how dependent on the precise understanding of some key Christian doctrines the answers to the usual ETI questions are. Returning to the situation from which we began, namely, the identification of radiation patterns from a distant source as definite evidence of the presence there of intelligence, we can see that Christian theologians would be far from agreement as to whether we should expect antecedently that the Creator would become incarnate in a member of that distant race. Their answers could range, as we have seen, from "yes certainly" to "certainly not." My own preference would be for a cautious "maybe." If our imaginations can scarcely encompass such features of our cosmic home as action at the quantum level or the first moment of cosmic expansion, we should be modest in what we have to say about the Creator who set those limits in the first place.

NOTES

1. P. Davies, *The Fifth Miracle: The Search for the Origin of Life* (London: Penguin, 1998).
2. F. Hoyle, *The Intelligent Universe* (London: Michael Joseph, 1983).
3. C. de Duve, *Vital Dust* (New York: Basic Books, 1995).
4. S. J. Gould, *Wonderful Life* (Cambridge, Mass.: Harvard University Press, 1989).

5. Favored by Hoyle in *Intelligent Universe*. See the chapter, "Panspermia," in Davies' *The Fifth Miracle*.
6. For a fuller account, see E. McMullin, "Introduction" in *Evolution and Creation* (Notre Dame, Ind.: University of Notre Dame Press, 1985), 1–56.
7. A. Plantinga, "When Faith and Reason Clash: Evolution and the Bible," *Christian Scholar's Review*, 21 (1991), 8–32; reprinted in D.L. Hull and M. Ruse, eds., *The Philosophy of Biology* (Oxford: Oxford University Press, 1998), 674–697.
8. E. McMullin, "Evolution and Special Creation," *Zygon*, 28 (1993), 299–335; reprinted in *The Philosophy of Biology*, 698–733.
9. S.J. Dick, *Plurality of Worlds* (Cambridge: Cambridge University Press, 1982), chapter 2.
10. Reformation theologians, on the other hand, tended to emphasize the uniqueness both of the Incarnation and of the Bible. Philip Melanchthon explicitly rejected the possibility of a plurality of inhabited worlds on these grounds. T.J. O'Meara, "Christian Theology and Extraterrestrial Life," *Theological Studies*, 60 (1999), 3–30; 6.
11. M.J. Crowe, *The Extraterrestrial Life Debate, 1750–1900* (Cambridge: Cambridge University Press, 1986).
12. T. Paine, *The Age of Reason*, in E. Foner, ed., *Thomas Paine: Collected Writings* (New York: Library of America, 1995), 704.
13. Ibid., *The Age of Reason*, 708.
14. Ibid., 710.
15. Ibid., 705.
16. Ibid., 709.
17. Ibid., 710.
18. R. Puccetti, *Persons: A Study of Possible Moral Agents in the Universe* (New York: Herder and Herder, 1969).
19. P.F. Strawson, *Individuals* (New York: Doubleday, 1963).
20. Puccetti, *Persons*, 139.
21. For a detailed critique, see E. McMullin, "Persons in the Universe," *Zygon*, 15 (1980), 69–89.
22. P. Ricoeur, *The Symbolism of Evil* (New York: Harper, 1967), 232–278; S.J. Duffy, "Our Hearts of Darkness: Original Sin Revisited," *Theological Studies*, 49 (1988), 597–622.
23. A few examples: G. Daly, "Theological Models in the Doctrine of Original Sin," *Heythrop Journal*, 13 (1972), 121–152; C. Duquoc, "New Approaches to Original Sin," *Cross Currents*, 28 (1978), 189–200. E.L. Mascall remarks: "The fact of original sin is undeniable, but its adequate formulation is the despair of theologians," *Christian Theology and Natural Science* (London: Longmans, 1956), 43.
24. Once again, there is a large literature in this area. See the bibliography appended in W.S. Brown, N. Murphy, and H.N. Malony, eds., *Whatever Happened to the Soul: Scientific and Theological Portraits of Human Nature* (Minneapolis: Fortress, 1998).
25. N. Murphy, "Non-reductive Physicalism," in *Whatever Happened to the Soul*, 127–148; E. McMullin, "Biology and the Theology of Human Nature," in P. Sloan, ed., *Controlling Our Destinies: Historical, Philosophical, and Ethical Perspectives on the Human Genome Project* (Notre Dame, Ind.: University of

Notre Dame Press, 2000), 367–393; Arthur Peacocke, *Science and the Christian Experiment* (London: Oxford University Press, 1971), 148–154.
26. M. Luther, *Sermons of Martin Luther*, ed. and transl. John N. Lenker (Grand Rapids, Mich.: Baker, 1988), 8, 376–377; quoted in James T. Burtchaell, *Philemon's Problem* (Grand Rapids, Mich.: Eerdmans, 1998), 75–76.
27. J.T. Burtchaell, "His Father's Son, Firstborn of Many Children," *op. cit.*, 59–84.
28. The view defended by J.J. Davis in "Search for Extraterrestrial Intelligence and the Christian Doctrine of Redemption," *Science and Christian Belief*, 9 (1997), 21–34.
29. E.L. Mascall, *Christian Theology and Natural Science*, 36–45.

George V. Coyne, S.J.

George V. Coyne, S.J. is the director of the Vatican Observatory. Long before NASA introduced its Ranger and Apollo programs, he studied the lunar surface, and his broadly-based research interests also include the birth of stars. He invented a special technique, known as polarimetry, as a powerful tool for astronomical investigation. He is currently studying cataclysmic variable stars. An abiding and parallel fascination with the interrelationship of science and religion led him to found a series of studies concerning controversies about Galileo and to organize several conferences around the theme "Scientific Perspectives on Divine Action." A graduate of Fordham University, where he majored in mathematics and earned his licentiate in philosophy, he received his Ph.D. in astronomy from Georgetown University in 1962 and a licentiate in theology from Woodstock College in 1966. Dr. Coyne joined the Vatican Observatory as an astronomer in 1969 and the next year began teaching in the Lunar and Planetary Laboratory of the University of Arizona at which he held several directorships. Dr. Coyne holds honorary degrees from St. Peter's University and Loyola University (Chicago) in the United States, the University of Padua, and the Pontifical Theological Academy of Jagellonian University in Cracow. He has published more than 100 scientific papers and edited a number of books.

The Evolution of Intelligent Life on the Earth and Possibly Elsewhere: Reflections from a Religious Tradition

George V. Coyne, S.J.

History records many instances in which scientific thought has influenced religious thought and vice versa. Newton required God so that his infinite, static universe would not collapse. He also would not accept that there was an active principle in the attractive force of gravity, because that would detract from God's omnipotence. Leibniz, on the other hand, made his monads active because it would be unbecoming of God to have to step in and keep things going in the universe.[1]

In fact, it has been proposed[2] that religious thought in the sixteenth and seventeenth centuries, at the very time when modern science was being born, was deceived by trying to establish its own rational foundations with the same rigor that characterized the sciences. Has our current scientific world view been so influenced by religious thought that, as Lee Smolin in this volume has suggested, there may be hidden influences from which we must be liberated to advance beyond Newton and Einstein to the unification of relativity and cosmology with quantum theory? I doubt that such is the case, but since the influences are suspected to be hidden, there is little we can do about it until they are uncovered.

There is, however, one overriding detrimental influence that science has had on religious thought and that in turn infects scientific thinking, namely, the assumption that God is Explanation, that God is needed to explain what we cannot otherwise explain. In recent times there has been a growing body of literature in which the religious implications of cosmology have been discussed. This has even led to the coining of a phrase, "to know the mind of God," as the ultimate attainment of scientific cosmology.[3] Scientific discussions of the evolution of intelligent life are particularly prone to exerting this influence

177

on religious thought. The evolution of intelligent life at least once here on Earth and possibly elsewhere, considered within the context of expanding universe cosmologies, is today one of the most poignant topics on which scientific and religious thought interpenetrate. The extraterrestrial intelligence debate is a salient example of the temptation to religious thought offered by the rigorous rationality of the scientific method and of the failure, in turn, of science to realize that the God of religious faith is not in the first place an explanation of as yet unanswered human queries.

INTELLIGENT LIFE: THE SCIENTIFIC ISSUES

Let us gather together, as a source for later reflection, those scientific ideas about the evolution of intelligent life that are most subject to religious implications.[4] Scientists are still groping for a clear understanding of how life began. Richard Dawkins, for instance, proposes the need for a chance event that initiated the cumulative selection process that led to intelligence.[5] Christian de Duve[6] in this volume argues that life is essentially chemistry and that, given enough opportunity for chemistry to work, it will inevitably lead to something like the human brain. Since astrophysics has found that the primordial chemistry required is abundant in the universe,[7] so must intelligent life be abundant. While the human brain is the most complex organism we know, all of life is one since it is based in ever-more complex systems on the same genetic code.

Astrophysicists have noted that the universe is fine tuned toward life.[8] John Leslie discusses this explicitly in this volume. Life is thought to have emerged about three billion years ago in its first microscopic forms. This was about twelve billion years after the Big Bang and about seven billion years after the formation of the first stars. Why did it take so long for life to emerge? To provide the chemical abundances required for life it is estimated that three generations of stars were required. It is only through nucleosynthesis in stellar interiors that the heavier elements can be created and at the death of a star this material is regurgitated to form the matrix for a new generation of stars. The lifetime of a star depends on its total mass and can vary from several millions of years for a very massive star to tens of billions of years for lower mass stars. It took about ten billion years of stellar evolution to produce carbon, nitrogen, oxygen, and the like. The universe had to evolve to be big and old before it could contain us. Considering the

fine tuning of the constants of nature and of physical laws that was required for life to emerge, we might ask how did it emerge at all. Life
would have been impossible should any one of several physical quantities have had a different value.

It is important to note that, as best we know, the value of each of
the constants of nature is empirically determined. They are, in a manner of speaking, determined in the laboratory. There is no overriding
physical theory that requires that they have precisely the value they
have. And if any one of them had been slightly different, life could not
have come to be. A tentative explanation of this fine-tuning toward life
is reviewed by Martin Rees in this volume with his discussion of a
"multiverse," an ensemble of many universes. An explanation is given
of the fine tuning in our universe as an accident that happened (even
had to happen statistically speaking) in one of the many universes of
the multiverse.

As to the presence of inhabitable planets elsewhere in the universe,
our scientific knowledge is very limited.[9] Planets, and even planetary
systems, have been discovered in recent years about nearby stars, but,
due to detection limits, no planet like the Earth about a star like the
Sun has been detected. Protoplanetary disks, in which there is indirect
evidence that planets are forming, have been observed with the Hubble
Space Telescope.

Our knowledge of star formation and of the subsequent formation
of planets is rather well established.[10] A large interstellar cloud, typically containing 10^3 masses of the sun, fragments due to an interplay
of kinetic, gravitational, and magnetic energy. Each fragment that is
sufficiently compact and stable begins to collapse by self-gravity and,
like any normal gas, as it collapses it heats up. If it is sufficiently massive (more than about 0.1 the mass of the Sun), it will raise the temperature in its interior sufficiently high, so that thermonuclear burning
begins. At this point a star is born. For a star with a mass equal to that
of the Sun this process takes about 10^7 years. For more massive stars it
is shorter, for less massive stars longer. The Sun will keeping shining as
it does today for about 10^{10} years, and then it will explode and become
a white dwarf. Note, therefore, that a star like the Sun is born relatively
(relating "gestation" to "lifetime") fast, about ten times faster than the
birth of a human being!

About the new born solarlike star we also have a rotating disk of
hydrogen gas and dust. Planets form within this disk. As the disk continues to rotate, the material in it begins to separate out into rings ac-

cording to the mass distribution. Within each ring conglomerates begin to form due to elastic collisions, gravity, and electrostatic binding. Eventually larger conglomerates, called planetesimals, of the order of 100 kilometers in extent are formed and then from these the planets are formed. Thus, for a star like the Sun we have after about 10^9 years a stable star with a planetary system about it.

Since there are about 10^{11} stars in the Galaxy and 10^{11} galaxies in the universe, there are 10^{22} stars in the universe. From our knowledge of the distribution of stars by mass in the galaxy, we can estimate that about 30% of stars are solarlike. We know that about 30% of stars are double or multiple, a fact that may, for dynamical reasons, exclude the formation of planets. It would be difficult to estimate the percentage of solarlike stars that would have developed a planetary system, but from our knowledge of the formation of the solar system we know that the probability is neither 0 nor 100 percent. Let us say it is 10 percent. How many of these planets would be like the Earth: its mass, distance from the Sun, an atmosphere, and so forth? This may be even more uncertain, but again from geological knowledge of the formation of the atmosphere, we know that there is a finite probability. Let us say it is 2 percent. Now, if we put all these considerations together, we have, from these statistical considerations, 10^{17} Earthlike planets in the universe.

It is important to note the nature of this conclusion. It is based on scientific facts combined with reasonable estimates that are themselves based on scientific facts. Unless our scientific thinking is drastically wrong, this conclusion is acceptable and merits our further considerations about what it implies: at a minimum the macroscopic physical conditions for life (an Earthlike planet in a "habitable zone" about a solarlike star) exist elsewhere in the universe.

FIRST REFLECTIONS

If we consider both how little we know of the origins of life and how much we know of the fine tuning of the physical universe and the intricate interplay in the world of chemistry of deterministic and chance processes in a universe prolific with the opportunities for ever-more complex chemistry, then life is truly a scientific marvel. It is awesome. If life has occurred only once in the universe, it is still marvelous. In fact, the verification of a second independent genesis of intelligent life elsewhere would add little to this marvel. It would, however, surely provide suasive evidence that, in whatever way it originated, it is most likely not a rare and unusual event in our universe.

An alternative to invoking a multiverse to explain the anthropic principle of course, would be to invoke God who fine tuned the universe with an intention that there be life. In addition to the fact that from the scientific point of view this a purely arbitrary answer, from a religious point of view it provides an arbitrary God. God would be somewhat like a master cook whose pinches of salt, sugar, paprika, and other ingredients are just right to produce the pudding—intelligent beings. It appears that this inevitable inclination to a certain arbitrariness in the religious concept of God-Creator could be removed only if the appropriate cosmological model had built into it all that was necessary to explain scientifically the actual combination of physical laws and constants of nature that we observe. God would, in such a model, not be needed to select the ingredients. Quantum gravity models that exclude initial boundary conditions are an attempt in this direction, but they have not succeeded in explaining the fine tuning. The religious thinker might, of course, be tempted to see such models as a threat to the very existence of God, or at least as the establishment of a solipsistic God, completely divorced from the universe. This would only be the case if one seeks to find God exclusively, or even primarily, through science or seeks to understand the universe through religious thought alone. I will discuss this confusion of science and religion shortly.

Multiverse theories appear to be more compatible with the religious concept of God. God would have seen his image and likeness emerge in one or many of the ensemble of universes, and he would have marveled, loved, and taken special care of it as he told us he did in his self-revelation in Scripture and tradition. Let us explore this self-revelation.

A RELIGIOUS TRADITION: GOD IS LOVE

The fundamental problem with all attempts to use the rational processes of science to either assert or deny the existence of God or to limit his action is that they primarily view God as Explanation. We know from Scripture and from tradition that God revealed himself as one who pours out himself in love and not as one who explains things. God is primarily *love*. Let us review the history of the tradition that leads to this assertion.

At the very beginning of human reflection on the universe, a primitive view that saw the universe as full of personal forces, the gods, and superpowers of nature dominated. We should, however, be careful not to attribute an exclusively negative character to the attribute, "primitive". Such primitive notions are typically very pregnant with meaning and, when purified of what is patently false, frequently serve into the future to achieve an integrated and unified view of our place in the universe.

With the civilizations that flourished around the Ionian Sea for more than a half century, there was a growing consensus that, rather than innumerable personal forces acting somewhat capriciously in the universe, the universe had an intrinsic rational structure and that all parts of it were interrelated to form a complex totality to whose rational structure human intelligence was attuned. But how precisely did this tuning come about?

Copernicus and those who followed within the century after him made a significant contribution to answering this very important question, a question that has a great deal to do with how we view ourselves as part of this complex universe. Relying on the intellectual traditions of Archimedes and Aristotle, Copernicus claimed that, through careful observations and mathematical analysis, we could come to understand how the universe really worked, how its parts were really related to the whole. It was not enough to have mere hypothetical constructs as an expedient to understand the appearances. Furthermore, no single view of how the universe really works could dominate forever by the sheer force of having prevailed for a very long time. If Copernicus was correct, Aristotle's physics was wrong, even though it had reigned for two thousand years.

At the crucial moment when mathematics and physics were maturing to become the essential ingredients of the sciences, we note an increasing tension, concretized in the persons of Descartes and Newton but already noted many times before, between what we might in simple terms describe as the downward and upward movements in our knowledge of the universe and ourselves in it. Do we come to a true understanding by starting, like Plato and Descartes, with clear and certain ideas, an eternal, preexisting, immutable, rational structure of all that exists? And do we then seek to find the revelation of this world of ideas in the adulterated concreteness of the visible universe to which we are consigned to wander in search of who we are in this seemingly complex and complicated agglomeration of concrete particular beings? Or is there a rational structure imbedded in the universe that we see and touch and breath? Were the apple on Newton's head and his knowledge of Galileo's observations of Jupiter's satellites necessary for him to have come to the discovery of the universal law of gravity? There appears to be no definitive answer to this question and, perhaps, the very posing of the question is somewhat inaccurate and tendentious. And yet we sense a kind of unavoidable impulse to ask it, because we feel within ourselves this same tension between ideas and lived experiences. We seek to unify and bring meaning to all that we experience in the universe. And this tension seems to be present in all our experiences, especially in those that we call religious.

In parallel with these diverse ways of thinking, religious experiences were becoming more structured and institutionalized, evolving into what are today the world's major religions. These identifiable religious institutions, such as Islam, Buddhism, Judaism, and Christianity, differ among themselves as to the relative emphasis they place on the two sides of the tension described above, between the "downward" and the "upward." All the world's major religions are revealed, i.e., they lay claim to have received from elsewhere the content of their beliefs. The Judeo-Christian religious tradition emphasizes from its very beginnings the workings of God in human history. God speaks in human beings chosen by him, the patriarchs and the prophets, and he also speaks in a burning bush, in water from a rock, and eventually in his own Son, who, having abided eternally with the Father, at a certain moment in human history becomes man. This is the assertion of religious faith.

A study of the Old Testament shows that the first reflection of the Jewish people was that the universe was the source of their praise of the Lord who had freed them from bondage and had chosen them as his people.[11] The Book of Psalms, written for the most part well before the Book of Genesis, bears witness to this: "The mountains and valleys skip with joy to praise the Lord"; "The heavens reveal the glory of the Lord and the firmament proclaims his handiwork." But if these creatures of the universe were to praise the Lord, they must be good and beautiful. On reflecting on their goodness and beauty, God's chosen people came to realize that these creatures must come from God. And so the stories in Genesis in which at the end of each day God declares that what he had created is good (beautiful). The stories of Genesis are, therefore, more about God than they are about the universe and its beginning.

They are not, in the first place, speaking of the origins of the created world. They are speaking of the beauty of the created world and the source of that beauty, God. The universe sings God's praises because it is beautiful; it is beautiful because God made it. In these simple affirmations some have traced the roots of modern science in the West.[12] The beauty of the universe invites us to know more about it, and this search for knowledge discovers a rationality innate in the universe.

There are two implicit assertions in the Book of Genesis that set the faith of these people apart from their predecessors, the Canaanites, on whose stories they rely. First, God is one and there is no other god; there is no struggle between God and some equal, even malevolent force. Second, everything else is not God but depends for its beauty on him. He made everything and declared it beautiful. It is very important to note that created things are first of all beautiful because God says they are; it is only on reflection in a second moment that they are seen as understandable, as having a rational structure.

Early Christian reflection on these lived, historical events, especially those recorded in St. John's Gospel, sees in them the insertion of God's plan, thought, word (St. John uses the word "logos," inherited from the Greeks) into our universe.[13] "The Word of God became flesh." This revelation, which the Judeo-Christian tradition believes is spoken by God through his chosen spokespersons, has enormous consequences for assuaging the tension between the downward and upward we have described in our scientific knowledge of the universe. There are surely similarities in the tension present in both the religious and scientific experiences. The Judeo-Christian experience affirms emphatically the enfleshment of the divine and, since God is the source of the meaning of all things, that meaning too becomes incarnate.

As noted, some see in this religious belief the foundations of modern science. A rigorous attempt to observe the universe in a systematic way and to analyze those observations by rational processes, principally using mathematics, will be rewarded with understanding because the rational structure is there in the universe to be discovered by human ingenuity. Since God has come among us in his Son, we can discover the meaning of the universe, at least it is worth the struggle to do so, by living intelligently in the universe. Religious experience thus provides the inspiration for scientific investigation.

What are we to make of these assertions? Have we succumbed to a too facile assimilation of religious and scientific experiences? Or, on the other hand, is there truly at the origins of modern science the religious inspiration that God and his plan for the universe are incarnate? At a minimum, these two experiences are not incompatible; and the history of religions and of the origins of modern science certainly appear to support the connection we have presented.

This, however, makes ever-more poignant the temptation that we have already addressed; namely, that religious belief be led astray to seek the same rational certitudes that we strive to obtain in the natural sciences. While religious belief may have played a key role in the inspiration of modern science, we now know that religious experience cannot be limited to that which science can discover. To use the concepts coined by Galileo, both the Book of Nature and the Book of Sacred Scripture can be sources of coming to know God's love incarnate in the universe. We might extend the Book of Scripture to include all that is contained in the lived experience of the believing community. But knowing God's love through rational means is not sufficient; his love must be experienced. Such experience of God exceeds the content of the Book of Nature, just as any author is much more than what he or she can put into a book. Such experience also exceeds the Book of Scripture, taken even in the broader sense, if we approach the Book of Scripture only as an exercise in reason. We know that there are many ways whereby we come to know the universe and ourselves as part of it. To seize on one experience to the exclusion of others or to confuse them by failing to realize their diversity is a betrayal of all experience. While religious experience in the Judeo-Christian tradition may have inspired the birth of the rational process peculiar to the natural sciences, it is mistaken to assume that rational processes exhaust the primordial experience of God, the source of both the Book of Nature and the Book of Scripture.

This brings us back to questions about intelligent life in the universe. Whether life is unique to the Earth in all the universe is insignificant to the following questions. Had we been given the initial physical parameters in an expanding universe at some time near the Big Bang (a few Planck times) could we have predicted that life would come to be? I assume that the honest quest for a unified theory means that we could have predicted the emergence and the exact nature and strength of the four fundamental forces and such fundamental physics as that. But is life the result of so many bifurcations in nonlinear thermodynamics that we could not have predicted, even if we possessed the theory of everything and knew all the laws of microscopic and macroscopic physics, that it would come to be? I am asking questions somewhat different than those raised by the anthropic principle, whether taken in the weak or strong sense. The questions there have to do with interpreting and/or explaining the fine tuning of all the physical constants and conditions required for the emergence of life. I am asking whether, given antecedently all the physical constants and conditions necessary for life from our *a posteriori* knowledge of it, could we have predicted that it would have come to be? Did life happen to be or, given the conditions for it, did it have to be?

As we noted, it is not unusual for cosmologists to speak of the "mind of God." In most cases, this is taken to mean that ideal Platonic mathematical structure from which the shadow world we live in came to be. Should we be able to fathom the mind of God, develop, that is, a unified theory and thus an understanding of all physical laws and the initial conditions under which they work, would we also fundamentally understand life? As I understand it, there is no intentionality associated with the mind of God of the new physics. Can life be understood without that intentionality?

In our age, perhaps more than at any other time, the scientific view of the world has been the principal spur to a more unified view of the world. It has opened our minds to the vast richness of the universe that cannot be appropriated by any one discipline alone. Science invites us to that vision. It also cautions us not to absolutize scientific results. We must beware of a serious temptation of the cosmologists. Within their culture, God is essentially, if not exclusively, seen as an explanation and not as a person. God is the ideal mathematical structure, the theory of everything. God is Mind. It must remain a firm tenet of the reflecting religious person that God is more than that and that God's revelation of himself in time is more than a communication of information. Even if we discover the Mind of God, we will not have necessarily found God. The very nature of our emergence in an evolving universe and our inability to comprehend it, even with all that we know from cosmology, may be an indication that in the universe God may be communicating much more than information to us. Through the limitations of science we might come to see the universe as a unique revelation of God, that He is Love.

On the other hand, the principal difficulty with revealed religions is not so much that they go beyond what human reason alone can attain, but that they are by necessity anthropocentric. God's revelation is to us; it could not be otherwise. The possibility of extraterrestrial intelligence strains these anthropocentric revelations of God to his people. The history of theology has shown, however, that anthropocentricism does not necessarily imply exclusivity. The anthropocentric revelation of Christianity is resilient. An example of such resilience is given by Ernan McMullin's discussion in this book of Augustine's notion of *rationes seminales* to explain the origin of the vast array of material beings.

From the scientific evidence, presented in summary above, the existence of extraterrestrial intelligence must be taken as a serious possibility with all its consequences. Let us look at some of those consequences for Christian theology. At the very beginning human beings did something bad. They revolted against the God who had made them. Theologians call this original sin. Even if we do not accept the Scripture story of Adam and Eve as historically true, original sin is an essential element in the theologians' view of the relationship of humans to God. Did our extraterrestrials sin in this way?

God freely chose to redeem human beings from their sin. Did he do this also for extraterrestrials? Now we are getting ever more hypothetical, since we are determining what God, who is absolutely free, would freely choose to do. In fact, there are serious theological implications here for our understanding of God. If God is good and passionate, the answer is "yes, God did save them." How could he be God and leave extraterrestrials in their sin? After all he was good to us. Why should he not be good to them? God chose a very specific way to redeem human beings. He sent his only Son, Jesus, to them and Jesus gave up his life so that human beings would be saved from their sin. Did God do this for extraterrestrials? Or did he choose another way to redeem extraterrestrials? The theological implications about God are getting ever more serious. Surely God is completely free to choose his methods. He certainly did not have to send his Son to us. But once he chose to do so, did he have to choose to redeem extraterrestrials in the same way? There is deeply embedded in Christian theology, throughout the Old and New Testament but especially in St. Paul and in St. John the Evangelist, the notion of the universality of God's redemption and even the notion that all creation, even the inanimate, participates in some way in his redemption.

After this whole sequence of hypotheses, increasingly more difficult to make, theologians must accept a serious responsibility to rethink some fundamental realities within the context of religious belief. What is the human being? Could Jesus Christ, fully a human being, exist on more than one planet at more than one time? We are obviously very limited today in our ability to answer such questions. We cannot rely, even theologically, solely on God's revelation to us in the Scriptures and in the churches, since that revelation was *to us* and was received, therefore, in a very anthropocentric sense. But God has also spoken in the Book of Nature. While we may not need him, in fact should not need him, as a source of rational explanation, we can learn much about the manner in which he loves and, indeed, much about ourselves, from the best of science, both the life sciences and the physical sciences.

NOTES

1. I have discussed these cases in "The Concept of Matter and Materialism in the Origin and Evolution of Life," in J. Chela-Flores and F. Raulin, eds., *Exobiology: Matter, Energy, and Information in the Origin and Evolution of Life in the Universe* (Dordrecht: Kluwer Academic Publishers, 1998), 71–80.
2. M.J. Buckley, *At the Origins of Modern Atheism* (New Haven: Yale University Press, 1988).
3. See, for instance, P. Davies, *The Mind of God* (New York: Simon and Schuster, 1992) and the closing sentences of S. Hawking, *A Brief History of Time* (New York: Bantam, 1988).
4. For an excellent recent review of the history of evolution see F.J. Ayala, "The Evolution of Life," in *Evolutionary and Molecular Biology* (Vatican City: Vatican Observatory Publications, 1998, distributed by University of Notre Dame Press, Notre Dame, Ind.), 21–57.
5. R. Dawkins, *The Blind Watchmaker* (London: Penquin Books, 1986), 140–141.
6. C. de Duve, *Vital Dust: Life as a Cosmic Imperative* (New York: Basic Books, 1995).
7. C.B. Cosmovici, S. Bowyer, and D. Werthimer, eds., *Astronomical and Biochemical Origins and the Search for Life in the Universe* (Bologna: Editrice Compositori, 1997), 5–89.
8. J.D. Barrow and F.J. Tipler, *The Anthropic Cosmological Principle* (Oxford: Oxford University Press, 1986).
9. C.B. Cosmovici et al., *Astronomical and Biochemical Origins,* 267–381.
10. F. Shu, *The Physical Universe: An Introduction to Astronomy* (Mill Valley, Calif.: University Science Books, 1982), 144–157 and 413–497.
11. J.L. McKenzie, *Dictionary of the Bible* (Milwaukee: Bruce Publishing Company, 1965), 157–160.
12. O. Pedersen, *The Book of Nature* (Vatican City: Vatican Observatory Publications, 1992), 25–32.
13. R.E. Brown, *An Introduction to the New Testament* (New York: Doubleday, 1997), 333–382.

STEVEN J. DICK

The historian of science at the United States Naval Observatory (USNO), **Steven J. Dick** is the author of three books on the debate over extraterrestrial life: *Plurality of Worlds* (1982) *The Biological Universe* (1996), and *Life on Other Worlds* (1998), all published by Cambridge University Press. He studied astrophysics at Indiana University and took a Ph.D. in the history and philosophy of science there in 1977. In 1979, he joined the scientific staff of the Naval Observatory as an astronomer, a position he held until being named historian of science in 1989. For three years in the mid-1980s, Dr. Dick was an astronomer at the USNO Southern Hemisphere Station in South Island, New Zealand. In the early 1990s, he acted as historian of NASA's High Resolution Microwave Survey-Search for Extraterrestrial Intelligence program. Currently president of International Astronomical Union's Commission 41 (History of Astronomy), Dr. Dick is the author of some seventy scientific and historical articles and a member of the editorials boards of the *Journal for the History of Astronomy*, the *Journal of Scientific Exploration*, and the new *Journal for Astronomical History and Heritage*.

Cosmotheology: Theological Implications of the New Universe

Steven J. Dick

It is important that we define what we mean by "the new universe" before we try to study its theological implications. The essential elements of the new universe may be emphasized by comparing the view of A.R. Wallace at the turn of the century with the Space Telescope's Hubble Deep Field at its end. The universe of Wallace, co-founder with Darwin of the theory of natural selection, was only 3,600 light years in diameter (Figure 1). It was static, gave humanity a central position, and harbored no extraterrestrials. The Hubble Deep Field (Figure 2), by contrast, reveals a universe some 12 billion light years in extent, whose central theme is cosmic evolution, full of billions of evolving galaxies floating in an Einsteinian space-time with no center. Cosmic evolution, it is conjectured, has produced not only planets, stars, and galaxies, but also life, mind, and intelligence.

THE BIOLOGICAL UNIVERSE

While the abundance of extraterrestrial life is by no means proven, it is the view accepted by many working on the origins of life, has seemed likely to most astronomers for thirty years, and is the working hypothesis of those in the growing hybrid fields of bioastronomy and astrobiology. More than that, it is the view widely accepted by the public, as conveyed over the past forty years by the astronomers Harlow Shapley, Carl Sagan, Frank Drake, Eric Chaisson, and Armand Delsemme, among many others. This new world view of a universe full of life, produced by cosmic evolution, I call "the biological universe." The central assumptions of the biological universe are that planetary systems are common, that life originates wherever conditions are favorable, and that evolution culminates with intelligence. Alien morphology and

191

FIGURE 1
DIAGRAM OF STELLAR UNIVERSE (PLAN)

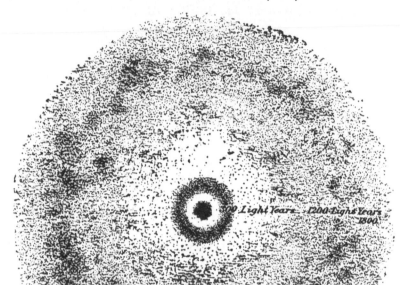

The universe of A. R. Wallace at the beginning of the twentieth century was only 3,600 light years in diameter, and the Sun was located very near the center. From Wallace, Man's Place in the Universe *(New York: 1903).*

intelligence may not be similar to that on Earth, but at least some who subscribe to the biological universe believe that compatible technologies (most commonly, radio astronomy) will allow us to communicate. Decipherment of an extraterrestrial message could take a slow or fast track, with diverging consequences depending on the nature of the message.[1]

Beyond the biological universe, the anthropic principle and other considerations lead us to believe that our universe may be only one of many. These, presumably, undergo their own forms of cosmic evolution, within a "multiverse" too vast to conceive.[2]

FIGURE 2

Hubble Deep Field
Hubble Space Telescope · WFPC2

The Hubble Deep Field represents the new universe, some 12 billion light years in extent, with billions of galaxies that may harbor life and intelligence. This Hubble Space Telescope image, taken over ten days in December 1995, is the deepest-ever view of the universe and covers an area of the sky only 1/30th the diameter of the full Moon. It is only the latest in a series of studies since the early twentieth century that show the noncentrality of our galaxy.

The transformation from the simple diagram of Wallace to the striking image presented by the Hubble Deep Field is a drastic change over one century, a new world view that theologies ignore at their peril and must eventually accommodate if they are to remain in touch with the real world. Although this accommodation took place over centuries for the Copernican world view, and is still in process for the Darwinian world view, a systematic study of the theological implications of the new universe is not only a task whose time has come, but one that is long overdue. Indeed, the decade of the 1990s has seen an upturn of interest in the general implications of the new universe, especially in connection with the existence of extraterrestrial life. In 1991–1992 NASA convened a series of workshops on the Cultural Aspects of SETI (Search for Extraterrestrial Intelligence), as it was about to launch its SETI program. Theology was only a small part of that discussion, but the Proceedings show the richness of the questions that remain to be asked. Such meetings have had little public impact, but in the wake of claims of fossil life in Martian meteorite ALH84001, media speculations about the implications of life reached a wide and receptive audience. The interest also extends to the highest levels of government; in 1996 Vice President Al Gore convened a meeting that included several theologians to discuss the implications of possible life on Mars and beyond. The current NASA Astrobiology Roadmap recognizes as one of its four Principles "a broad societal interest in our subject, especially in areas such as the search for extraterrestrial life and the potential to engineer new life forms adapted to live on other worlds."[3]

The awareness that these questions need to be addressed, and the rudimentary discussion thus far, ought to inspire increased thought, word, and action at many levels in the near future. In this essay I emphasize the importance of history in informing this discussion and providing a foundation for it. I then indicate what elements might constitute a "cosmotheology," the need to rethink our conception of God in light of the new universe, and the implications for human destiny.

HISTORICAL APPROACHES TO STUDYING THEOLOGICAL IMPLICATIONS

Among the possible approaches to studying theological implications of the new universe, I confine myself here to historical approaches. From the point of view of the history of science, at least three areas may contribute to the study of the theological implications of the new universe.

First, the history of science allows us to place the new universe in the context of past scientific world views and to make cautious use of the trajectories of these scientific world views as analogs or guides for our thinking about the potential impacts of the biological universe. Other historical analogs also may be illuminating. Second, ideas discussed during the development of the concept of cosmic evolution, including the implications of extraterrestrial life, form a background for further discussion that should be neither forgotten nor dismissed. Third, the imaginations of the best science fiction writers provide ample food for thought in the theological realm.

The latter two approaches bear on the content of a possible cosmotheology, while the first addresses its diffusion. In addition to these approaches, a knowledge of history also contributes in broader ways, notably by careful attention to the history and evolution of religions and their accompanying theologies.

The Trajectories of World Views and Other Analogs

As I suggest in *The Biological Universe*, the idea of a universe full of life is more than just another theory or hypothesis; it is rather a kind of world view, which we may call the biophysical cosmology or simply the biological universe. The Gallup polls tell us that the majority of well-educated Americans today subscribe to the biological universe, and a large number even believe the aliens have arrived. At one extreme, in 1996, thirty-nine people in the Heaven's Gate cult went so far as to willingly give up their lives to the supposed aliens; millions more believe in alien abductions, and still more hold an extraterrestrial interpretation for UFOs. Nor is interest in these ideas by any means confined to the United States. We need not agree that aliens have arrived on Earth to believe that cosmic evolution may end in intelligence throughout the universe, that this may be seen as a world view analogous to Copernicanism and Darwinism, and that we would naturally expect the biological universe to have implications for many fields, just as Copernicanism and Darwinism have.

This, then, is my first conclusion: studying the rich literature in history of science of the implications of the Copernican, Darwinian, and other world views may help guide us in discussing the implications of the biological universe. Studies have shown, for example, how Darwin's theory had distinctive impacts over the short term and the long term, and among scientists, theologians, and other segments of the population.[4] The exploration of implications, including theological implications, is a stage in the development of any major world view and is also for the biological universe (Table 1). At the same time it is important to emphasize that in no way can these analogs predict an outcome, which will depend in any case on the circumstances of discovery.

TABLE 1
STAGES IN WORLD VIEW DEVELOPMENT

Stage	Geocentric	Heliocentric	Galactocentric	Extraterrestrial/ Biophysical
Motivation	motion of planets anthropocentrism	motion of planets Neoplatonism geocentric problems	globular cluster distribution	Copernican theory cosmic evolution
Presentation Based on Observation	Eudoxus/ Aristotle 4th century BC	Copernicus 1543	Shapley 1917	Kepler (disproven) Lowell (disproven) Viking (unlikely) radio signal? Martian meteorite?
Elaboration	Ptolemy et al.	Galileo, Kepler, Newton, et al.	Trumpler, Oort, et al.	scientists
Opposition	antirationalists	geocentrists religious	Curtis, et al.	religious philosophical scientific
Exploration of Implications Outside Field	anthropocentric religions and philosophies	philosophical literary scientific	further proof of nonanthropo-centrism	all aspects of human knowledge
General Acceptance	4th century BC	1700	1930s	widely accepted 1750
Final Confirmation	disproven	1838 (stellar parallax = Earth motion)	1950s (radio maps of galaxy)	deciphered signal? UFO identified? life on Mars/ Europa, etc.? Martian meteorite?

Every scientific world view traverses broad stages, as seen in this sample of cosmological world views. Galactocentric refers to the solar system's peripheral location with respect to the center of our Milky Way galaxy; Extraterrestrial/Biophysical is the world view that posits a universe full of life. Every major world view has broader implications, and so will the biological universe that may be the ultimate outcome of cosmic evolution. In many ways the biological universe is an extension of the Darwinian world view from the terrestrial to the cosmic realm. Adapted from Dick: "Consequences of Success in SETI," San Francisco: Astronomical Society of the Pacific, 1995 (see note 4).

Other historical analogs also are possible. If the contact is remote intellectual contact rather than physical contact, one might invoke the transmission of Greek knowledge to the Latin West via the Arabs in the twelfth and thirteenth centuries. What historian Arnold Toynbee called "encounters between civilizations in time" are particularly apt comparisons because they deal with the transmission of knowledge from non-contemporary civilizations across time. If the contact is physical, there are ample cases (usually negative) of culture contact on Earth. Each of these contact scenarios also carries theological implications.[5]

Of course, we might argue that no historical analogs are valid, because the information acquired will be unlike anything that has ever happened on Earth before. While this is possible, it assumes substantive message content and rapid decipherment, neither of which is assured. Historical analogs provide a starting point, grounded in human behavior and experience, for discussion of a whole range of issues.

Issues from the Extraterrestrial Life Debate

As cosmic evolution has become more widely accepted in the twentieth century, a variety of philosophical and ethical questions have been discussed.[6] The role of chance and necessity in the context of the origin of life, for example, received a classic treatment in Jacques Monod's *Chance and Necessity* (1971) and is a constant theme running through the extraterrestrial life debate. The problems of self-organization in the origin of life, directionality in evolution, and the nature and possibility of objective knowledge are intrinsic to the matrix of questions surrounding the biological universe. We need to be aware of this history as background for any further discussion of theological implications.

Furthermore, as a subset of the history of cosmic evolution, the history of the extraterrestrial life debate is a rich source of ideas on theological implications. The concept of life on other worlds has been a religious challenge, at least in the Christian world, since the fifteenth century, when it was asked in one of the numerous commentaries on Aristotle's works "Whether Christ by dying on this earth could redeem the inhabitants of another world." The standard answer was that he could, because Christ could not die in another world. Because the medieval Scholastics did not believe other worlds actually existed, however, the whole exercise for them was academic.

A more serious phase began in the late sixteenth and seventeenth centuries, under the impetus of the Copernican theory. The Roman Inquisition burned Giordano Bruno at the stake in 1600 in part because of his belief in an infinite number of worlds. Galileo's observations hardly had been committed to print when Kepler wondered, "If there are globes in the heavens similar to our earth, do we vie with them over who occupies a better portion of the universe? For if their globes are nobler, we are not the noblest of rational creatures. Then how can all things be for man's sake? How can we be the masters of God's handiwork?" (If that sounds familiar, it may be because H.G. Wells used it as the prelude to his *War of the Worlds* in 1897). Seventeenth-century writers weighed scriptural objections to the idea of life on other worlds against the benefits to natural theology in a Newtonian universe that otherwise seemed to have little need for God. In the end natural theology largely won out, so that extraterrestrials were widely accepted by the beginning of the eighteenth century, resulting in what William Derham (1715) termed "astrotheology."[7]

By the end of the eighteenth century, Thomas Paine bluntly stated in his *Age of Reason* that extraterrestrials and Christianity did not mix, and "he who thinks he believes in both has thought but little of either." Paine made no secret of the fact that he accepted other worlds. A great deal of thought subsequently went into analyzing the relationship between the two; during the numerous nineteenth century discussions of the subject some rejected Christianity, others rejected a plurality of worlds, and still others found ways to reconcile the two.[8]

In the twentieth century the discussion has, until recently, been more muted or expressed in science fiction. Nevertheless, a pattern begins to emerge in the twentieth century. In interviews with twenty-one religious authorities from a variety of religions, one researcher found that none of the authorities believed extraterrestrial intelligence created a theological or religious problem, not even the seventeen who were virtually certain extraterrestrial intelligence existed. Internal to religions, flexibility seems to be the watchword, whereas those external to religion proclaim the imminent death of religions after such a wrenching discovery as extraterrestrial intelligence. Either way, it is difficult to disagree with Arthur C. Clarke, who wrote in his 1951 volume *The Exploration of Space* that some people "are afraid that the crossing of space, and above all contact with intelligent but nonhuman races, may destroy the foundations of their religious faith. They may be right, but in any event their attitude is one which does not bear logical examination—for a faith which cannot survive collision with the truth is not worth many regrets."[9]

Role of the Imagination

Although science fiction is often dismissed by serious scholars (and much of it should be), the best of it is a source of original thought that should not be ignored. And of course the alien has been one of the perennial themes of science fiction.

Among authors who should be considered in this category are David Lindsay, whose *A Voyage to Arcturus* (1920) uses alien beings in a search for deeper reality; the British philosopher Olaf Stapledon, whose *Star Maker* (1937) universe was full of aliens seeking the meaning of life and mind in the universe; C.S. Lewis, whose *Silent Planet* trilogy placed Christianity in a cosmic context; and Arthur C. Clarke, whose *Childhood's End* (1953) also involved a religious vision. Carl Sagan's *Contact* not only depicted one possible theological reaction to the discovery of extraterrestrial intelligence, but also broached the question of theological versus scientific truth. Most recently, Mary Dorrit Russell's *The Sparrow* (1997) and its sequel *Children of God* (1998) delivered a wrenching story about a Jesuit mission of first contact.

All these science fiction stories, and many more, contain well-considered ideas in the context of the new world view of cosmic evolution. When transferred onto the medium of television or film, they reach an even broader audience with higher emotional impact, although not always with facts that should be viewed as confirming the biological universe. The popularity of *Star Wars* (1977), *Close Encounters of the Third Kind* (1977), *Alien* (1979), *E.T.: The Extraterrestrial* (1982), and *Independence Day* (1996); the more cerebral ideas of *2001: A Space Odyssey* (1968) and *Contact* (1997); and the growing numbers of Star Trekkers and *X-Files* fans around the world represent a phenomenon that is more than just entertainment. These stories of mythic proportion broaden our horizons; they force us to consider our place in the universe; they make us wonder whether the universe is full of good, as in *E.T.*, or evil, as in *Alien*. And they make us realize that terrestrial concepts of God and theology are only a subset of the possible.

COSMOTHEOLOGY

Some might argue that we should not change our theologies until we know with more certainty the ultimate outcome of cosmic evolution. That is why so much now hinges on the search for planetary systems, on experiments and observations related to the origin of life, and on studies of the evolution of life and intelligence. But the probable truth we now face is that cosmic evolution ends with the biological universe, although one can certainly argue how abundant intelligence might be. That the origin of terrestrial life occurred 3.8 billion years ago, shortly after the heavy bombardment of the Earth ceased, may be a clue that single-celled organisms originate rather easily, perhaps with the help of organic molecules from space. But the fact that for two billion years bacteria ruled the Earth until even the nucleated (eukaryotic) cell was evolved and that another billion years passed until multicellular life proliferated in the Cambrian explosion, might argue for a universe full of bacteria. On the other hand, optimists argue that in a universe more than twelve billion years old (even though some of that time was needed to generate the elements for life in several generations of stars), not only has intelligence had time to evolve, but it is likely to be immensely older and therefore more advanced than *homo sapiens*. Even if it turns out that intelligence is not abundant, it is clear that we will never return to Wallace's small universe, much less the anthropocentric universe extant when many of the world's major religions were born.

It is prudent, then, to proceed with what I call "cosmotheology." Cosmotheology, as I define it, means using our ever-growing knowledge of the universe to modify, expand, or change entirely our current theologies, whatever they may be. In short, cosmotheology takes into account what we know about the cosmos. Let us begin with some general principles of any cosmotheology, examine the possible role of God in cosmotheology, and broach the implications of extraterrestrials for human destiny. Finally, I suggest that a "roadmap for cosmotheology" would encourage more systematic study.

Principles of Cosmotheology

Cosmotheology is to be distinguished from Derham's eighteenth-century astrotheology in that the main thrust of the former is not to offer proof of God or God's attributes, but to use Nature to inform a much broader range of theological discussion. The history of the extraterrestrial life debate gives us some idea of the elements of a cosmotheology as perceived by our predecessors. Although we need not be bound by their limits, the problems of the new universe for Christianity are fairly clear, and will become clearer for other religions as their attitudes toward life on other worlds become better known. Whatever the tenets of a specific religion, we offer five general principles for cosmotheology.

1. Cosmotheology must take into account that humanity is in no way physically central in the universe; we are located on a small planet around a star on the outskirts of the Milky Way galaxy. Although we have known this now for most of the century, and although it gives urgency to the religious questions (especially the Incarnation) raised in the wake of the Copernican theory, this revelation has resulted in no change of doctrine to any of the world's anthropocentric religions.

2. Cosmotheology must take into account that humanity probably is not central biologically. We may be unique in the sense that Loren Eiseley so poetically wrote when he said:

Nowhere in all space or on a thousand worlds will there be men to share our loneliness. There may be wisdom; there may be power; somewhere across space great instruments, handled by strange, manipulative organs, may stare vainly at our floating cloud wrack, their owners yearning as we yearn. Nevertheless, in the nature of life and in the principles of evolution we have had our answer. Of men elsewhere, and beyond, there will be none forever.[10]

But uniqueness of form does not make us central to the story of the universe. Nor, one would think, should it make us the special object of attention of any deity.

3. Cosmotheology must take into account that humanity is most likely somewhere near the bottom, or at best midway, in the great chain of intelligent beings in the universe. This follows from the age of the universe and the youth of our species. The universe is in excess of ten billion years old. The genus *homo* evolved only two million years ago, and archaic *homo sapiens* only 500,000 years ago. *Homo sapiens sapiens* is considerably younger than that, and terrestrial civilization and history cover only a few millennia. Even taking into account that the universe needed billions of years to generate the ingredients for life, if nature does select for intelligence, it has probably been doing so at numerous sites long before we arrived on the scene. Surely this has relevance to the question of our relation to any universal deity.

4. Cosmotheology must be open to radically new conceptions of God, not necessarily the God of the ancients, nor the God of human imagination, but a God grounded in cosmic evolution, the biological universe, and the three principles stated above.

5. Cosmotheology must have a moral dimension, extended to include all species in the universe—a reverence and respect for life that we find difficult enough to foster on Earth. While the challenge of this

principle should not be underestimated, it will perhaps also make us realize that *homo sapiens* is one, after all, despite superficial differences.

In my opinion, religions will adjust to these cosmotheological principles because the alternative is extinction. The adjustment will be most wrenching for those monotheistic religions that see man in the image of God (Judaism, Christianity, and Islam), a one-to-one relationship with a single Godhead. It will be less wrenching for Eastern religions that teach salvation through individual enlightenment (Buddhism and Hinduism) rather than through a Savior, or that are this-worldly (Confucianism) rather than otherworldly. The adjustment will not be to the physical world, as in Copernicanism, nor to the biological world, as in Darwinism, where man descended from the apes but still remained at the top of the terrestrial world. Rather the adjustment will be to the biological universe, in which intelligences are likely to be superior to us for reasons stated above.

A Natural God? The Role of God in Cosmotheology

It is entirely possible that in contemplating changes to current theological doctrines of particular religions we are too parochial in our thinking. In a chapter on "The Meaning of Life" in *The Biological Universe*, I wrote:

> In the end, the effect on theology and religion may be quite different from any impact on the narrow religious doctrines that have been discussed during the twentieth century. It may be that in learning of alien religions, of alien ways of relating to superior beings, the scope of terrestrial religion will be greatly expanded in ways that we cannot foresee.[11]

This is, in fact, very likely, and nowhere more than in our basic concept of God, which may need to undergo wholesale transformation. The basis for this new concept might be found in the discussion of extraterrestrial intelligence; indeed, in some ways SETI may be seen as a religious quest. This is not a characterization that SETI proponents favor, but SETI is, after all, a search for a superior intelligence, for knowledge (omniscience?), for wisdom, and perhaps for power (omnipotence?). The major difference is that the intelligence is not supernatural. This brings us to the concept of a "natural God" as opposed to the supernatural God of the Judeo-Christian and Islamic traditions.

The concept of a natural God—a God *in* the universe rather than outside it—seems so unnatural to human minds (especially in the

Western world) because we have been conditioned to believe otherwise; indeed, it is heretical to most established monotheistic religions. This idea of a supernatural God is, of course, a historical artifact, a product of the evolution of human thought. It was the great innovation of the Judaic tradition, which began about four thousand years ago, to conceive over the course of centuries a single, omnipotent, and supernatural Yahweh. That concept was developed in the context of the political, economic, and social conditions of the ancient Near East. Although it has proven a resilient and flexible concept, a supernatural God is no different from other powerful ideas developed throughout history, in the sense that it is useful, persistent, and subject to change. Moreover, considering the divergence of human ideas of God, there is no basis for expecting convergence of theistic ideas by intelligences on other planets throughout the universe. Unless, that is, there is some scientific basis for it.

The subsequent spread of the idea of this supernatural God, and its reforms in the Christian and Islamic traditions, has been the subject of numerous books over the centuries.[12] It need hardly be said, however, that the historical evolution of this idea, and its widespread acceptance in Judaic, Christian, and Islamic cultures, does not necessarily make it true. Why, we may well ask, could God not be natural? Although this raises the specter of pantheism, the natural God we have in mind is not the God of Spinoza for whom God was indwelling in nature. Our natural God is compatible with the concept of Einstein, for whom God "does not play dice" nor concern himself with the fate and actions of men. But Einstein's God "appears as the physical world itself, with its infinitely marvelous structure operating at atomic level with the beauty of a craftsman's wristwatch, and at stellar level with the majesty of a massive cyclotron."[13]

Closer to what we mean by a natural God is the concept raised fifteen years ago in a popular work of the iconoclastic British astronomer Fred Hoyle. In his volume *The Intelligent Universe* Hoyle proposed that God may be a superior but worldly intelligence, and he used the concept to explain why the universe is fit for life and why life increases in complexity, in contrast to everything around it, which is in chaos or decay.[14] We need not accept that interpretation to posit the existence of a natural God with many of the same characteristics as the God of Judaism, Christianity, and Islam, with the major exception that the God of nature is, by definition, not supernatural, not transcendent in the sense of being outside the world.

A major effect of the concept of a natural God is that it has the capacity to reconcile science and religion. For those with a vested interest in the supernatural God of most standard religions, this may be too great a sacrifice for reconciliation. But consider the benefits. A *natural* God is an intelligence in and of the world, a God amenable to scientific methods, or at least approachable by them. A *supernatural* God incorporates a concept all scientists reject in connection with their science. For some, this may be precisely the point: that God cannot be, and should not be, approachable by science. But for Einstein and many other scientists (perhaps expressed in a different way for the latter) "the cosmic religious feeling is the strongest and noblest motive for scientific research."[15]

Such a radical change in the concept of God raises the question, "Is God necessary?" In other words, if we "retreat" to a natural God, why have God at all? This is analogous to the question asked in the wake of Newton's theory of gravitation: if gravitation kept the solar system working, what need was there of God? This was a difficult question to answer, but Newtonians countered by promoting natural theology—the idea that the magnificence of the universe was a reflection of the magnificence and power of the Creator. We need not adopt a similar strategy; the point is that advanced extraterrestrial intelligence could possess many of the same characteristics now attributed to the supernatural God of the Judeo-Christian and Islamic traditions. Such advanced intelligence could have fine tuned the physical constants, thus explaining the conundrum of the anthropic principle. In principle, it could even "intervene in human history," the touchstone principle of the Christian faith, not to mention of the UFO and alien abductee advocates.

But, I hasten to add, there is no accepted evidence for alien intervention on the cosmic or terrestrial level. It may be that God is necessary only from a social or psychological point of view; if that is the case, we may as well have a natural God within the realm of the real world, rather than a supernatural one with attributes so often the source of personal agony, guilt, and religious wars. Whether or not God is necessary, it may well be that another thousand years of evolution of theology will show the futility of the current division between the Heavens and the Earth—one the home of God, the other of humanity—in the same way that it took two thousand years to reject Aristotle's celestial-terrestrial dichotomy in science. The idea of the "holy," the "numinous," and the "divine," and the quest for the otherworldly, however, will likely remain as a part of human nature.

The success of a SETI program in which information is exchanged is bound to accelerate this evolution in human thought. In *The Biological Universe* I speculated that "it may be that religion in a universal sense is defined as the never-ending search of each civilization for others more superior than itself. If this is true, then SETI may be science in search of religion, and astrotheology [equivalent to cosmotheology in this passage] may be the ultimate reconciliation of science with religion." The need for a superior, but not supernatural, intelligence may remain at the heart of the religious quest, with the relationship between humanity and the superior intelligence radically altered in terms of today's theologies.

BEYOND COSMOTHEOLOGY: HUMAN DESTINY

In the end, theology addresses questions of meaning and purpose, and thus questions of our place in the universe. In asking whether we will be "at home in the universe," in the words of Stuart Kauffman, the answer must be that we do not know, because we still do not know where we fit in the great chain of being.[16] We know nothing about good and evil in the universe in the context of extraterrestrial civilizations. Thus, the meaning and purpose of the universe will not be known until we know more about whether or not there is a biological universe. The famous passage of Nobel physicist Steven Weinberg that "the more the universe seems comprehensible, the more it also seems pointless," did not take into account the possibilities inherent in the biological universe.[17] Surely meaning and purpose in the universe would be quite different if we are its only life rather than one of many sentient races. And therefore theologies would be quite different. Human destiny would be quite different also; if we are alone, it may be our destiny to fill the universe with life. If extraterrestrial intelligence is abundant, it will be our destiny to interact with that intelligence, whether for good or ill, for life seeks out life.

It is here that the fifth cosmotheological principle comes into play. The moral dimension—a reverence and respect for extraterrestrial intelligence that may be morphologically very different from terrestrial life forms—will surely challenge a species that has come to blows over superficial racial and national differences. If we are wise, humanity will realize that our species is one, a necessary realization before we have any hope of dealing with extraterrestrial beings in a morally responsible way.[18] Whether intelligence is rare or abundant, whether life is of a lower order or a higher order than *homo sapiens*, human destiny is intimately connected with cosmic evolution. Our earlier message, reinforced by Arthur C. Clarke, bears repeating: any theology that ignores the facts of cosmic evolution as understood over the last century does so at the peril of being divorced from reality.

Summary: The Way Ahead

I suggest the time is ripe for us to take cosmotheology seriously, to consider how religions and their accompanying theologies should change in light of what we now know about the universe, and what we are likely to know in the future: we are not the only intelligent creatures in the universe, most likely not the most superior, and most likely not unique in any way except in biological details. It may even be time for an entirely new theology based on a transformed concept of God.

The question is how to proceed. No one will disagree that all past discussions amount to sporadic suggestions, not systematic cosmotheologies. No Thomas Aquinas for cosmotheology has yet appeared to reconcile current doctrine with new world views. Nor is it clear that such reconciliation is our primary task. As I have suggested, perhaps we need to move beyond current theology, to step back and ask what we would do if we started over, given what we now know about the universe.

Unlike space projects with deadlines, theology is unaccustomed to roadmaps to lead the way. But in the sense of encouraging a systematic discussion, something analogous to a roadmap for cosmotheology, an outline of important questions and possible approaches to them, is perhaps not out of hand. In this paper I have given possible approaches to cosmotheology as a historian of science. But a more comprehensive roadmap must originate from many points of view. An important desideratum for any discipline is systematic discussion without, however, exclusion of well-considered ideas. It is important that we consider discussion in a broad way, according to the outlines of some roadmap, feeling free to wander the unexpected byways off the main freeways. At least we can define the parameters of the problem, point to the major areas of concern, and perhaps set an agenda for the future.

The year 2000 is the four hundredth anniversary of the death of Giordano Bruno, burned at the stake in February 1600. Bruno's burning occurred little more than a half century after the introduction of the Copernican theory, which fed his vision of the new universe. We now stand at about the same point after the first stirrings of the new world view known as cosmic evolution, the beginnings of the biological universe. Bruno's anniversary, a symbol of the need for science and theology to engage in rational discussion at all levels, is an appropriate time to take stock of the implications of the new universe for theology. Bruno will be looking over our collective shoulders, amazed himself at the new universe, but hopeful that its implications will be accepted in a more rational way than in his day, when the scientific world view was dawning on the Western world. Pope John Paul II gave impetus to this hope when, on the occasion of the four hundredth anniversary of the Gregorian reform of the calendar, he wrote:

> . . . it is necessary for [the] relationship between faith and science to be constantly strengthened and for any past historical incidents which may be justly interpreted as being harmful to that relationship, to be reviewed by all parties as an opportunity for reform and for pursuing more harmonious communication. In brief, it must be the sincere desire of all to learn from history so as to gain insight into the positive direction that we must take together in the future.[19]

The lessons of history and of science may take us further than the pope intended, but we should not shrink from the responsibility of rational thought.

For those who would argue that theology exceeds the boundaries of rational thought, I end with the closing words of Karen Armstrong's magisterial *A History of God*:

> Human beings cannot endure emptiness and desolation; they will fill the vacuum by creating a new focus of meaning. The idols of fundamentalism are not good substitutes for God; if we are to create a vibrant new faith in the twenty-first century, we should, perhaps, ponder the history of God for some lessons and warnings.[20]

Surely the modern cosmos may serve as a new focus of meaning; it already has for many, and the numbers are increasing. Surely the history of God teaches us that the concept will persist, but that it ought to be adjusted to our knowledge of the universe. Surely history demonstrates that the true meaning of God is not grounded in any single human culture, but in the best elements of otherworldly thinking of all of them. To this body of thought we must now add the scientific world view, wherein the universe, or the multiverse, is large enough to encompass God. As we learn more about our place in the universe, and as we physically move away from our home planet, our cosmic conscious-ness will only increase. With due respect for present religious traditions whose history stretches back four millennia, the natural God of cosmic evolution and the biological universe, not the supernatural God of the ancient Near East, may be the God of the next millennium. Humanity in the year 3000 will undoubtedly be transformed scientifically in ways we can only dimly perceive. Considering the fractious nature of reli-gions and their accompanying theologies today, one can only hope that *homo religiosus* also will be transformed.

NOTES

1. I treat the origins of the new world view in detail in S.J. Dick, *The Biological Universe: The Twentieth Century Extraterrestrial Life Debate and the Limits of Science* (Cambridge: Cambridge University Press, 1996), and *Life on Other Worlds* (Cambridge: Cambridge University Press, 1998). For a recent statement of extraterrestrial life in the context of origins of life, C. de Duve, *Vital Dust: Life as a Cosmic Imperative* (New York: Basic Books, 1995). On the conveyance of the new universe to the public, H. Shapley, *Of Stars and Men* (Boston: Beacon Press, 1958); C. Sagan, *Cosmos* (New York: Random House, 1980), among others; F. Drake and D. Sobel, *Is Anyone Out There: The Scientific Search for Extraterrestrial Intelligence* (New York: Delacorte Press, 1992); E. Chaisson, *Cosmic Dawn* (Boston, 1981); and A. Delsemme, *Our Cosmic Origins* (Cambridge: Cambridge University Press, 1998). S.J. Dick, "The Biophysical Cosmology: The Place of Bioastronomy in the History of Science," in C.B. Cosmovici et al., eds., *Astronomical and Biochemical Origins and the Search for Life in the Universe* (Bologna: Editrice Compositori, 1997).
2. On the multiverse and the anthropic principle J. Leslie, *Universes* (London and New York: Routledge, 1989); L. Smolin, *The Life of the Cosmos* (Oxford: Oxford University Press, 1997); and M. Rees, *Before the Beginning: Our Universe and Others* (Reading, Mass.: Addison-Wesley, 1997).
3. The results of the 1991–1992 NASA meetings are recorded in J. Billingham et al., eds., *Social Implications of the Detection of an Extraterrestrial Civilization: A Report of the Workshops on the Cultural Aspects of SETI* (Mountain View, Calif.: SETI Press, 1999; available from the SETI Institute, 2035 Landings Dr., Mountain View, CA 94043). The vice president's meeting is discussed in A. Lawler, "Origins Researchers Win Gore's Ear, Not Pocketbook," *Science*, 274 (1996), 2003. The Astrobiology Roadmap is at http://astrobiology.arc.nasa.gov/roadmap/.
4. In addition to *The Biological Universe* and its update *Life on Other Worlds*, see S.J. Dick, "Consequences of Success in SETI: Lessons from the History of Science," in G.S. Shostak, ed., *Progress in the Search for Extraterrestrial Life* (San Francisco: Astronomical Society of the Pacific, 1995), 521–532; I. Almar,

"The Consequences of a Discovery: Different Scenarios," Ibid., 499–505. On the impact of Darwinism, P.J. Bowler, *Evolution: The History of an Idea* (Berkeley: University of California Press, 1989); D. Hull, *Darwin and His Critics: The Reception of Darwin's Theory of Evolution by the Scientific Community* (Cambridge, Mass.: Harvard University Press, 1973); and, for the short-term impact, P.J. Vorzimmer, *Charles Darwin: The Years of Controversy: The Origin of Species and its Critics, 1859–82* (Philadelphia: Temple University Press, 1970).

5. Dick, "Consequences of Success in SETI," 521–532; A. Toynbee, *A Study of History*, vol. 9 (London: Oxford University Press, 1954).

6. P. Davies, *Are We Alone? Philosophical Implications of the Discovery of Extraterrestrial Life* (New York: Basic Books, 1995); Dick, *The Biological Universe* and *Life on Other Worlds*; E. Regis, ed., *Extraterrestrials: Science and Alien Intelligence* (Cambridge: Cambridge University Press, 1985); R.O. Randolph, M.S. Race, and C.P. McKay, "Reconsidering the Theological and Ethical Implications of Extraterrestrial Life," *CTNS* [Center for Theology and the Natural Sciences] *Bulletin*, 17, no. 3 (1997), 1–8.

7. S.J. Dick, *Plurality of Worlds: The Origins of the Extraterrestrial Life Debate From Democritus to Kant* (Cambridge: Cambridge University Press, 1982); William Derham, *Astro-Theology: Or a Demonstration of the Being and Attributes of God from a Survey of the Heavens* (London, 1715).

8. M.J. Crowe, *The Extraterrestrial Life Debate, 1750–1900: The Idea of a Plurality of Worlds from Kant to Lowell* (Cambridge: Cambridge University Press, 1986); M.J. Crowe, "A History of the Extraterrestrial Life Debate," *Zygon*, 32 (June 1997), 147–162.

9. M. Askenazi, "Not the Sons of Adam: Religious Response to ETI," *Space Policy*, 8 (1992), 341–350; R. Puccetti, *Persons: A Study of Possible Moral Agents in the Universe* (London: MacMillan, 1968). The history of twentieth century discussions of theological implications has been given in Dick, *The Biological Universe* and *Life on Other Worlds,* and T. Peters, "Exo-Theology: Speculations on Extra-Terrestrial Life," *CTNS Bulletin*, 14, no. 3 (1994), 1–9.

10. L. Eiseley, *The Immense Journey* (New York: Random House, 1957).

11. Dick, *The Biological Universe*, 526.

12. Most recently, K. Armstrong, *A History of God: The 4,000-Year Quest of Judaism, Christianity and Islam* (New York: Ballantine Books, 1993).

13. R.W. Clark, *Einstein: The Life and Times* (New York: Avon Books, 1972), 38; A. Einstein, "Religion and Science," in *Ideas and Opinions* (New York: Bonanza Books, 1954), 36–40.

14. F. Hoyle, *The Intelligent Universe* (New York: Holt, Rinehart and Winston, 1983), especially chapters 8 and 9. Hoyle based his concept of a "large-scale intelligence" on quantum mechanics. Chapter 8 describes this intelligence as one that works in a reversed time sense, from future to past, controlling individual quantum events and giving rise to the "information-rich universe" that biology represents. Chapter 9 describes an intelligence that works, like ourselves, from past to future but is superior to us. This intelligence, which in Hoyle's view created carbon-based life, "is firmly within the universe, and is subservient to it" (p. 236).

15. Einstein, "Religion and Science," 39.

16. S. Kauffman, *At Home in the Universe: The Search for the Laws of Self-Organization and Complexity* (New York and Oxford: Oxford University Press, 1995).

17. S. Weinberg, *The First Three Minutes* (New York: Basic Books, 1977), 154–155.

18. On the problem of morality in relation to extraterrestrials, see M. Ruse, "Is Rape Wrong on Andromeda? An Introduction to Extraterrestrial Evolution, Science and Morality," in E. Regis, Jr., *Extraterrestrials: Science and Alien Intelligence* (Cambridge: Cambridge University Press, 1985), 43–78.

19. G.V. Coyne, S.J., M.A. Hoskin, and O. Pedersen, eds., *Gregorian Reform of the Calendar* (Vatican, 1983), XXI.

20. K. Armstrong, *A History of God*, 399.

SELECT BIBLIOGRAPHY

Barrow, John D. and Frank Tipler, 1986. *The Anthropic Cosmological Principle* (Oxford: Clarendon Press).

Davies, Paul, 1983. *God and the New Physics* (New York: Simon and Schuster).

Davies, Paul, 1988. *The Cosmic Blueprint: New Discoveries in Nature's Creative Ability to Order the Universe* (New York: Simon and Schuster).

Davies, Paul, 1992. *The Mind of God: The Scientific Basis for a Rational Universe* (New York: Simon and Schuster).

Davies, Paul, 1995. *Are We Alone? Philosophical Implications of the Discovery of Extraterrestrial Life* (New York: Basic Books).

Davies, Paul, 1998. *The Fifth Miracle: The Search for the Origin of Life* (London: Penguin Press).

Dawkins, Richard, 1976. *The Selfish Gene* (Oxford: Oxford University Press).

Dawkins, Richard, 1996. *Climbing Mount Improbable* (London: Viking).

De Duve, Christian, 1995. *Vital Dust: Life as a Cosmic Imperative* (New York: Basic Books).

Dick, Steven J., 1982. *Plurality of Worlds: The Origins of the Extraterrestrial Life Debate from Democritus to Kant* (Cambridge: Cambridge University Press).

Dick, Steven J., 1996. *The Biological Universe: The Twentieth Century Extraterrestrial Life Debate and the Limits of Science* (Cambridge: Cambridge University Press).

Dick, Steven J., 1998. *Life on Other Worlds: The Twentieth Century Extraterrestrial Life Debate* (Cambridge: Cambridge University Press).

Dyson, Freeman, 1988. *Infinite in All Directions* (New York: Harper and Row).

Dyson, Freeman, 1997. *Imagined Worlds* (Cambridge, Mass.: Harvard University Press).

Dyson, Freeman, 1999. *Origins of Life* (Cambridge: Cambridge University Press).

Gold, Thomas, 1999. *The Hot Deep Biosphere* (New York: Copernicus).

Hoyle, Fred, 1983. *The Intelligent Universe* (New York: Holt, Rinehart and Winston).

Küppers, Bernd-Olaf, 1985. *Molecular Theory of Evolution* (New York: Springer-Verlag).

Küppers, Bernd-Olaf, 1990. *Information and the Origin of Life* (Cambridge, Mass.: MIT Press).

Kauffman, Stuart, 1995. *At Home in the Universe: The Search for Laws of Self-Organization* (New York and Oxford: Oxford University Press).

Leslie, John, 1989. *Universes* (London and New York: Routledge).

Leslie, John, 1996. *The End of the World: The Science and Ethics of Human Extinction* (London and New York: Routledge).

Leslie, John, ed., 1998. *Modern Cosmology and Philosophy* (Amherst, N.Y.: Prometheus Books).

McKay, Christopher, P.J. Thomas, and C.F. Chyba, 1997. *Comets and the Origin and Evolution of Life* (London: Springer-Verlag).

McMullin, Ernan, 1992. *The Inference That Makes Science* (Milwaukee: Marquette University Press).

Monod, Jacques, 1972. *Chance and Necessity* (London: Collins).

Peacocke, Arthur, 1996. *From DNA to Dean: Reflections and Explorations of a Priest-Scientist* (London: Canterbury Press).

Peacocke, Arthur, 1996. *God and Science: A Quest for Christian Credibility* (London: SCM Press).

Polkinghorne, John, 1994. *Quarks, Chaos, and Christianity* (London: Triangle Press).

Rees, Martin, 1997. *Before the Beginning: Our Universe and Others* (Reading, Mass.: Addison-Wesley).

Smolin, Lee, 1997. *The Life of the Cosmos* (Oxford: Oxford University Press).

Index